CONVERSATIONS ON PHILANTHROPY

Emerging Questions on Liberality and Social Thought

Volume IX
Law & Philanthropy

The Philanthropic Enterprise, Inc.
©2012

CONVERSATIONS ON PHILANTHROPY

Emerging Questions on Liberality and Social Thought

Volume IX 2012 • Law & Philanthropy

EDITOR'S INTRODUCTION
Lenore T. Ealy & G. M. Curtis III v

SYMPOSIUM ON TAX EXEMPTION

ESSAYS
A Radical Reform for Nonprofit Tax Exemption: A Thought Experiment
William C. Dennis 1

Philanthropy and the Federal Income Tax: Should our Republic Subsidize Tocqueville's Democracy?
Robert E. Atkinson, Jr. 9

COMMENTS
The Good, the Bad, and the Charitable
Adam G. Martin 22

Trading in Tocqueville: Philanthropy in an Era of Philanthrocapitalism, LC3s, and Social Innovation Bonds
Robin Rogers. 29

Tocqueville or Austerity? Health Care and the Social Compact
John T. Thomas 36

Second Thoughts on Tax Treatment of American Philanthropy
John E. Murray 46

ARTICLES
Philanthropy, Law, and Associational Liberty: A Few Remarks on Gierke's *Genossenschaftsrecht*
Steven Grosby. 53

Charity and Religion: Historical Connections in our Law
Richard H. Helmholz. 74

Towards a Modern Idea of Charity
Joseph Isaac Lifshitz 84

Philanthropy and Research Biobanks: The Model of Biotrust
Ilaria Anna Colussi. 105

Philanthropic Institutional Design and the Welfare State
David F. Hardwick and Leslie Marsh. 118

Charity, Reciprocity, and the Moral Law
Todd Breyfogle 138

RESEARCH NOTE
"Philanthropy," "Nonprofits," and the IRS Master Data File for Massachusetts
George McCully. 153

BOOK REVIEWS

**The Man Who Sold America: The Amazing (But True!) Story of
Albert D. Lasker and the Creation of the Advertising Century**
By Jeffrey L. Cruikshank and Arthur W. Schultz
Reviewed by Martin Morse Wooster. 164

The Two Narratives of Political Economy
By Nicholas Capaldi and Gordon Lloyd
Reviewed by Art Carden. 168

Ten Ways to Destroy the Imagination of Your Child
By Anthony Esolen
Reviewed by Tony Woodlief. 171

Adam Smith's Marketplace of Life
By James R. Otteson
Reviewed by Samuel Gregg. 176

Philanthropy in America: A History
By Olivier Zunz
Reviewed by George McCully. 180

The Information: A History, A Theory, A Flood
By James Gleick
Reviewed by Heather Wood Ion. 187

Bad Students, Not Bad Schools
By Robert Weissberg
Reviewed by George Leef. 190

**Western Culture at the American Crossroads:
Conflicts Over the Nature of Science and Reason**
By Arthur Pontynen and Rod Miller
Reviewed by Troy Camplin 194

Aims and Scope

Conversations on Philanthropy: Emerging Questions on Liberality and Social Thought aim is to promote inquiry and reflection on the importance of liberality—in the dual sense of generosity and of the character befitting free individuals—for the flourishing of local communities, political societies, and humanity in general. As such we seek to open new perspectives on the roles, theories, and practices of philanthropic activities ranging from charitable giving, the actions of eleemosynary organizations, trusts, foundations, voluntary associations, and fraternal societies to volunteerism, mutual aid, social entrepreneurship and other forms of social action with beneficent intention (whether or not also combined with commercial and/or political purposes). To facilitate conversations among traditional academic disciplines, *Conversations on Philanthropy* will include papers from a number of fields, including history, political science, economics, sociology, anthropology, philosophy, philanthropic studies, religious studies, belles lettres, law, and the physical sciences, as well as from philanthropic practitioners. Published comments on feature essays are a means of providing a transparent peer-review process to enhance interdisciplinary understanding.

Editorial Correspondence

Material published in *Conversations on Philanthropy* is typically solicited by the Editors. Authors who would like to submit material for consideration should first submit a brief abstract to *Lenore T. Ealy, Ph.D., PO Box 4449, Carmel, IN 46082*; E-mail:*editor@conversationsonphilanthropy.org*. For detailed instructions concerning the submission of manuscripts, please contact the Editor.

Subscription Rates

The electronic version of the journal (ISSN 2150-0959) is updated as new material is ready for publication. The printed version of the journal (ISSN 1552-9592) is published annually. The electronic archive of the journal can be accessed on the internet (http://www.conversationsonphilanthropy.org). Individual and institutional print subscriptions to *Conversations on Philanthropy* are available through http://www.conversationsonphilanthropy.org/subscribe/.

ISBN 978-0-9761904-8-6

INTRODUCTION

This volume of *Conversations on Philanthropy* grew out of papers presented at a 2011 scholarly colloquium on *The Law of Charity: History, Theory, and Social Practice*. It was unintentional, but the papers gathered for this conference seemed, upon reflection, both to amplify the importance of and reveal a lacuna in Harold Berman's magisterial study of the Western legal tradition presented in *Law and Revolution: The Formation of the Western Legal Tradition* and *Law and Revolution II: The Impact of the Protestant Reformations on the Western Legal Tradition*. To identify the lacuna requires a careful look at Berman's focus on the implications of the Lutheran Reformation; consider this passage from the first volume of Berman's study:

> The key to the renewal of law in the West from the sixteenth century on was the Lutheran concept of the power of the individual, by God's grace, to change nature and to create new social relations through the exercise of his will. The Lutheran concept of the individual will become central to the development of the modern law of property and contract. To be sure, there had been an elaborate and sophisticated law of property and contract, both in the church and in the mercantile community, for some centuries, but in Lutheranism its focus was changed. Old rules were recast in a new ensemble. Nature became property. Economic relations became contract. Conscience became will and intent. The [individual's] last testament, which in the earlier Catholic tradition had been primarily a means of saving souls by charitable gifts, became primarily a means of controlling social and economic relations. By the naked expression of their will, their intent, testators could dispose of their property after death, and entrepreneurs could arrange their business relations by contract. The property and contract rights so created were held to be sacred and inviolable, so long as they did not contravene conscience. Conscience gave them their sanctity. And so the secularization of the state, in the restricted sense of the removal of ecclesiastical controls from it, was accompanied by a spiritualization, and even a sanctification, of property and contract (2006, 29-30).

Property and contract, however, are only two of the three legs of the stool upon which the modern world has been constructed. Perhaps, to fully ground property and contract as unassailable features of our jurisprudence, we must turn our attention to a theory of *association*, which can be cast as the third leg of the stool. The Reformation, as Berman convincingly argues, precipitated a revolution in the legal nature of property and contract. Nevertheless, Berman leaves largely out of the narrative of *Law and Revolution* the story of the changes that were also transpiring in our understanding of the legal nature of associations and corporations, those formal and informal entities through which people coordinate their social and economic activities. And yet, the emergence of the *jus commune* Berman describes, a "pan-European estate of jurists" engaged in developing a new legal science, was itself an epiphenomenon of the new phenomenon of associational liberty that would set the Western legal tradition on a new course. Broadening legal recognition of nonpolitical associations gave rise not only to the early forms of incorporated commercial activity but also ushered in a new age of philanthropy anchored in grassroots, private charities.

The belief that people could associate together outside of the state or the church to create positive social and commercial benefits would eventuate in the settlement of the American colonies on a new political economy of the covenanted, and later the constitutional, society. The reader of the Mayflower Compact, John Winthrop's *A Model of Christian Charity*, much of the writings of Benjamin Franklin, Alexander Hamilton's *Federalist 1*, and much more in the literature of the American colonial and early republic periods will readily assent to the conclusion that America was also conceived of as a charitable and philanthropic society, a society in which rich lateral and voluntary associations among people promoted the general welfare, as well as a society whose members self-consciously believed themselves to be modeling a new hope for human freedom and flourishing.

Puzzling over the nature of democracy in America, which he did not believe could be easily grafted onto the Old World, Alexis de Tocqueville penned his famous lines outlining the emergence of a new science of association: "Americans of all ages, all conditions, all minds constantly unite. . . . In democratic countries the science of association is the mother science; the progress of all the others depends on the progress of that one. Among the laws that rule human societies there is one that seems more precise and clearer than all the others. In order that men remain civilized or become so, the art of associating must be developed and perfected among them . . . ."

By science, Tocqueville may have had in mind less a positivist science in the modern sense than a deeper study and clearer articulation of the *phronesis* already embodied in the Americans' legal procedures, associational habits, and conversational traffic (not only the conversation in homes, taverns and inns but that which transpired through circular letters and a robust free press as well). If they failed to understand their unique associational practices, Tocqueville speculated that Americans would drift into "soft despotism," unable to balance their hopes for liberty and their fierce belief in equality. In this prediction, Tocqueville seems to have prophesied the emergence of the modern welfare state and its enervating effects on the philanthropic enterprise.

The present quest for "social justice" shifts us further away from an understanding of and trust in the positive social effects of private charity and independent voluntary association and seems to tighten the link between our philanthropy and our politics. A deeper examination of the philosophy of social justice suggests that the processes of secularization and sacralization are far from over, and it highlights more than ever our need to understand better our history and our present aspirations and to reflect more carefully about how each finds, or should find, expression in our legal institutions and traditions.

The papers collected in this volume thus serve as signposts back to many of the questions Tocqueville explored. They help us not only fill in missing pieces of the legal history of the role of philanthropic (and commercial and political) associations but also advance Berman's call for an integrative jurisprudence and a social theory of law that recognizes not only the inevitability of progress (revolution in Berman's sense) but also the value of tradition in helping us renew and recreate the foundations of order.

The first set of papers in this volume, comprising a symposium on "The Political Economy of Tax Exemption," should be read as a thought experiment rather than a direct move toward a policy prescription. We were intrigued when William Dennis and Robert Atkinson, beginning with divergent presuppositions about the nature of American political economy, converged in seriously questioning the desirability of exempting charitable entities from taxation.

As this volume goes to press, there is much ink being spilled in protest against President Obama's continuing efforts to cap the charitable deduction. Much more empirical study should be done on the potential impacts of such a policy, but the papers in this symposium approach the questions of the entanglement of philanthropy and state from a different, more normative, perspective. The President's intent certainly is to raise more tax revenue and draw welfare provision even further into the domain of the national government. It may be that we have lived with the Sixteenth Amendment authorizing the national income tax too long for those who would defend charitable giving to recall that Tocqueville witnessed a robust voluntary spirit in America long before the tax exemption or the charitable deduction existed. Incentives are important, but if our current tax regime has reduced our charitable system to one in which the central government increasingly establishes the proper ends of welfare and the people support these ends primarily as a means of tax avoidance, we may have already lost our ability to imagine together, as Tocqueville thought we must, our self-interest, rightly understood. We leave it to the reader to explore our authors' arguments and to reflect, as our symposium commentators have done, on the validity and implications of their arguments.

The second group of papers—those by Joseph Isaac Lifshitz, Richard Helmholz, and Steven Grosby—sheds further light on the contemporary political economy of philanthropy by way of historical examinations of legal theory and practice in three distinct contexts. Lifshitz orients us to the treatment of property and charity in the Jewish legal tradition and questions whether modern scholars are justified in reading today's concerns with distributive or social justice back into this tradition. Helmholz opens a window into the late medieval and early modern European laws of charity, with special attention to the negotiation between church and state of jurisdictional boundaries over wills and trusts. Grosby's examination of the early legal and political theory of associations, especially as presented in the works of Otto von Gierke and Pollock and Maitland, highlights tensions and questions about the legal foundations of associational liberty.

A third group of papers turns our attention to the implications of legal frameworks for practical applications in modern philanthropic entities. Neither the law nor philanthropy is a static institution, and Ilaria Colussi introduces us to the complexities surrounding the development of a workable legal theory to guide jurisprudence in the relatively new world of human tissue banks. David Hardwick and Leslie Marsh argue that institutional design, in theory and practice, matters, and they provide a case study of how one Canadian hospital has navigated the space between philanthropy and the welfare state. Todd Breyfogle concludes this group of papers with a literary reflection on Willa Cather's *Death Comes for the Archbishop* which is suggestive of the ways our deeply embedded and often unexamined cultural understandings of both law and philanthropy shape our expectations of charity and our practices of giving.

Finally, we are pleased to present here a research note by George McCully of the Catalogue for Philanthropy discussing preliminary findings of a program he is pursuing to explore how the legal designations of "nonprofit" entities utilized by the Internal Revenue Service actually confuse our categorical understanding of the true meaning of philanthropy and cloud both our charitable practices and our research on the philanthropic sector.

Our cover art for this volume is a painting of *Founder's Hall* at Girard College in Philadelphia, which was founded as a school for poor, white, male orphans in 1833 by a bequest from Stephen Girard, one of the wealthiest men in America in the early nineteenth century. The development of American law regarding philanthropic trusts has proved a complex legal process, as English statutes, including the Elizabethan Statute on Charitable Uses (1601), were repealed after the Revolution, and the courts had both to look for precedents in Common Law and to align decisions with the new Constitutional order. Girard's legacy stands out, both as one of the largest charitable bequests in American history to that time and as the subject of legal contests around the law of charitable trusts in two succeeding centuries.

First, in the litigation that resulted in a U.S. Supreme Court decision in *Vidal v. Girard's Executors* (1844), Girard's heirs argued that the stipulation that the City of Philadelphia serve as trustee for Girard's trust could not be upheld and sought to take control of the estate themselves. The decision also stands among the earliest church-state rulings by the Court, which held that despite Girard's stipulation that no ecclesiastics or ministers could be employed by the school it nevertheless remained incumbent on the City to ensure that Girard's desire for instruction in the "purest principles of morality" be honored through Biblical instruction by lay teachers.

In the 20th century, in the wake of *Brown v. Board of Education*, Girard's bequest was again the subject of Supreme Court attention in *Pennsylvania v. Board of Trusts*, 353 U.S. 230 (1957). The Court ruled that the continuing enforcement of Girard's will by denying admission to Negro boys by the City of Philadelphia constituted a violation of the Fourteenth Amendment. Subsequently, a new board of trustees was appointed, effectively privatizing the trust, which was then free to set its own admissions policies. Girard College thus became an important target for Civil Rights activists, who effected integration of the school in 1968 through popular protests and continuing litigation, which culminated in a decision by the Third Circuit Court of Appeals that the case should be decided on Constitutional rights rather than state law.

Such contestations over the fulfillment of donor intent continue into our present century, fueled by twentieth-century welfare state experiments, increasingly contentious politics regarding entitlements and social regulation, and, after the ratification of the Sixteenth Amendment establishing a federal income tax, new statutory treatments of tax-exempt entities in both Washington and the states. A judiciary increasingly prone to activism from the bench contributed to confusions about the legal place of philanthropy. The result is that American philanthropy, having become increasingly an adjunct of the state, has too often relinquished its standing as a fundamental source of social power.

—Lenore T. Ealy
G. M. Curtis III

SYMPOSIUM ON TAX EXEMPTION

ESSAYS

**A Radical Reform for Nonprofit Tax Exemption:
A Thought Experiment**
William C. Dennis

**Philanthropy and the Federal Income Tax: Should our Republic
Subsidize Tocqueville's Democracy?**
Robert E. Atkinson, Jr.

COMMENTS

The Good, the Bad, and the Charitable
Adam G. Martin

**Trading in Tocqueville: Philanthropy in an Era of
Philanthrocapitalism, LC3s, and Social Innovation Bonds**
Robin Rogers

Tocqueville or Austerity? Health Care and the Social Compact
John T. Thomas

Second Thoughts on Tax Treatment of American Philanthropy
John E. Murray

ARTICLES

**Philanthropy, Law, and Associational Liberty:
A Few Remarks on Gierke's *Genossenschaftsrecht***
Steven Grosby

Charity and Religion: Historical Connections in our Law
Richard H. Helmholz

Towards a Modern Idea of Charity
Joseph Isaac Lifshitz

Philanthropy and Research Biobanks: The Model of Biotrust
Ilaria Anna Colussi

Philanthropic Institutional Design and the Welfare State
David F. Hardwick and Leslie Marsh

Charity, Reciprocity, and the Moral Law
Todd Breyfogle

RESEARCH NOTE

**"Philanthropy," "Nonprofits,"
and the IRS Master Data File for Massachusetts**
George McCully

*Conversations on Philanthropy Volume IX:
Law & Philanthropy*
©The Philanthropic Enterprise, Inc. 2012

CONTRIBUTORS

ROBERT E. ATKINSON, JR. (ROB) is a native of Kingstree, South Carolina, and a graduate of Washington and Lee University (History and Philosophy, 1979). After receiving his law degree (Yale 1982), he clerked for Judge Donald Stuart Russell of the United States Court of Appeals for the Fourth Circuit. He practiced estate planning and nonprofit organizations law with Sutherland, Asbill & Brennan's Washington, D.C., office before joining the faculty at the Florida State University College of Law, where he has taught property, professional responsibility, law and literature, and nonprofit organizations, and where he writes and lectures on philanthropy and on the legal profession.

TODD BREYFOGLE is Director of Seminars for the Aspen Institute. He earned a BA in Classics-History-Politics from Colorado College before attending Corpus Christi College, Oxford (as a Rhodes Scholar), where he read Ancient and Modern History (BA) and Patristic and Modern Theology (MSt). He earned his PhD as a Century Fellow and Javits Fellow at the University of Chicago's Committee on Social Thought. He is the editor of *Literary Imagination, Ancient and Modern: Essays in Honor of David Grene* (University of Chicago Press, 1999), and has authored articles ranging from Augustine to J. S. Bach to contemporary political theory. Before joining the Aspen Institute, he directed the Honors Program at the University of Denver. He has lectured at universities in the US, Canada, the UK, and India, including Oxford, Cambridge, Princeton, Dartmouth, and the University of Chicago. He serves on several non-profit boards and is a Senator of the Phi Beta Kappa Society.

ILARIA ANNA COLUSSI is a PhD Candidate in Public Law at the Doctoral School of Comparative and European Legal Studies, University of Trento (Italy). She also collaborates with the European Centre for Law, Science and New Technologies (Pavia) and is a member of the project "Biolaw" within the Department of Legal Science of the University of Trento. Her main research interests concern the legal aspects of synthetic biology, the relationship between genetics and the law, with a specific attention to biobanks and forensic DNA databanks. She has published several articles in Italian Law journals and chapters within books (such as "Biotech Innovations and Fundamental Rights," published by Springer, 2012). Moreover, she has participated, as a speaker, at conferences and seminars all over the world. She has recently carried out research periods at the Oxford Uehiro Centre for Practical Ethics (Oxford, UK) and at the Inter-University Chair in Law and the Human Genome, University of Deusto (Bilbao, Spain).

WILLIAM C. DENNIS, now an independent consultant in philanthropy in McLean, Virginia, has spent most of his career working at nonprofit tax-exempt institutions. He has also gifted conservation easements on family property to a nonprofit organization.

STEVEN GROSBY is professor of religion at Clemson University. His recent books include *Nationalism: A Very Short Introduction* (Oxford, 2005) and, as editor, *Edward Shils, A Fragment of a Sociological Autobiography* (Transaction, 2006). He is also a contributing editor to *Conversations on Philanthropy*.

DAVID F. HARDWICK is Professor Emeritus, Pathology and Pediatrics at The University of British Columbia; the Secretary of the International Academy of Pathology and Associate Editor of *Modern Pathology*. He currently serves on the Board of Governors of British Columbia Children's Hospital Foundation and has been intimately involved in the interrelationship of Government and the British Columbia Children's Foundation in the creation of new Children's Hospital facilities. He has published numerous books and papers on organizational and administrative systems the latest being a series of papers (co-authored with Leslie Marsh) on the relationship between the market and science, notably "Science, the Market and Iterative Knowledge" (*Studies in Emergent Order*, Vol. 5, 2012) and "Clash of the Titans: When The Market and Science Collide" (in press, *Advances in Austrian Economics*, Vol. 17, Emerald).

RICHARD H. HELMHOLZ is Ruth Wyatt Rosenson Distinguished Service Professor in the Law School of the University of Chicago. A legal historian, he has specialized in the study of Roman and canon laws. His principal contribution has been to show their relevance to the development of the Anglo-American common law. Among his publications on the subject, the two most recent are *Volume One of the Oxford History of the Laws of England: The Canon Law and Ecclesiastical Jurisdiction from 597 to the 1640s* (2004), and *Three Civilian Notebooks, 1580-1640* (Selden Society 2010).

JOSEPH ISAAC LIFSHITZ is a Senior Fellow in the Department of Philosophy, Political Theory, and Religion. He received his PhD in Jewish Thought from Tel Aviv University. In his study of Jewish philosophy and history, his main focus is on the philosophy and history of Ashkenaz in the high Middle-Ages. His book *Judaism, Law and the Free Market*, was published by Acton Institute on May, 2012.

LESLIE MARSH is a Research Associate in the Dean's Office (Medical School) at The University of British Columbia and was previously Assistant Director of The New England Institute for Cognitive Science and Evolutionary Studies. His work is primarily located at the interface of mind, sociality and liberality with an active interest in the philanthropic world. He is the founder of the journal *EPISTEME: Journal of Individual and Social Epistemology* (Cambridge); is currently working on a monograph *Stigmergic Cognition: Socializing Cognition and "Cognitivizing" Sociality* (Springer); is the co-editor of *A Companion to Michael Oakeshott* (forthcoming, Penn State); and is the editor of Hayek in Mind: *Hayek's Philosophical Psychology*.

ADAM G. MARTIN is a lecturer in political economy at King's College, London. After receiving his PhD in Economics from George Mason University in 2009, he was a post-doctoral fellow at the Development Research Institute at New York University. He can be reached at adam.martin@kcl.ac.uk and more information can be found on his website, adamgmartin.com.

GEORGE McCULLY served for twenty years as professor of European intellectual and cultural history, from the Renaissance to the Enlightenment, and for twenty-five years as a professional philanthropist—fundraiser, strategic planner, executive director, trustee, and advisor to charities, foundations, families and individual donors. In 1997 he created the highly respected and influential Massachusetts Catalogue for Philanthropy, to promote charitable giving and strengthen the culture of philanthropy through donor education. His book, *Philanthropy Reconsidered* (2008), presents a comprehensive overview of the "vocabulary, conceptualization, and rhetoric" of philanthropy from the ancient coinage of the term in *Prometheus Bound*, to its essential role informing the American Revolution and Constitution, to the paradigm-shift transforming philanthropy today. His latest work is the *Massachusetts Philanthropic Directory*—an on-line, systematically taxonomized, analytical directory to all the philanthropic charities of (initially) Massachusetts, which comprise only 1/7th of the state's "nonprofits." This dramatically innovative Directory system will be extended nationwide over the next two years. He is also a contributing editor to *Conversations on Philanthropy*.

JOHN E. MURRAY is Joseph R. Hyde III Professor of Political Economy at Rhodes College in Memphis, Tennessee. He has written on public and private approaches to poverty, poor relief, and income maintenance in a variety of places and times. His books include *Origins of American Health Insurance* (Yale University Press, 2007), *Children Bound to Labor* (Cornell University Press, 2009), and *The Charleston Orphan House* (University of Chicago Press, 2013).

ROBIN ROGERS is an associate professor of sociology at the City University of New York and has served as a Congressional fellow on public policy.

JOHN T. THOMAS, Esq., J.D. Vanderbilt University School of Law, 1990, is health care executive and a tax lawyer by training and practice. He has served as in-house counsel to both the Sisters of Mercy Health System and Baylor Health Care System and has represented other nonprofit health care organizations. While serving as general counsel for Baylor, he testified before the U.S. House of Representatives Ways and Means Committee on May 23, 2005, about the structure of the Texas charity care law and the differences between nonprofit hospitals and taxable hospitals in their service to the community.

A RADICAL REFORM FOR NONPROFIT TAX EXEMPTION: A THOUGHT EXPERIMENT

William C. Dennis

Already in America, government is tightening its grip on the independent sector. It is challenging the tax-exempt status of foundations making new efforts to "regulate" almost all private groups. An independent sector "regulated" by its competition has, at best, an uphill fight on its hands. . . . The foundation is an instrument forged by citizens who transfer profit from the commercial sector and put it directly to work as risk capital for the general betterment of the society. To say or imply that the foundation exists only on the sufferance of government is to reason from the premise that government is the whole of society.
—Richard C. Cornuelle, *Reclaiming the American Dream*

The late economist Benjamin A. Rogge used to talk of "Rogge's World," that ideal arrangement of institutions which he would have established had he been in charge (not that he would have agreed to be put in charge if asked). This was a thought experiment he used to consider the implications of better social configurations from a free-market perspective. Rogge, I think, was aware of how difficult and even dangerous it is to approach social reform in a constructivist mode, because of unintended consequences and secondary effects. Institutions have been built up over long periods of time, and countless individuals have made life choices on the basis of existing arrangements. For many, radical changes will bring unexpected and undesired difficulties that will not be obviously balanced by the theoretically improved institutional setting.[1] Nevertheless, thought experiments exploring ideal worlds can demonstrate interesting possibilities and help guide more incremental change.

With this in mind, let us look into the institutional setting of tax-exempt philanthropy, with improvements in mind. This is a good time to do so, because various congressionally sponsored reforms of nonprofits—reforms which are not always friendly toward philanthropy—are circulating in political circles. A list of these proposals includes: requiring greater annual payouts from charitable endowments; requiring philanthropies to spend more on politically favored minorities or minority-managed enterprises; requiring minority and female "representation" on foundation boards; and increased auditing of philanthropic accounts. Most recently, some politicians have been considering limiting the tax deductibility of charitable giving by "the rich."

Government Entanglement

This is a thought experiment about an ideal world. It is not a plea to increase taxes on nonprofits. Indeed, this writer believes that all of America is vastly overtaxed. What is needed, however, at whatever level of taxation we settle on, is a new consideration of the effect of tax exemption on the status of American philanthropy. Upon such examination, I think we will find that the tax-exempt status cannot be justified and is not needed in order to have a vibrant nonprofit sector.

Congress grants tax exemption to certain nonprofits on the condition that they spend their resources on activities in the public interest. This tax-exempt status of philanthropic organizations and other nonprofits sets them apart from other institutions of civil society, most notably families and for-profit businesses. From the point of view of the philanthropies, this suggests that they have some superior status, and it too often produces a "do-gooder complex" that separates them from the world of getting and spending that produces the wealth off of which they live. From their perspective, they are endowed by law with a lofty public purpose that leaves them unsullied by crass materialism. In recent years this status has encouraged many philanthropies to identify closely with the actions of government, because government, whatever its real purposes, always boasts of its special devotion to serving the public good. Note how many philanthropic leaders now argue that the main purpose of their organizations is to develop a case for the further expansion of government programs. Yet as recent scholarship indicates, government on net is an insatiable consumer of personal wealth far beyond what its positive effects on the public good can possibly justify. Furthermore, government actions, more often than not, actually promote explicit and identifiable private interests in opposition to any possible public good. This is one aspect of the problem of faction, famously discussed by Madison in the *Federalist Papers* and under scrutiny today both in public choice theory and in the investigation of cronyism.

To put this point more bluntly, both donors and recipients, whether acting privately or through public institutions, face the temptation of moral corruption in their efforts to do good. They do not need the added endorsement of tax exemption to increase this danger.

The growing alliance between philanthropy and government is unfortunate, for we should view our diverse nonprofit organizations as constituting just one aspect of the vast civil society outside the realm of government, where work, savings, and private endeavor provide the great bulk of resources necessary for personal and social well-being and for economic and cultural progress. It is civil society, not government, that provides most of the heavy lifting that produces public goods. From this perspective, government, when confined to its proper role, should be viewed as a limited-purpose agent, or utility (as Dick Cornuelle often put it), of the larger civil society, a true servant of the people and not the dominant force in social life.

Seen in this light, it is clear that tax exemption for private philanthropy helps sustain a false sense of separateness that detracts from a proper understanding of the true place of philanthropy in a free society. It encourages the state to believe it has the power and the duty to give tax exemptions only to those nonprofits it deems as working in the public interest as defined by the state itself. It permits the government to funnel money to those nonprofits it favors (a sort of Solyndra-ization of philanthropy; see Husack 2011), while increasing the nonprofits' dependency on the state.

A Host of Harms

There are additional harmful and less philosophic elements in the favored tax treatment of philanthropic enterprise. First, Government views Philanthropy, with its growing wealth, as a potential source of new tax funds, and the threat of the loss of tax-exempt status undermines philanthropy's independence.

Politicians continually threaten philanthropy with new taxes and regulations unless the philanthropies conform to what the politicians deem to be socially useful projects. Congressional hearings and IRS investigations of philanthropic wealth and expenditure have happened in the past. Political demagogues will surely be tempted to turn again to such tactics one day, especially if Congress really gets serious about government debts and deficits. The possibility of such threats may encourage philanthropies to be too complicit with the explicit pronouncements of their political supervisors. Because of the constant possibility of increased government supervision and regulation, many philanthropy executives govern more on the basis of unduly cautionary advice from their attorneys than by creative and bold thinking about how to carry out their philanthropic mission. In this they are not too different from many for-profit firms also fearful of government notice and greater regulation.

Second, tax-exempt philanthropies, with their ability to buy and sell securities free of the capital gains tax and the income tax paid by individuals and for-profit corporations, are able to unfairly compete with private taxable endeavors. This is a growing problem as the business wings of nonprofits increasingly engage in commerce (such as bookstores and museum shops) and the provision of social services, widely conceived (including hospitals and educational institutions), and compete directly with private, for-profit ventures. If business income is to be taxed at all, it should be taxed everywhere.

Third, the tax-exempt status of philanthropies promotes ill-considered philanthropic investments and institutional arrangements. For instance, a property owner who gives land or buildings to a historical preservation or conservation nonprofit only to avoid burdensome taxation takes valuable property out of productive enterprise and freezes in place the status quo at the cost of some economic benefit to the society at large. Family fortunes may be turned into hastily conceived foundations run by non-family philanthropic professionals with purposes of their own, different from those of the original donor. Or worse, perhaps, run by family members with large salaries. Without tax-exempt status and death duties, such largely irreversible decisions would be less attractive, and fewer resources would be spent devising complicated trust arrangements.

These two problems—unfair competition and inflexible institutional arrangements—increase the suspicion with which both government officials and private individuals view the operations of many nonprofits.

Fourth, a related question is the problem of perpetuities, a suspect category under common law. Times change, but nonprofits, in theory at least, can go on forever. For-profit corporations appear also to be immortal, but they can be bought and sold, merged with other corporations, go bankrupt, or distribute their assets to their shareholders. Subject to competitive pressures, in practice no American for-profit corporation has the lifespan of a Harvard University, a Carnegie Endowment, or a Chicago Symphony Orchestra. Only one company on today's Dow Jones Index of thirty stocks, General Electric, was there at the beginning of the Dow Jones Averages. Without tax-exempt status, a philanthropic-minded individual might be willing to develop more flexible and less permanent institutional arrangements for his financial legacy, situations in which complexity and contingency could be more easily dealt.[2]

Fifth, as nonprofits increasingly become subjects of political controversy, civil peace should be improved by removing their tax-exempt status. People opposed to a particular group would no longer feel aggrieved that it was getting favored tax treatment at their expense, and the controversial group could no longer be threatened by hostile politicians seeking to punish them by removing their tax-exempt status. Consider, for instance, the controversy in the 2011 budget surrounding the government funding of Planned Parenthood.[3] Many hundreds of other tax-exempt groups get government grants as well.

Sixth, without annual payout requirements, both donors and recipients would be released from the pressure of annual deadlines to complete gifting and expenditures and could be expected to make more considered judgments on what projects to fund or develop.

Looking at philanthropies as if they are categorically different from other institutions of civil society generates such problems. If we instead view philanthropies as more generically part of the civil order, engaged in many of the same endeavors as private individuals and businesses, we begin to see that they are not as different from the for-profit world and from private families as usually assumed. Like businesses, philanthropies provide jobs and social services (employment bureaus, credit counseling, retirement plans); purchase and sell goods (museum calendars or "fair trade" coffee); run medical care and research facilities (hospitals and laboratories); and provide cultural and environmental amenities (fine architecture, art collections, universities, libraries, golf courses, nature preserves, and office parks). Both may charge fees for goods and services, though the nonprofit may give away many of its services. However, for-profit businesses also donate many goods and services to worthy causes and persons and contribute time and money to nonprofit entities. The nonprofit, like the heavily taxed family, may provide most of its goods free of charge, yet the family in a free society is by far the more important social service "agency," providing most of our education, cultural upbringing, medical care, food, clothing, and shelter. We usually think of these as private goods, and truly they are, but the successful delivery of such goods also has profound social implications for the overall health and well-being of the social order. Considering the family's greater contributions to society, it is not clear why they should bear the brunt of taxation while nonprofits, which are much less important to society, remain tax-exempt. It would be better to tax both at some low, uniform rate.

Tax Reform for the Philanthropic Sector

A tax structure that acknowledged the similarities between the philanthropic sector and the rest of the private sector, indeed the overlapping and intertwined functions and duties of the two forms of corporations, as well as the associations, clubs, and families (which taken altogether constitute civil society), would look much different from what we have today. By reforming the tax structure, we would bring the activities of the two sectors into harmony instead of continuing to perpetuate rivalry between them, and would serve, over time, to blend them together into the one sector that they truly constitute, different from government, because they are based on voluntary rather than coerced relationships. Such a harmonization of interests would strengthen the institutions of the free society in general while restraining the tendency of government toward unchecked growth. Philanthropies should stop being the compliant handmaidens of government and resume their rightful place in the civil society.

Another benefit of moving the nonprofit, for-profit, and private institutions closer together would be the mitigation of various troubling social conflicts. For example, consider the following questions, a few from a long list: By what criteria are 501(c)3 applications for tax-exempt status to be judged? What institutions deserve 501(c)3 status by these criteria? Who determines which organizations these are? Does the IRS harass politically unpopular nonprofits, or do Congressmen, through threats of their own, implicit or explicit, attempt to influence nonprofit giving? How far may nonprofits go in advocating social change or proposing or opposing a particular political agenda without calling their tax-exempt status into question? Do political leaders use the IRS to investigate and intimidate their political enemies among the nonprofits? For taxation purposes, what is a church? What government regulations should be applied to church activities? What revenues of tax-exempt entities should be designated "unrelated business activities?" What actions of foundations should be prohibited as self-dealing? Should the names of donors to nonprofit organizations be publicly disclosed?

All these questions are frequent subjects of public controversy. Absent tax exemption, none of these questions would need answers. With tax exemptions, the chance of inflammatory political and partisan answers to these questions becomes increasingly likely.

When we begin to think about such issues, the usefulness of our thought experiment becomes clear. In the ideal world of the thought experiment, there should be no nonprofits. All income on investments and sales of goods and services by any entity would be taxed at the same low, flat tax rate. Nonprofits would pay local sales and property taxes like any other organization. Groups without endowments, living off of annual giving alone, would still be largely de facto tax exempt because there would be no retained profits to tax. The main tax revenues they would generate would come from taxes on the income of their employees, as is the case today. Churches might have to pay property taxes, if any existed, but local governments could provide property tax exemptions to churches, museums, open space, nature preserves, and historic properties if they cared to do so, on a nondiscriminatory basis. An even better policy would be to attempt to keep property taxes controlled at some low level through constitutional restraints, in order to reduce political meddling and social engineering. To maintain equal tax treatment, there would be no death duties and no capital gains taxes on anyone. In order to make this new system of taxation work and to keep income tax rates low enough to encourage productive endeavor and discourage new reasons to create tax-favored entities, deductions on personal income taxes for charitable giving, mortgage interest, medical expenses, and so forth should be abolished also. Only deductions for local and state taxes paid would remain, in order to avoid double and triple taxation of income. There could also be some "basic living" exemption for each member of a family.

Time and careful design would be necessary in order to engineer the transition to this new system with a minimum of disruption and unfairness. No doubt tax policy experts would perceive other problems and difficulties in this proposal that should be addressed. There probably are some undesirable and unintended consequences that would emerge. A serious discussion of such matters should lead to a more complete understanding of needed reform.

More Money for Philanthropy

Would such a radical reform mean the death of nonprofits and the loss of their important contributions to overall public well-being? Not at all. "Nonprofit" need not be synonymous with "not taxed." Increased national wealth from a more efficient tax system and the elimination of the huge economic loss created by estate planning, tax avoidance schemes, income tax preparation, and consultant fees to accountants and lawyers would leave both individual donors and nonprofit organizations with more money to spend on charitable activities. Here in the United States, at least, the amount of personal disposable income, not tax avoidance, is the primary determining factor in the amount of charitable giving. Certainly the removal of tax exemption would change the nature of nonprofit activity in unpredictable ways. Nonprofits might be more willing to spend down their resources. They might be more adaptable to changing circumstances. Public charities might come to rely more on annual giving and become less concerned with building endowments. Most Americans with discretionary income would continue to support their favorite philanthropic institutions and would be able to do so more generously than before.

Viewed in this way, reform of the tax-exempt portions of the tax code becomes one phase of the larger question of reform of American taxation in general. Everyone acknowledges that whatever the total incidence of taxation should be, our tax code needs radical simplification. Despite this widely held understanding, so far politicians have largely remained unwilling to do much about this scandalous situation, surely in violation of the spirit of the Constitution. They appear to believe that handing out tax advantages to favored groups is a key to their political success. In recent years a few members of Congress, political candidates, and public intellectuals have questioned this conventional political wisdom and have begun to advocate a major overhaul of the structure of our tax system, though there is hardly a strong movement in this direction. This may be the right time to reconsider the issue of tax exemption for nonprofits as well.

Perhaps only constitutional reform can ever bring major changes in the nation's tax structure. In the meantime, further research and thought experiments may help, over time, to influence the public discussion of the place of nonprofits in our society. While we contemplate, as Professor Rogge would have had it, the ideal structure of larger institutional changes, we should be sure to include in this discussion an investigation of the tax status of the nonprofits. Indeed, this would be a good project for a forward-looking foundation to fund as part of its own philanthropic reform efforts.

NOTES

[1] For instance, making mortgage interest deductible ostensibly to help homeowners probably increases the listing prices of home sales, and whatever financial benefit exists may largely accrue to the lender, seller, and the real estate agents rather than the homebuyer. Once such a system is in place, however, it becomes difficult to unwind it in a fair way.

[2] Some foundations have dealt with this problem by intentionally sun-setting their operations.

[3] For instance, this appeared on *National Review Online* while I was revising this essay: Planned Parenthood to Be Investigated September 27, 2011 4:07 P.M. By Charmaine Yoest. Sarah Kliff of *Newsweek* just broke the news that Cliff Stearns (R., Fla.), chairman of the subcommittee on oversight and investigations for the House Energy and Commerce Committee, has launched an investigation into Planned Parenthood. She links to a detailed two-page letter that outlines eight in-depth questions the abortion giant must respond to, including a release of all of their internal audits for national Planned Parenthood and their affiliates since 1998.

REFERENCES

Husack, Howard. 2011. "The Solyndra-ization of Philanthropy." *The Wall Street Journal* (October 28, 2011). http://www.manhattan-institute.org/html/miarticle.htm?id = 7569#.UT9rqFetqM0

PHILANTHROPY AND THE FEDERAL INCOME TAX:
SHOULD OUR REPUBLIC SUBSIDIZE TOCQUEVILLE'S DEMOCRACY?

Robert E. Atkinson, Jr.

The U.S. Internal Revenue Code's charitable exemption and deduction clearly treat philanthropy favorably; the question for tax theory has always been why, and how well. The traditional subsidy theory has offered no means of comparing the relative goodness of one philanthropic purpose with another, or of comparing philanthropic providers of a good or service with alternative suppliers in the for-profit or governmental sectors. It simply has accepted that all philanthropy, whatever that is, is good, and deserving of favorable tax treatment.

This seems, on its face, to be a serious deficiency, if not an outright vice. On closer inspection, however, we can see it to be an odd virtue born of the need to fit our understanding of charity to our capitalist market economy on the one hand and our liberal democratic polity on the other. If our philanthropy is to be both consumerist and populist, it must be agnostic about both human need and human excellence; it must leave the specification of philanthropy's dual traditional aims to the market and the electorate. That is the implicit genius of the traditional subsidy theory: it does not fail to specify the goodness of particular philanthropic purposes; it simply leaves that decision to the philanthropic participants themselves, bowing deeply to Tocquevillean democracy.

But we also need to see that that obeisance is a choice our republic need not make—indeed, should not make, if it is to honor both philanthropy's better traditions and its own. We need not conform our philanthropy to the two-sided mold of our current economics and politics if we prefer other politics and other

AUTHOR'S NOTE: This article radically abbreviates a longer article of the same title, which in turn comprises two chapters of a book manuscript, "Tax Favors for Philanthropy: Should our Republic Underwrite deTocqueville's Democracy?" For full citations and fuller development of the argument, please refer to the original article, now available on SSRN.

Atkinson, Jr., Robert E. 2012. Philanthropy and the Federal Income Tax: Should our Republic Subsidize Tocqueville's Democracy? *Conversations on Philanthropy IX*: 9-21. ISSN 1552-9592 ©The Philanthropic Enterprise.

economics. Borrowing from deep traditions in our philanthropic sector, we can, instead, see this mold as an iron maiden, profoundly damaging to what we believe best in both our society and ourselves. The function of philanthropy, from this neo-classically republican perspective, is not to conform to this world but to transform this world into its own image. At the very least, that would give both market capitalism and liberal democracy a human face and a humane spirit; at the very best it would move our whole society past self-congratulating self-aggrandizement toward the public virtues of the American founders and the classical philosophers. Toward that goal, removing the federal tax code's underwriting of Tocquevillean democracy would not be the worst place to start (nor, alas, the easiest).

The Function of Tax Exemption

From a functional perspective, tax exemption subsidizes individuals' ideas about the public good. This new perspective on the traditional subsidy theory looks neither at the products charities provide nor at anything special about the way they provide them, beyond the fact that they are provided by philanthropic-sector organizations that are, by definition, forbidden to distribute net profits to any owning or controlling group. Instead, this perspective focuses on the way those goods and services are chosen by those who support their provision; that way of choosing is, in a word, individualistic. Citizens decide for themselves what charities to give to and, more basically, what charities to found. This very individualism is the focus of Alexis de Tocqueville's oft-quoted observations about Americans' inclination to form associations for what they take to be publicly beneficial functions:

> In no country in the world has the principle of association been more successfully used or applied to a greater multitude of objects than in America. Besides the permanent associations which are established by law under the names of townships, cities, and counties, a vast number of others are formed and maintained by the agency of private individuals.
>
> ... If a stoppage occurs in a thoroughfare and the circulation of vehicles is hindered, the neighbors immediately form themselves into a deliberative body; and this extemporaneous assembly gives rise to an executive power which remedies the inconvenience before anybody has thought of recurring to a pre-existing authority superior

to that of the persons immediately concerned. If some public pleasure is concerned, an association is formed to give more splendor and regularity to the entertainment. Societies are formed to resist evils that are exclusively of a moral nature, as to diminish the vice of intemperance. In the United States associations are established to promote the public safety, commerce, industry, morality, and religion. There is no end which the human will despairs of attaining through the combined power of individuals united into a society (1972, 1:191-192).

On this view, individual Americans, acting in voluntary collaboration, both define social problems and offer solutions to those problems. Americans define the good, that is, not by a nationally shared sense of "goodness" nor by the national recognition of social need, but rather by their joint action in voluntary associations. From this observation we can derive a Tocquevillean definition of charity: whatever nonprofit activity citizens say is in the public interest and put their time, money, or other resources into. As a matter of both liberal principle and constitutional law, the state cannot discourage this kind of associational activity unless the ends themselves can be made illegal.

But to say that the state cannot ban such associational activity is not to say that it should encourage it; to define Tocquevillean charity is not to prove that it is good. And so, too, the question of whether to relieve such public-spirited private initiatives from the burden of taxation, and further to relieve their donors to the extent of their donations is, necessarily, a normative question. Another critical feature of the Tocquevillean understanding of charity is this: the majority's decision on that normative question is conclusive. Thus the functional definition of Tocquevillean charity—whatever nonprofit project anyone wants to undertake in what they take to be the public interest—is matched with is normative justification: a majority of citizens believe that this kind of social action, even by political minorities, is good in general, and also worthy of particular favor in the tax system. In a democracy, as democracy, there is no other measure of the good. A majority can decide to grant this favor, or not; ours has granted it, and therefore it is good. The people in a democracy are, in principle, like God in a theocracy: their will is the law, and their law is right and good.

Subject to constitutional constraints (which are themselves subject to democratic revision), a majority of citizens can choose to support not only particular goods or services they themselves favor, but also those that their neighbors, even their neighbors in a minority, favor. This is, in effect, what it means, in the context of the special tax treatment of charity, to say that it promotes the values, or meta-benefits, of "pluralism" and "diversity." The traditional subsidy theory's odd inability to provide a substantive definition of the public benefit that it holds to be the basis of the exemption and deduction can thus be seen not as a failure but as a virtue, a bow toward Tocquevillean philanthropy.

A Critique of Tocquevillean Democratic Philanthropy

The people's will in a democracy, we have conceded, is like God's will in a theocracy: whatever it is, is right; whatever it seeks, is good. In classical normative philosophy, however, another question can always be put, to both the people and the deity: Is it good because they favor it, or do they favor it because it is good (Plato 1956)? A majority of Americans, at some level, must favor our Tocquevillean system of charitable tax exemption and deduction; they are entirely entitled to change it whenever they like, and presumably, if they disliked it enough, they would.

But that still leaves open this question: Is our system of exemption and deduction *really* good, or good for any reason other than its having been democratically chosen? Unless one is a radically reductionist kind of democrat, one can question its merits, in whole or in part. One's meat is, proverbially, another's poison. So, in classical political theory, one system's virtues are another's vices (Plato 1968; Aristotle 1943; see also Montesquieu 1977). And so it is, this section will show, with Tocquevillean philanthropy. We begin by identifying the kind of state that Tocquevillean philanthropy implies as its ideal complement, the minimalist state of libertarianism. We then note two critical biases that this libertarian leaning implies for philanthropy and its tax treatment. The first is a bias toward philanthropic as opposed to government providers; the second is a bias toward private contributions as opposed to public finance. But this relationship between Tocquevillean philanthropy poses a puzzle: Wouldn't a consistently libertarian position favor abolition of all tax subsidies to philanthropy?

This question, in turn, brings us to two fundamental points about the much-vaunted value that Tocqueville placed on philanthropy in America: he saw it not as the ideal but as a distinctly second-best arrangement. And he saw it not as a means of advancing the people's will, whatever that might be, but as the only means available to move the America of his day toward what he implicitly took to be the proper end of all societies, what he called "civilization." As we shall see, his desired civilization was distinctly neoclassical and republican.

As noted earlier, the current system offers no guidance to individual donors or voters regarding comparisons among charities or between charity provision and other provision. From a liberal democratic perspective, that silence may be golden. The point to note is simply that it leaves a normative gap here, as is the tendency of liberal democracy in general, under the liberal principle of neutrality toward life-plans. And here that silence is nearly total, which puts the liberalism reflected in our tax treatment of charity near the libertarian, minimal-state pole of the spectrum of liberal theory. Libertarians prefer the state to be silent on the relative merits of citizens' individual ethical systems.

This libertarian tendency of Tocquevillean charity is at least as evident in two other respects, by embodying unmistakable preferences on two very important issues. The for-profit, the governmental, and the cultural sectors are, to a very large extent, capable of producing the same goods and services. Thus, for example, organizations in each sector can and do operate elementary schools. So, more generally, funding for subsidized goods and services can come from voluntary contributions or coerced transfers, primarily taxes. Schools for those who cannot afford tuition can thus be funded by taxes or by gifts (or cross-subsidies). Tocquevillean philanthropy embodies a strong preference for both nongovernmental provision and donative financing. We need look at each bias, then at their interaction.

A charity need neither prove its superior efficiency in advance nor demonstrate it in operation in order to qualify for the exemption of its income; a charity is in effect simply presumed to be more efficient, economically or productively, than government provision. This implicit preference for charity over the state, in turn, shapes our culture; if we get what we cannot find or afford in the market from charity rather than the state, we come to expect it from charity rather than from the state. Thus the charitable sector grows, qualitatively and quantitatively, at the expense of the state. Predictions of the superiority of charity—its greater efficiency, its higher quality—become self-fulfilling prophecies. The tax system's preference for philanthropic provision, then, reflects demonstrably anti-statist, even libertarian, tendencies, tendencies not wholly apparent on its face but profoundly important in their cultural implications.

The tax system's preference for voluntary financing is, if anything, even more troubling. Tocquevillean philanthropy is biased against not only state provision of goods and services through its own agency, but also public financing of goods and services without regard to the provider. The basic problem with financing through voluntary contributions is this: that system taxes civic virtue and, conversely, subsidizes social shirking. Consider, again, the case of public elementary schools. Every fall, in schools across the land, the call goes out from individual teachers and from central administrations for basic school supplies or the money with which to buy them. Presumably, those who respond to the call are those who can afford to; so far, so good. Let's focus, instead, on those who do not respond. Some, of course, are simply too poor; others are quite able to respond but not especially forthcoming. They are, in effect, free-riding on the parents who do pay. Those paying parents are, then, paying twice: not just their "share" but also the share of parents who are able but not willing to pay (or thrice, if we count the share of those parents who cannot afford to pay). If, by contrast, the schools' necessary supplies were paid for with tax revenues, the poor could be exempted and the burden placed on all parents who are able, whether or not they are willing. Voluntary financing shifts the burden to parents both willing and able; it is thus a peculiar, if not perverse, surtax on their civic virtue.

Such examples could, of course, be multiplied almost at will; it does not strain credulity too much to imagine that the same parents who supplied chalk and construction paper yesterday are the ones shipping body armor today to their sons and daughters in Iraq. These are not, however, worst-case scenarios; both these cases involve at least some measure of public provision. Few openly doubt we should have a public army; only a vocal minority questions whether we should have public schools. As this last example suggests, opposition to public financing of goods and services may well coincide with opposition to public provision of those services. Behind proponents of vouchers for privately operated schools, at least some suspect opposition to public financing of education as well.

This last critique is the most significant. Here we need to see that Tocqueville's own praise of American philanthropy was profoundly qualified. It was, he quite clearly believed, the best we Americans could do; it is not at all clear that he believed it best by any other standard. Tocqueville wrote *Democracy in America* in the 1830s, nearly a century before the New Deal, not to mention the GI Bill and the *Brown* decision; he cannot fairly be faulted for failing to foresee these later developments. By his lights, America was, in its very essence, a democracy, free from the mixed blessings of England's hereditary nobility or France's always powerful, sometimes terrible, state apparatus. And ours, of course, was not a very liberal democracy at that: women were disenfranchised, African Americans were enslaved, and states had established religions. Tocqueville's praise of the central role of voluntary associations in American culture was grounded, we need to note, on the premise that Americans could get the goods and services they provided no other way. He saw America's dependence upon private associations not as the best imaginable social order but only the best that America could possibly achieve.

Behind what he remarked to be Americans' astonishing inclination to form associations as the response to the full range of perceived social problems, Tocqueville noted a distinctive element of the American national character:

The citizen of the United States is taught from infancy to rely upon his own exertions in order to resist the evils and the difficulties of life; he looks upon the social authority with an eye of mistrust and anxiety, and he claims its assistance only when he is unable to do without it. This habit may be traced even in the schools, where the children in their games are wont to submit to rules which they have themselves established, and to punish misdemeanors which they have themselves defined. The same spirit pervades every act of social life (1972, 1:191).

It was this engrained sense of self-reliance and distrust of government that made the promotion of private associations, in Tocqueville's view, critical to American democracy:

Nothing, in my opinion, is more deserving of our attention than the intellectual and moral associations of America. The political and industrial associations of that country strike us forcibly; but the others elude our observation, or if we discover them, we understand them imperfectly because we have hardly ever seen anything of the kind. It must be acknowledged, however, that they are as necessary to the American people as the former, and perhaps more so. In democratic countries the science of association is the mother of science; the progress of all the rest depends upon the progress it has made.

Among the laws that rule human societies there is one which seems to be more precise and clear than all others. If men are to remain civilized or to become so, the art of associating together must grow and improve in the same ratio in which the equality of conditions is increased (2:110).

Given American culture's entrenched dislike of government and American law's Constitutional rejection of a hereditary aristocracy, promoting private associations was, in his view, America's only way out of a kind of Cyclopean semi-barbarism. Reliance on private associations, then, was not just America's best way to become, or remain, civilized; it was our only way, a Hobson's choice, not a utopian alternative. In that, Tocqueville's thinking was implicitly Aristotelian; his virtues were functions of the institutional arrangements he thought we Americans could not transcend (Aristotle 1943; see also Plato 1968). He knew that the "ought" implies the "can"; surely he also knew that *le mieux est l'ennemi du bon.*

Democracy and Meritocracy

We now need to see another, much more significant, sense in which Tocqueville's vision of both American democracy and its philanthropy is, at bottom, Aristotelian. The phrase "to remain civilized or to become so" necessarily implies that Tocqueville has an end in view, a goal for all societies, including our democratic society, which is not to be reduced, even in our democracy, to what the people, or the majority of the people, want. For Tocqueville, child of the Enlightenment and the classics that he was, that end is civilization, "to be or become civilized." In giving content to that end, he most assuredly looked beyond America's Jacksonian democracy, back to Europe and back to Europe's past, particularly to its classical Greco-Roman past.

Tocqueville wrote, we must remember, in the era of Jackson's racist and rowdy populist democracy, scornful of both Hamilton's Bank of the United States and Marshall's principle of judicial review. Had he looked only a bit further back in America's own past, he would have seen evidence of quite a different culture, a culture itself more supportive of both classical and Enlightenment values. In recounting Americans' aversion to government, he seems not to have noticed the role of the state in the early development of some of the most "Ivy" of our universities, not least Harvard and Yale. In that respect, they quite closely, and consciously, reflected similar synergies and hybrid origins in the histories of all of the great universities of Europe—Oxford, Cambridge, Edinburgh, and the Sorbonne.

More significantly for America's future, Tocqueville might have taken greater notice of Thomas Jefferson's alma mater, the College of William and Mary, and his fondest legacy, the University of Virginia. William and Mary was founded very much on the European university model, as a hybrid of public and private funding and control. The University of Virginia was both more neo-classical and more republican. It was a creature of the Commonwealth of Virginia, and it was to be the capstone of a universal system of publicly funded education (Malone 1981, 243). It became the model, within a very few years, for state universities across much of the South.

Perhaps, we can now appreciate, Tocqueville should have looked ahead as well. From the perspective of the populist era in which he wrote, even as Tocqueville could not see back to Jefferson the Democratic-Republican, so he could not see ahead to Lincoln the Whig, advocate of an activist government, state and national, much less Lincoln the Republican, public opponent of popular sovereignty on the question of slavery (and probably private opponent of popular sovereignty *tout court*). His Grand Army of the Republic neither defended America against foreign invaders nor secured its independence from a distant prince; it crushed the effort of the legally enfranchised voters of the Southern states to establish, by majority vote, an independent nation of their own, even as their forebears and Lincoln's had done.

Lincoln may have had a vision of government "of the people, by the people, and for the people," but not without serious qualifications. He meant not to follow popular whim but to lead the people to a higher sense of themselves, individually and collectively. On the eve of the Union's unconditional triumph, in his second inaugural address, he commended the people to "the better angels of our natures." To ensure that the Union triumphed, and triumphed unconditionally, Lincoln's administration suspended the writ of *habeas corpus*, aggressively suppressed the rival press, and dispatched troops to New York and other Northern cities to press reluctant citizens into the Grand Army of the Republic.

And Lincoln the Republican, remember, was not only the author of the Emancipation Proclamation and the savior of the Union. He was also the signer of the Morrill Act, which established the land-grant college system. Remember, too, that the land grant colleges now count among their number not just my grandfather's Clemson and my brother-in-law's North Carolina State, but also the Ivy League's Cornell. Designed to focus on agricultural and mechanical subjects, very much as Tocqueville would have recommended (1972, 2:154)[1], all land grant colleges eventually developed liberal arts majors and required humanities courses even for students in their more "practical" programs. Nor did this development cost them their popular support or public subsidies.

The federal court order that admitted James Meredith to the University of Mississippi, like the GI Bill that funded my father's veterinary studies and flooded the Ivy League with students far more diverse than their pre-war Yankee clientele, was, in one sense, distinctly egalitarian: both struck down or at least diminished, directly or indirectly, distinctions of race, creed, ethnicity, and even wealth.

And yet, in an even deeper and more significant sense, the GI Bill and the desegregation orders were neither egalitarian nor democratic, but meritocratic and republican. The doors that they opened, literally and figuratively, were the doors of universities. Even after the invidious, extraneous bars of race, religion, and poverty had been removed, one essential, salutary bar remained: individual talent. To attend the college of their choice, James Meredith, my father, and your parents or grandparents had to pass more or less rigorous admissions requirements. In that sense, universities are distinctly undemocratic; no adult citizen can be denied a vote in a liberal democracy, but many are regularly denied seats in our public universities. Even after admission, a student's success depends on nondemocratic, as well as nonmarket, criteria. The student body does not vote on the curriculum, nor are individual students entirely free to choose what courses they will take. They follow a prescribed course, a course traditionally set to include at least a basic knowledge of the culture of the West and the world, all the way back to their beginnings.

That tradition of liberal education, of course, has been gravely damaged by the cultural radicalism of the 1960s and 1970s and the fundamentalism and multiculturalism of the 1980s and 1990s; it may well succumb to the consumerism and fiscal crises of the 2000s and 2010s. But, at least for now, the great bulk of our universities, public and private, secular and religious, are recognizable as the lineal descendants of Plato's academy and Aristotle's lyceum, of either Jefferson's University of Virginia or the Puritans' Harvard and Yale Colleges. Our universities, that is to say, have long been supported, quite generously until relatively recently, by a majority of our citizens, including many who never had the ability or the opportunity to attend university themselves.

My point? American democracy need not be indifferent to merit, even excellence. Our democracy, in our parents' time if not our own, has proved itself capable of promoting a distinctly non-populist, non-consumerist institution, the traditional Western university. And that gives us reason to hope, if not expect, that our democracy, properly prompted by "the better angels" of our philanthropic sector, may yet choose still further to distance itself from Jacksonian populism and modern consumerism, yet more fully to remake itself in the image of Jefferson and Lincoln's neoclassical republicanism.

A Neoclassical, Republican Philanthropy

On the foundation of this solidly American tradition, it is eminently possible to build a model of neoclassical, republican philanthropy. This alternative vision of philanthropy is neoclassical in two related senses. First, it adopts the traditional subsidy theory's two-part understanding of philanthropy's publicly beneficial function: on the one hand, to ensure that the most needy receive the basic necessities of life; on the other, to encourage the highest forms of human excellence. Second, it interprets both halves—relief of need and promotion of excellence—in neoclassical terms, terms traceable back through America's republican origins to the Greco-Roman classics themselves.

This second kind of neoclassicism has several implications. For one thing, it focuses on a particular vision of human excellence, the most fully developed individuals in service of the public good. This is, of course, the model of Plato and Aristotle, and one could find no better exemplars than Thomas Jefferson and Abraham Lincoln. For another, the principal focus of its relief program would be to ensure that no Lincoln fails to achieve his or her potential on account of humble origins. Every Lincoln, on this model, would be the beneficiary of the kind of subsidized public education that Jefferson envisioned. With Jefferson, in other words, neoclassical philanthropy would reject the libertarian myth that Lincoln was born in a log cabin he built with his own hands. Thus the relief of distress and promotion of excellence are essentially different aspects of the same neoclassical republican goal: enable everyone in the Republic to become a leader of the Republic.

As this reference to Jefferson's educational ideal suggests, this neoclassical version of philanthropy would have no particular preference for philanthropic as opposed to state provision of essential services, either in the form of the relief of distress or the promotion of excellence. It would, in other words, seek the most efficient provider in terms of real productive efficiency, without the current system's heavy hand on the private side of the scale. And it would have a preference for public rather than private funding, taking into account the analysis, above, of the fundamental unfairness of private funding's "double tax" on virtue.

Finally, like both classical republican philosophers and the founders of the American republic, neoclassical republican philanthropy would be essentially secular, although not necessarily atheistic.[2] Any argument in favor of a particular form of relief or promotion of excellence would have to be made in secular terms. Private religious opinions and purported divine revelations would be respected, even legally protected, but they could not form the basis of the laws of the Republic.

The neoclassical republican philanthropy outlined here implies a very different treatment under the federal income tax code from the code's present preferential treatment of Tocquevillean philanthropy. The most salient differences would be on the points at which our neoclassical critique found the current system to be problematic: its explicit embrace of alternative visions of the public good, its implicit assumption of the efficiency of private service providers, its implicit preference for funding public benefits with private donations instead of progressive taxes, and, as taken up in a longer treatment of these problems, its constitutionally suspect subsidy of religion (Atkinson 2011a).

The net effects of moving from the present subsidy of Tocquevillean philanthropy to a system of neoclassical republican philanthropy would be both a substantially smaller philanthropic sector and a substantially more restricted charitable exemption and deduction. Both would be displaced by the expansion of direct state provision of publicly beneficial goods and services, financed by appropriately increased and properly targeted taxes. This should mean both more publicly beneficial goods and services, as taxation addresses the free-rider problem of private contributions, and more equitable sharing of their costs, as taxation based on ability to pay replaces the current system's implicit double tax on virtue.

But here we must sound a serious, even proverbial reservation: The best is the enemy of the good, or will be, in the case of philanthropy, if we are not careful. Moving from the present system of Tocquevillean philanthropy to a neoclassical republican alternative poses a serious problem of the second-best. In the face of that blunt reality, the second-best solution, sad to say, is that the present system of subsidizing Tocquevillean philanthropy will have to stay pretty much as it is until the climate for progressive tax increases improves.

This is not to say that we who would advance Lincoln's republic have nothing to do but await the political millennium. In the neoclassical republican ideal, a primary function of both private philanthropy and the state is to educate citizens about public affairs. Promoting public debate about the dubious subsidy of Tocquevillean democracy is thus at least a step in the neoclassical republican direction. It will be a long haul, but all hauls begin the same way: shouldering the burden, striding forward with clear directions about the right path.

NOTES

[1] Tocqueville's views on education in a democracy were hardly what we would call democratic:

> It is evident that in democratic communities the interest of individuals as well as the security of the commonwealth demands that the education of the greater number should be scientific,

commercial, and industrial rather than literary. Greek and Latin should not be taught in all the schools; but it is important that those who, by their natural disposition or their fortune, are destined to cultivate letters or prepared to relish them should find schools where a complete knowledge of ancient literature may be acquired and where the true scholar may be formed. A few excellent universities would do more towards the attainment of this object than a multitude of bad grammar-schools, where superfluous matters, badly learned, stand in the way of sound instruction in necessary studies (1972, 2:63).

[2] As I argue elsewhere, the same values that inform neoclassical republicanism can easily be found in the Scriptures and traditions of the West's three Abrahamist faiths, Judaism, Christianity, and Islam. See Atkinson, "The Future of Philanthropy" (2011b).

REFERENCES

Aristotle. 1943. *Politics*. Trans. Benjamin Jowett. New York: Random House.

Atkinson, Jr., Robert E. 2011a. "Tax Favors for Philanthropy: Should Our Republic Underwrite de Tocqueville's Democracy?" (working papers series, FSU College of Law, Public Law Research Paper No. 541). http://papers.ssrn.com/sol3/papers.cfm?abstract_id = 1924474

______. 2011b. "The Future of Philanthropy: Questioning Today's Orthodoxies, Re-Affirming Yesterday's Foundations." (working papers series, FSU College of Law, Public Law Research Paper No. 542). http://papers.ssrn.com/sol3/papers.cfm?abstract_id = 1924479

Malone, Dumas. 1981. *Jefferson and His Time: The Sage of Monticello*. Boston: Little, Brown.

Montesquieu, Charles de. 1977. *The Spirit of the Laws 13*. Trans. Thomas Nugent. Berkeley: University of California Press.

Plato. 1956. *Euthyphro*. Trans. F. J. Church. 2nd revised ed. New Jersey: Prentiss Hall.

______. 1968. *The Republic of Plato*. Trans. Allan Bloom. New York: Basic Books, Inc.

Tocqueville, Alexis de. 1972. *Democracy in America*. 2 vols. New York: Alfred A. Knopf.

THE GOOD, THE BAD,
AND THE CHARITABLE

Adam G. Martin

Robert Atkinson and William Dennis both critique the philanthropic tax exemption in the United States in a manner reminiscent of Augustine's early pleas for chastity: "IRS, grant me taxation, but not yet." Although both essays point to current problems generated by the exemption, the writers recognize that when bad policies are deeply entrenched, the exemption might serve as a coping mechanism. Each of the two essays thus sketches out an (effectively) ideal fiscal regime in which the tax exemption for charities is no more, as well as a few preliminary steps toward the author's ideal. Dennis helpfully dubs this sort of thought experiment "Rogge's World," in which we consider what the merits of a policy might be in a more sensible overall policy regime.

Like Atkinson's World and Dennis' World, my ideal policy regime lacks a tax exemption for charitable organizations. But I remain unconvinced of significant portions of their arguments, taking issue with aspects of each author's depiction and ordering of alternative policy regimes. In the interest of brevity I focus on the areas of sharpest disagreement. That means offering a critique of Atkinson's ideal (the Good) and a counter-critique of Dennis' appraisal of the current regime (the Bad).

In engaging with both authors, I think it is fair to refer to Atkinson's preferred approach as state-centric and Dennis' as market-centric. In using this terminology I do not mean to reduce important questions to a market-state dichotomy, but merely as shorthand for the distinction between charitable activities undertaken with public funds as opposed to those for which revenue comes from private property and the competition for donations. Whereas Atkinson wants to eliminate the tax exemption to bring charity and the state closer together, Dennis wants to do so in order to push them further apart.

Martin, Adam G. 2012. The Good, the Bad, and the Charitable. *Conversations on Philanthropy IX*: 22-28. ISSN 1552-9592
©The Philanthropic Enterprise.

Atkinson's Good Ain't So Good

Atkinson's World—his ideal of a Neoclassical Republic—is one in which the state abandons any "liberal neutrality towards various life plans" and instead actively promotes the cultivation of human excellence. He contrasts the value-neutral or pluralistic market model of philanthropy with a state-centric model that works toward a definite hierarchy of values, tightly linking underlying moral visions with the institutions that determine how philanthropic resources are allocated. To support the market model of philanthropy, he argues, is to affirm both value neutrality and the goodness of individuals' philanthropic decisions.

This position fundamentally misconstrues the nature of the market and of voluntary activity more generally. Correcting that misunderstanding exposes some deep cracks in the institutional foundations of Atkinson's World.

The driving force of the market is not the affirmation of individual choices, but the ceaseless push to eliminate error and discover better ways of accomplishing ends (Kirzner 2000). The relentless process of weeding out failed enterprises can hardly be described as equating given choices with the good. The market model of philanthropy is not identical with the market of profit and loss, but the freedom to experiment with various projects and the competition for charitable dollars allow for a significant measure of social learning and adaptation. Markets ultimately rely on dissent and critique rather than popular approval.

The problem of grappling with failure is the first crack in the foundation of Atkinson's World. Even well-meaning men who correctly discern Atkinson's favored hierarchy of values can make mistakes about the best way to achieve those values, and changing technology and circumstances can make today's effective solutions into tomorrow's clumsy failures. How, in his state-centric system, are such errors to be detected and corrected? The absence of any discussion of opportunity costs or tradeoffs is especially troubling here. Within the context of his paradigmatic philanthropic project of education, for example, every dollar spent widening the net to find a potential paragon of civic virtue is a dollar *not* spent deepening the education of potential paragons so identified. In Atkinson's story about double taxation there are only two groups: the civically virtuous who give and the free riders who do not give to causes that are assumed to be the wisest use of resources. He nowhere recognizes that someone might not give to project A because they believe that project B is more worthwhile, even according to a given system of ends.

Atkinson's only nod to concerns of effectiveness is his blithe assertion that "this neoclassical version of philanthropy would ... seek the most efficient provider in terms of real productive efficiency" (2012, 19). This is begging the question. More troubling, the next sentence goes on to admit that this regime "would have a preference for public rather than private funding." Far from enabling error correction, public funding has a strong tendency to entrench errors (Pennington 2011, ch. 6). It eliminates the opportunity for donors to divert their funds elsewhere and the incentive for competing philanthropic entrepreneurs to detect those errors in the first place. Public funding likewise slackens the incentive of the public-spirited to monitor the effectiveness of projects. Even if they know that services are being provided poorly—say in the case of ineffective public schools—that knowledge does nothing unless they can create a sufficient political groundswell to overcome the entrenched interests of current providers. In an attempt to solve the free-riding problem of funding, state provision creates a free-riding problem in project evaluation (Tullock 1971).

But even if the competitive pressure of the market for philanthropy does better at eliminating failures, Atkinson may object that there is no guarantee it will do so according to his preferred hierarchy of values. Some individuals will even choose to give little or not at all. All of this is true. There is no guarantee that private donors will choose according to a given scale of values. But this is equally true of his preferred regime.

A second crack in the foundation of Atkinson's World is this: once the power to subsidize his favored values is handed over to the state, there is no guarantee it will actually be used to support them. Any freedom of choice over means entails a freedom of choice over ends. This is no less true of discretionary authority given to political agents. Any set of decision rights allows the individuals holding those rights to pursue a variety of ends with them. Why should we expect a state empowered to pursue ends deemed public benefits to secure a Neoclassical Republic and not Imperial Tyranny or mere Petty Cronyism?

Imbuing high offices with wide powers is a dangerous price to pay for any vision of human excellence. But setting aside the obvious problems of power—that it can be abused, draws the ambition of the vicious, and can corrupt the virtuous—there is still something deeply troubling about the hierarchy of values that Atkinson extols. The "particular vision of human excellence" that he wishes to enshrine is "the most fully developed individuals in service of the public good" (2012, 19). This means, unambiguously, that the best and the brightest wield political power. The role of philanthropy in this regime is thus to "enable everyone in the Republic to become a leader of the Republic." The exercise of political authority is not merely instrumental to the realization of human excellence, but is constitutive of the highest forms of that excellence.

The deeply troubling exaltation of state authority is a cavernous rupture in the moral foundations of Atkinson's Neoclassical Republic. Whatever one may think of the possibility or desirability of a given hierarchy of values underpinning the institutional regime of a nation, this is the wrong set of values. At its *best*, political leadership is a weapon against tyranny or injustice. No weapon has ever been the key to human flourishing or civilization, but only a means to protect it from other destructive forces.

Excellence in commercial, philanthropic, spiritual, artistic, scholarly, and even routine domestic activities—the most meaningful sphere of life for most individuals—far outweighs the excellence of political life. There is a crucial difference between the exercise of political power and these other activities: it is by nature rivalrous. One individual can only lead the Republic to the extent that other individuals follow, and thus do not lead. By contrast with excellence in leading, and its corollary of servility (Wagner 2007, ch. 8), excellence in private endeavors leaves other individuals free to pursue their own excellence. Often—as is the case in market endeavors—the excellence of one individual even lays the foundation for the excellence of others. There is a telling omission in Atkinson's essay: for all his talk of merit, he does not mention the merit or excellence of the philanthropist. The good of charitable giving is subsumed to the political good as interpreted by agents of the state. That is no ideal worth striving for.

Dennis' Bad Ain't So Bad

Dennis' World is likewise not my ideal, but it is in the same neighborhood. Whereas Atkinson advocates abolishing the philanthropic tax exemption in order to expand the state's influence over philanthropy, Dennis more wisely hopes to diminish state control. He qualifies his call for abolition by imagining a regime of low, flat, and uniform taxes levied on all organizational and family income. In such a regime, making philanthropic enterprises tax-exempt would distort civil society more than it would nourish it. I concur.

However, some of the effects of charitable tax exemption in the current regime that Dennis dubs disadvantages are arguably—at least in that current regime— advantages. Dennis' arguments against the efficiency of the exemption basically boil down to two deleterious effects he claims it has. First, it leads to "ill-considered philanthropic investments" designed to minimize tax burdens rather than effectively achieve their putative ends. Second, it allows nonprofit organizations to "unfairly compete" with both for-profit businesses and families who offer competing services.

Kirzner (1985, ch. 6) distinguishes between entrepreneurial discoveries borne out of a normally functioning market process and *superfluous* discoveries engendered by fiscal and regulatory burdens. Superfluous discoveries are profitable only because of some government policy, and they are wasteful compared to options that would be profitable in the absence of said policy. For example, if the United States were to ban the importation of cars from Mexico, an intrepid entrepreneur might establish factories just south of the U.S. border in which cars are *nearly* assembled. The almost-finished work could then be quickly shipped across the river to factories on the U.S. side for final assembly. Although such production methods are wasteful compared to what would obtain were there no import restrictions, the cross-border workaround would still save resources compared to other plans that are proportionately more domestic.

The logic of superfluous discovery implies that Dennis' first and second deleterious effects of the tax exemption may in fact be advantages. It's true that charitable projects designed to minimize tax burdens are unlikely to be the wisest use of dollars toward advancing some genuinely charitable end. However, one must also consider where the tax money being sheltered would be spent once taxed. Economists are apt to worry about marginal units, the last additions to or first subtractions from a stock. Eliminating the tax deduction means eliminating some marginal philanthropic projects (projects their initiators deem just barely worth doing at present). Without the deduction, these resources would be shifted toward marginal tax-funded projects (projects presently considered just outside the scope of government budgets). Does the marginal poorly chosen, tax-minimizing charitable project tend to enhance human flourishing more or less than the marginal tax-funded project? One need not be a raving libertarian to recognize that, in the world we live in, such "distortions" which may be due more to motives of tax avoidance than beneficence may nevertheless improve welfare on net. On the other hand, one could imagine a regime in which the marginal tax dollar is not merely wasted but rather actively retards human flourishing or is used to violate human dignity. In such a scenario, maybe even the most wasteful charitable activities undertaken for the most self-interested of reasons could be seen as morally salutary. Han Solo is a smuggler, rogue, and scoundrel, but we cheer for him because he is not the Evil Empire. That intuition is surely right.

The same basic logic applies to Dennis' concern about "unfair" competition between tax-exempt and non-exempt enterprises. Fairness may be a concern in and of itself, but as a practical matter uneven hurdles to competition are better than uniformly high hurdles. When rules retard human flourishing, it is better that they *not* be uniformly applied, because exceptions allow at least some liberty. Corrupt license czars are preferable to principled ones, and a lax and uneven prohibition on imports is better than a rigorously enforced one. The same is true of an onerous tax burden. Generality is a quality of good rules, but it does not follow that it is a good quality of all rules. Only under a more benign fiscal state would generality—including eliminating the exemption—positively contribute to human flourishing.

But concerns about waste and competition, I surmise, are secondary to Dennis' deeper, third concern that special treatment makes philanthropy beholden to the state. Even if the tax exemption is a release from state control at any given point in time, it fundamentally politicizes charitable activity in a way that breeds servility and undermines the natural connection between philanthropy and other branches of civil society, especially markets. Tax-exempt status is a grant given by state agents, a boon to be bestowed on those who are willing to dance to the tune called by the state. The politicization of philanthropy is the most serious concern on which Dennis has put his finger. Unfortunately, the picture here is rather grim. Even if practitioners seeking favors did not politicize charitable activity, states throughout history have intruded on the domain of charity by making largesse a tool of social control (Jacobs 1992). The wall separating charity and the state has probably never been very high.

The silver lining is that, despite this omnipresent historical trend, there still exists a vibrant private philanthropic sector in the modern United States. Concerned liberals should seek ways to bolster its robustness in the short and medium run while seeking to make practitioners aware of the symbiotic relationship between market making and charitable giving. Without such recognition there is unlikely to be any lasting separation, much less a full divorce, between philanthropy and the state. For now, though, it is wiser to leave the tax exemption in place, even if it means living with nonprofit organizations of less than perfect charity.

REFERENCES

Atkinson, Jr., Robert E. 2012. "Philanthropy and the Federal Income Tax: Should our Republic Subsidize Tocqueville's Democracy?" *Conversations on Philanthropy* (The Philanthropic Enterprise) IX: 9-21.

Dennis, William C. 2012. "A Radical Reform for Nonprofit Tax Exemption: A Thought Experiment." *Conversations on Philanthropy* (The Philanthropic Enterprise) IX: 1-8.

Jacobs, Jane. 1992. *Systems of Survival.* New York: Random House.

Kirzner, Israel. 1985. *Discovery and the Capitalist Process.* Chicago: University of Chicago Press.

_____. 2000. *The Driving Force of the Market.* London and New York: Routledge.

Pennington, Mark. 2011. *Robust Political Economy.* Cheltenham: Edward Elgar.

Tullock, Gordon. 1971. "Public Decisions as Public Goods." *Journal of Political Economy* 79: 913-918.

Wagner, Richard. 2007. *Fiscal Sociology and the Theory of Public Finance.* Cheltenham: Edward Elgar.

TRADING IN TOCQUEVILLE: PHILANTHROPY IN AN ERA OF PHILANTHROCAPITALISM, LC3s, AND SOCIAL INNOVATION BONDS

Robin Rogers

William Dennis opens "A Radical Reform for Nonprofit Tax Exemption: A Thought Experiment" with a compelling quote from Richard C. Cornuelle's *Reclaiming the American Dream*: "Already in America, government is tightening its grip on the independent sector. It is challenging the tax-exempt status of foundations, making new efforts to 'regulate' almost all private groups. An independent sector regulated by its competition has, at best, an uphill fight..." (2012, 1).

Cornuelle's concern about foundations losing tax-exempt status provides the backdrop for Dennis' thought experiment on federal taxation and philanthropy: *What if the tax subsidy for nonprofits was eliminated?* Would this be a good thing? The answer, Dennis posits—at least in theory—is yes. But he recognizes that an abrupt end to tax advantages for the nonprofit sector might do more harm than good. Much of the infrastructure of the independent sector and the life choices of those involved with it, he notes, are dependent on the current constellation of tax incentives. Thus he offers this as a thought experiment with policy implications, but not as a policy prescription.

In 2012, substantive conversation about philanthropy, democracy, and taxation is important. There are numerous and controversial congressional proposals to alter the tax treatment of nonprofits and charitable giving. Nonetheless, there is a critical flaw in Dennis' execution of his thought experiment: it is based on an understanding of the nonprofit sector that no longer maps to reality. Most critically, Dennis omits any mention of philanthrocapitalism, B-Corps, LC3s, Social Innovation Bonds (SIBs), and the rise of billionaire philanthropists, all of which blur the boundaries between business, government, and nonprofits.

Rogers, Robin. 2012. Trading in Tocqueville: Philanthropy in an Era of Philanthrocapitalism, LC3s, and Social Innovation Bonds. *Conversations on Philanthropy* IX: 29-35. ISSN 1552-9592 ©The Philanthropic Enterprise.

Even in a thought experiment, these developments are too profound to be set aside. Many of the new developments in philanthropy have little to do with the idea of voluntary associations on which Dennis focuses his attention. Above all, these changes invert the power relations between philanthropy and government that Cornuelle identified. Instead of relying on government grants and subcontracts, as nonprofits have commonly done since the 1960s, philanthrocapitalism is premised on large foundations, such as the Gates Foundation, setting agendas and partnering only with governments that accept their agenda and match funds or promise to do so in the future. Foundations are arguably now "subcontracting" the state.

Blurring Lines

The New Philanthropy has profound implications for civil society in the United States. Bruce Sievers, in "The Philanthropy/Civil Society Paradox," persuasively argues that civil society emerged in response to the rise of the state. He writes, "[T]his emergent civil society, with its emphasis on individual rights, rule of law, pluralism, tolerance among diverse belief systems, and a commitment to the commonweal, provided a platform for the evolution of liberal democracy. Inherent in the scheme was a delicate balance of public and private power—an eternally unresolved tension between the public and the private poles of life. Without institutions and norms of civil society, and its underlying polarity, there would be no democracy as we know it" (2012, 4).

Concern about the death of civil society spans the political spectrum. But what Sievers contributes to a discussion of philanthropy and taxes is the idea that we move among different worlds in different spheres of social life—worlds with different rules, expectations, and incentives. A recent political exchange may help to illustrate the point. Mitt Romney recently suggested that taxes are a form of charity. The Cato Institute's Michael Tanner concurred: "Taxes are a form of charity.... We tax people because there's some use, some public good, for which they're needed" (*Washington Post 2012*). Garrett Gruener, a wealthy activist for higher taxes on the rich, countered, "Democracy is not a charity. It's an enterprise of all Americans to accomplish things that we democratically decide are important" (*2012*). The debates over taxation and the nonprofit sector, therefore, are as much about the nature and independence of the different sectors as they are about efficiency and fairness.

Sievers usefully borrows the concept of "the colonization of the life-world" from the German philosopher Jürgen Habermas to make the point that the "life-world" of civil society is different from that of government or business—and always in jeopardy of being colonized by either. This is very much in line with the concern expressed by Cornuelle that the nonprofit sector was at risk of being consumed by the government sector.

The new movements in philanthropy, however, could amount to a colonization of the nonprofit sector by the market rather than by the government. Therefore, the question of taxing the nonprofit sector should not be looked at as simply affecting the efficacy of solving social problems or maintaining the autonomy of the independent sector from the government, but as a quest to reestablish the appropriate tensions and power relations between the nonprofit sector, the government sector, and the business sector in order to maintain some form of liberal democracy in a very changed world. This balance goes beyond the question of how much to tax nonprofits and expands out into the new tax structures being developed to accommodate the blurring of the line between the nonprofit and for-profit sectors.

Assumption of Goodness

Discussions of the nonprofit sector tend to assume that philanthropy is by definition good. Within some strands of philanthropy—particularly the emerging mega-donor philanthrocapitalism—there is an astonishing code of non-criticism. Michael Edwards of Demos noted its "mock civility that turns honest conversation into Jell-O" (2010, 92). William Schambra, a lonely voice of caution, observes that one of the largest and most "successful" early philanthropic initiatives was to support eugenics, a fact rarely mentioned in polite philanthropic circles (2012). If Schambra focuses on the fact that human fallibility is a factor in even philanthropic acts, Robert Atkinson, in the second lead essay of this symposium, is focused on a much more procedural aspect of what is "good," asking how we can know that our current system of giving tax preferences for charities is good just because it has been democratically decided upon. Atkinson's well-argued essay "Philanthropy and the Federal Income Tax: Should Our Republic Subsidize Tocqueville's Democracy?" touches this third rail of charity, questioning what constitutes "the good" while also posing the more academic and theoretical question of the proper role of the state in taxation and subsidies. He further questions why there is an implicit assumption that nongovernmental provision of services is better than governmental. Within that discussion, he talks about a "free-rider effect" in which people who do not give may be able to unfairly profit off of those who do. He uses the example of public schools. Even in schools that are publicly funded, parents are often asked to give—and do give—school supplies. These supplies, however, are often then used by children whose parents did not contribute; this, he argues, amounts to two taxes—one voluntary and one mandatory. Few would blame the children, or the parents who could not give for legitimate financial reasons. Nonetheless, it is true that there are always some who will not give even when they can, but will always gladly take.

As an alternative to a taxation system that favors nonprofits based on the assumption that the "good" is whatever the people say it is, either through individual philanthropy or democratic vote, Atkinson argues that we should reject a preference for philanthropy over government provision, to promote merit, and institute a preference for public (tax) funding over philanthropy, to reduce the free-rider problem.

Innovations in Philanthropy

Although it is important to think about the impact and desirability of changing preferential tax treatment for nonprofits and philanthropy, we ought to make sure that discussions reflect the independent sector as it is and not as it was or as we merely imagined it to be. There are developments occurring now in the philanthropic sector that are changing the world.

Philanthrocapitalism, as I note in "Why Philanthro-policymaking Matters," the lead essay in *Society's* 2011 symposium, The Politics of Philanthrocapitalism, is a new movement that fuses large-scale charitable giving with business practices. Its core tenets are: (1) Economic elites should assume leadership in global social change through philanthropy. (2) Philanthropic money should be used to leverage other money (primarily government) in support of its goals. (3) Market tools can be used to improve the philanthropic sector. (4) The boundaries between for-profit and nonprofit should be blurred to enable the most resources to go toward the social good.

This movement is supported by many of the most powerful people in the world. Billionaires Bill Gates, Warren Buffett, and David Rockefeller have been organizing a group of the ultra-wealthy to give away half of their money during their lifetimes in what is known as the Giving Pledge. So far, ninety-one of the wealthiest four hundred people in the United States have signed on. Others, including the Koch brothers and Walton family, are actively involved in hands-on philanthropy. Bill Clinton's Global Initiative has facilitated and stumped for many of the changes advocated by philanthrocapitalists, including greater giving by the very wealthy and new financing structures such as Social Innovation Bonds (SIB)[1]. This unprecedented private wealth is being used for public policy purposes largely without accountability to voters or taxpayers even in cases, such as the following, where philanthropic donations are matched with taxpayer dollars to fund philanthropists' policy agenda.

Philanthropy has long exerted an influence on public policy, but today it is transpiring in many new ways. In 2011, George Soros partnered with Michael Bloomberg to give a combined $60 million (matched by city tax dollars) to start a comprehensive program to change government policies in eighteen agencies in New York City, called the Young Men's Initiative. Goldman Sachs then put in a $10 million investment-loan in an anti-recidivism portion of the program. This form of investment/loan is known as a Social Innovation Bond (SIB), and this was the first ever granted in the United States. Pierre Omidyar has pioneered new for-profit philanthropies. Eli Broad has famously and controversially set about changing American public education. Jeffery Skoll has been active not only in philanthropy but also in building an intellectual network to support the work of new philanthropists across the nonprofit, business and government sectors.

There are also new legal frameworks that bridge the nonprofit and for-profit sectors. LC3s are perhaps the most innovative. They permit socially oriented for-profit companies to have some of the legal and tax flexibility of an LLC but also to attract investments from foundations and private investors. Similarly, the B-Corps provide a framework that permits a for-profit company—start-ups primarily have utilized this—to put its social mission at the core of its business. B-corps seem to be focused more on building workable industry standards and practices for socially oriented businesses than LC3s.

Tax policy creates and changes institutions. Will the existence of LC3s change the relationship between for-profit organizations and foundations? Will B-corps and Social Innovation Bonds prove a double win by providing capital for social "good" and returns for investors, or will they permit for-profit investors to skim money from social programs that can be run cheaply, though not necessarily more effectively, while leaving financially burdensome programs and knotty social problems at the feet of taxpayers and depleted governments?

These changes in philanthropy correspond with the development of a global economy in which wealth is becoming concentrated among a small group of well-networked businessmen (and they are nearly all men). These men changed the nature of business and markets over the last twenty years by expanding technology's capacity and reach and creating what Thomas Friedman has called "the flat world" of international competition and cheap goods (2005). In part because of these changes, governments have become less powerful, allowing the market to begin to "colonize" the nonprofit sector as the leaders of the sector are increasingly men like Bill Gates rather than foundation professionals or the wives of wealthy men dedicated to tending to the female sphere of domestic problems with the money earned in the male sphere of commerce.

I'd like to see the conversation on nonprofits, philanthropy, civil society, and taxation initiated in the essays by Dennis and Atkinson continue. I propose, however, that we put Tocqueville, brilliant as he was, in the background and bring forward the issues of civil society raised by Sievers and Edwards. Let's take a page from Atkinson and Schambra and question the idea that everything done in the name of philanthropy is good by definition. Finally, I want to invite challenges to my assertion that the power relationship between nonprofits and government is reversing, with some nonprofits setting the agenda, in some cases even policy, for governments. Let's look at the complexity of philanthrocapitalism and what it means for civil society. Are the new mega donors, such as Gates and Buffett really doing anything different from the old corporate liberalism and philanthropy? I argue yes. LC3s, Social Innovation Bonds and other philanthrocapitalist innovations and ideas are significantly different from older forms of philanthropy. The world in which they operate is different too; its highest economic strata are more tightly networked and separated from local communities than they have ever been before. They are able to fund global change with a speed and breadth that their predecessors could not have done. Perhaps it is time to focus less on a Tocquevillean framework derived from a bygone social order and more on constructing new models that reflect the realities of the 21st century but also retain the values of liberty and democracy.

NOTES

[1] The first Social Innovation Bonds (sometimes called Social Impact Bonds) were granted in the UK in 2010 for a pilot program to reduce recidivism. The goal of the SIB is to provide private funding for new public programs and then generate a profit for the investors if the programs are successful.

REFERENCES

Atkinson, Jr., Robert E. 2012. "Philanthropy and the Federal Income Tax: Should our Republic Subsidize Tocqueville's Democracy?" *Conversations on Philanthropy* (The Philanthropic Enterprise) IX: 9-21.

Dennis, William C. 2012. "A Radical Reform for Nonprofit Tax Exemption: A Thought Experiment." *Conversations on Philanthropy* (The Philanthropic Enterprise) IX: 1-8.

Edwards, Michael. 2010. *Small Change: Why Business Won't Save the World.* San Francisco, CA: Berrett-Koehler Publishers.

Friedman, Thomas L. 2005. *The World is Flat.* New York, NJ: Farrar, Straus and Giroux.

Roger, Robin. "Why Philanthro-policymaking Matters." *Society* 48, no. 5 (Sept., 2011): 376-381.

Schambra, William. 2012. "Philanthropy's War on Community." *Nonprofit Quarterly* (March 12). http://www.nonprofitquarterly.org/philanthropy/21012-philanthropys-war-on-community.html

Sievers, Bruce. 2012. "The Philanthropy/Civil Society Paradox." http://www.hudson.org/files/publications/civilSocietyParadox.pdf

Washington Post. 2012. http://www.washingtonpost.com/politics/romneys-equating-of-taxes-and-charitable-giving-sparks-debate/2012/08/18/63bea3e6-e891-11e1-936a-b801f1abab19_story.html

TOCQUEVILLE OR AUSTERITY?
HEALTH CARE AND THE SOCIAL
COMPACT

John T. Thomas

Aboard the *Arbella* in 1630, John Winthrop composed "A Modell of Christian Charity," outlining a social compact by which the Puritan settlers in the New World might "be all knit more nearly together in the Bond of brotherly affection." Almost four centuries later, America's democratic society still rests on a tacit social compact enjoining us to seek to balance and maximize individual liberty, personal responsibility, and the public good. These essays by Robert Atkinson and William Dennis invite us to reconsider the function of government and the impact of modern tax policy on our long-lived social commitment to justice and mercy.

Atkinson and Dennis both take a narrow, but very important, focus on the role of tax policy on philanthropy. They reach the same conclusion: each would eliminate tax subsidization of philanthropy through exemptions (and probably through deductions), even perhaps the tax subsidization of all "nonprofit" organizations. Yet they differ greatly in their rationales for this conclusion and in their positive suggestions for how to better realize the American social compact. In place of the current system of tax subsidization of charity, Atkinson proposes a more progressive tax system that increases taxation and government management to provide the "public good." Dennis promotes a more market-based approach to both philanthropy and the identification and funding of the "public good." Both conclusions have noble and virtuous grounding, yet each author raises, but does not answer, questions that lie at the very heart of the social compact.

The "academic" questions the authors present include whether to end tax subsidization of Tocquevillean philanthropy and whether to continue government protection of family-funded perpetuities (such as those established by Carnegie, Ford, and Rockefeller in the early 20th century or those of Gates, Buffet, Broad, Soros, and Koch today). These questions can and should be evaluated through the volumes of more than 100 years of tax data and the history of a charitable tradition

Thomas, John T. 2012. Tocqueville or Austerity? Health Care and the Social Compact. *Conversations on Philanthropy* IX: 36-45. ISSN 1552-9592 ©The Philanthropic Enterprise.

in Christian cultures extending over two millennia. Perhaps looking at the historical record can help shape a serious, much-needed, and more broadly political debate on the role of government in realizing the social compact. Politics and social influence prevent strictly data-driven conclusions, but volumes of data are available to assess the comparative efficiency of private and public expenditures required by the social compact, and the historical record should inform our reflections on the present recommendations to eliminate federal subsidies for charitable activities.

I would like to explore the questions raised by Atkinson and Dennis by examining in detail health care provision in the United States.

The Fog of Accounting for Health Care Provision

Currently, the United States spends $3.0 trillion on health care each year; that constitutes 17 percent of total GDP and is heading toward $4 trillion (20 percent of GDP). The difficulty of comprehending the complex mix of government funding (direct and indirect), charitable donations, and private payments that fuels American health care clouds honest, transparent debate on the subject.

It is not easy to determine exactly what government spends on health care provision. In addition to direct federal government payments for health care, which comprises almost 25 percent of the federal budget,[1] the Internal Revenue Code currently provides for more than $1 trillion per year in "tax expenditures" (Congressional Research Service). A "tax expenditure" occurs when the government doesn't collect tax revenue otherwise due under the applicable federal, state, or local tax laws and regulations because another law either provides a deduction for defined expenses of the taxpayer (e.g., the charitable deduction) or an exemption from taxation of certain property or transactions as a result of the status of the taxpayer (such as property or sales tax exemptions). The Congressional Research Service and Joint Committee on Taxation have identified more than 250 categories of federal tax expenditures, with the ten largest representing more than $700 billion in "foregone" tax revenue to the federal government (CRS 2010 at 6).

To get at the whole story about government's role in funding health care, we have to dig deeper to understand the impact of tax expenditures. For 2010, the deduction for charitable contributions by individual taxpayers was only the ninth largest tax expenditure, at $36.8 billion (CRS 2010 at 6).[2] The largest tax expenditure of all, the exclusion of the cost of health insurance from taxable compensation, was $106 billion in 2010, and the exclusion of Medicare benefits from taxation was 8th, at $54.6 billion in 2010 (CRS 2010 at 6).[3] In addition to subsidizing health care by foregoing almost $200 billion annually in federal tax revenue from individual and corporate taxpayers, the federal government also foregoes approximately $32-35 billion per year by exempting interest received by taxpayers from tax-exempt bonds from federal income taxation, the bond proceeds of which benefit many nonprofit health care and educational institutions (CRS 2010 at 781 and 951). Government also provides direct capital investment reimbursement through Medicare and Medicaid payments, HUD, USDA, FNMA, and other GSE subsidized debt for nonprofit hospitals, nursing homes, and senior housing. Indeed, the vast majority of hospital beds in the United States were built with Hill-Burton Act subsidies to nonprofit hospital organizations. Further, these are only the *federal* tax expenditures; state and local governments forego tens of billions of dollars in property and sales tax revenue from churches and nonprofit health care and educational institutions.

It is thus clear that government subsidies and direct expenditures far exceed philanthropic contributions to health care provision. The Giving USA Foundation and its research partner, the Center for Philanthropy at Indiana University, estimated that charitable contributions from individuals, corporations, bequests, and foundations in 2009 totaled $303 billion (CRS 2010 at 762). Even assuming that a portion of the donations to religious organizations (approximately one-third of all giving) went to provision of health care by faith-based entities, charitable provision comprises only a small portion of overall health care spending.

With the federal and state governments providing more than $1.1 trillion in Medicare and Medicaid compensation, and tax subsidies for the private insurance markets, we must consider whether charitable donations, or more material, federal tax-exemption of nonprofit organizations, are required to protect and further the social compact embodied in health care provision. Another way to frame this question is to consider whether the nonprofit status of a health care entity allows it to fulfill the social compact promise better or differently than a commercial hospital or health care organization. Would health care be provisioned less, or worse, without nonprofit providers?

What Distinguishes a Nonprofit Health Care Entity?

Some of the largest publicly traded companies in the United States—-to be clear, taxable, for-profit companies—are hospitals or other health care organizations.[3] Some of the largest nonprofit corporations in the United States are also hospitals and health care organizations. On what criteria do we distinguish the two or find one preferable to the other?

Nonprofit health care entities do not have to meet an objective mathematical standard to qualify for tax exemption. To qualify for the federal tax exemption, a health care organization must commit to provide "community benefit." Historically, that specifically meant and generally still requires a commitment to treat all who present for care, regardless of their ability to pay (IRS Revenue Ruling 69-545, 1969-2 C.B. 117). But that does not mean the nonprofit hospital must provide free care; it merely requires a commitment to care for all, without socioeconomic discrimination, and to have documented charity care policies that provide discounts or free care, based on a patient's ability to pay.

Many states (but still a small minority) have specific, objective, charity care requirements. Texas, perhaps the best example, requires nonprofit hospitals to document and prove that they provide at least 5 percent of net patient revenue in Community Benefit each year. "Community Benefit" includes "pure" charity care and the unreimbursed cost of treating Medicare and Medicaid patients, and must equal at least 4 percent of net patient revenue (Texas Health and Safety Code, Section 311.045.). Dollars invested in community education, medical education, and research can be included in the remaining 1 percent. Unfortunately, even with objective standards and requirements, it is difficult to account for the true "public benefit" of Texas nonprofit hospitals, because hospitals are allowed to self-define income thresholds for qualification for free or reduced-cost services, making it difficult to apply a uniform definition of "charity care," in contrast to, say, "bad debt." Hospitals and charities are not incented or given legal or political credit for having poor business practices; thus it is important to measure "bad debt" as amounts hospitals didn't collect for their services from patients with insurance or the resources to pay compared to "charity care" as most purely defined.

Unlike Texas and other states, Congress has not adopted objective legal standards to justify a health care organization's tax exemption. Upon evaluating this question, the American Hospital Association and other lobbying groups urged Congress to require more reporting of Community Benefit provided by tax-exempt health care organizations. This led the IRS to adopt and require tax-exempt health care organizations to file Form 990 Schedule H reporting their Community Benefits. This policy and requirement for disclosure is an evolution of the policy and laws adopted by Texas and other states. It remains questionable whether meeting the minimal threshold of community benefit as defined by legislatures makes provision of health care by tax-exempt entities more efficient or more efficacious than provision of health care by taxable entities.

Likewise, mandatory data collection and transparency may help politicians and tax-exempt organizations "justify" the concept of the various tax-exempt health care "tax expenditures," but does it establish or prove greater access to health care services than if there were no "tax exemptions" at all? There is little evidence assimilated to validate whether the subsidies through tax exemption of health care entities actually do much to expand access.

Is Tax Exemption Necessary for Charitable Health Care Provision?

We might shed further light on the supposed necessity of tax-exemption for health care provision by looking at the history of charitable provision of health care. Perhaps the greatest philanthropists in health care and education in the history of the world are William and Catherine Callaghan, a childless couple from Dublin, Ireland. In 1822, upon Mr. Callaghan's death, he left his entire fortune, about £25,000 at the time, to a young orphaned girl who had lived with the Callaghans for twenty years before their death. This young lady, orphaned at age five, was named Catherine McAuley. She used her inheritance to start the Sisters of Mercy, an organization dedicated to the health, education, and general welfare of women and children.

The Sisters of Mercy was formed without any tax incentive and grew until 1913 without tax-deductible charitable contributions. Since the introduction of the federal charity tax deduction and tax-exemption, they have utilized and maximized philanthropy and tax-exemption to continue their growth. Today, Sisters of Mercy ministries are worldwide, and they include six of the largest health care systems in the United States. Combined, the health care systems sponsored by the Sisters of Mercy own billions of dollars of assets, earn billions of dollars of revenue, and treat millions of people annually, with faith-based health care services, regardless of the patient's ability to pay or faith background (see www.sistersofmercy.org).

There are countless other examples of successful health care philanthropy predating tax-exemption. Colonel C. C. Slaughter, an iconic cattle baron, at the urging of the pastor of the first Baptist Church of Dallas, Texas, provided the land and funding for a Baptist-sponsored sanatorium, medical school, and nursing school in downtown Dallas. That sanatorium is now Baylor University Medical

Center, the flagship hospital of the Baylor Health Care System, a multibillion-dollar health care system that provides hundreds of millions of dollars of community benefit each year. The medical school, now located in Houston, known as the Baylor College of Medicine, is generally recognized as one of the best and most important medical education and research organizations in the world. The Baylor University Nursing School continues to train nurses near its original location.

Tax policy had no impact on the creation of the Sisters of Mercy or Baylor Medical, nor on their indisputable success for decades. Tax policy, over time, certainly has had an impact on their growth and prosperity, specifically through the ability to issue tax-exempt debt and benefit from direct government subsidies for indigent care. Nevertheless, we certainly should question, as Bill Dennis suggests, whether these entities would, even today, have "net taxable income" after deducting all of their charity care and calculable community benefits over their long histories. Perhaps the greatest subsidy each has enjoyed is a "tax expenditure" equal to the amount of state property tax exemption received annually, as each organization owns millions of square feet of expensive real estate in high-property-tax jurisdictions. Interestingly, however, we might note that this tax expenditure comes at the direct cost of public education, as schools across the United States are financed primarily through property taxes.

In any case, we should consider whether, in the end, these charitable entities are markedly different in operation from those of their for-profit, taxable competitors. Is the cost of their services to payers and those that can pay any lower than among taxable, commercial entities? No. Do they hold to the business principle of "No Margin, No Mission?" Absolutely. Do they provide tremendous Community Benefit? Yes, and Baylor, based in Texas, has to document and prove it every year. But does this mean that commercial hospitals do not provide similar contributions to the provision of the public good?

Comparing Market, Philanthropic, and Government Provision

Atkinson and Dennis raise provocative arguments and models for eliminating government subsidies for philanthropy and tax-exempt benefits for charitable entities. Here I have tried to raise questions, not answers, about the potential implications of such a change in tax policy. The data and history prove, if nothing more, that path dependence must be considered and the issues are complicated.

Dennis' "Thought Experiment" has appeal, and as documented above, provision of health care has and can be supported by a market in which both commercially and philanthropically motivated entities operate side by side. Could market forces and more efficient payment systems in the market address the broader "requirements" of the Social Compact, allowing us to substantially reduce or eliminate indirect tax expenditures? The U.S. health care market, including its "nonprofit" players, today has so much private capital that it is debatable whether it is necessary to subsidize hospitals and large physician organizations (Mayo, for example, is a nonprofit, tax-exempt physician organization that owns hospitals) to provide access to health care services for the vast majority of the U.S. population.

The elimination of tax-exemption for health care entities would not mean the end of government's role in health care. It is not tax policy alone that defines and enacts societal obligations. There are always at-risk individuals and populations that may need help accessing care, and it may be that government "management" of this access through taxing and paying for care is desirable. The law that requires all Medicare providers to screen and treat all patients, including specifically women in active labor, who present to a hospital seeking emergency medical care (known as "EMTALA"), is a requirement for participating in the Medicare program and is not a requirement for tax-exemption—it applies equally to for-profit taxable hospitals and nonprofit hospitals such as those owned and operated by the Sisters of Mercy. Could such non-fiscal legislation combined with market forces be sufficient to address the basic needs of the at-risk population (emergency care). Dennis' thought experiment asks us to consider just such questions.

Turning to Atkinson's argument for replacing federal tax subsidies of philanthropy with a more progressive tax system, we are asked to consider a path leading to more direct government funding of health care. Direct government subsidies of health care through programs such as Medicare now have a long history, but it remains debatable that direct government funding and provision of health care services, in and of itself, has provided a high-quality, low-cost, efficient model to address the needs of society's at-risk population. It is difficult to contemplate federal and state budgets and expenditures well in excess of $1.25 trillion (at least half of the U.S. GDP dedicated to health care products and services) and not question whether there isn't already enough tax revenue and government spending in the system to honor the Social Compact, and to wonder instead whether these funds are being spent most efficiently and with the objective of maximizing access to care.

The question is not whether Atkinson and Dennis are on to something in questioning the necessity of preferential tax treatment for charitable entities; I would submit that *the* question is to clarify the role of government, which should hinge in part on an evaluation of the efficiency and efficacy of government-funded care and better delineation of where the market can fairly honor the Social Compact and where we may in fact need either "incented" philanthropy or "coerced" progressive taxation to achieve the greater public benefit of a population with broad access to the best medical care in the world.

The Interesting Case of Medical Research

Medical research funding provides a concise case study for delineating where incented philanthropy or taxation may be desirable to supplement market activity. Free-market (i.e., private) investment for basic, bench, early-stage medical research and clinical trials is all but nonexistent today. Due in large part to an inefficient, slow, and very expensive regulatory approval process combined with allies in the plaintiff's bar and a broken U.S. tort system, there is no financial return for private investment in early stage research. Indirect government subsidy through incented philanthropy and/or direct government subsidy from taxation are currently the only fuel for early stage medical research. Fortunately, Gates, Buffet, Broad, and Koch all take advantage of current U.S. tax policy and give generously to medical research, but even their large foundations do not supply sufficient fuel for this effort. Is there a danger in relying upon a few enlightened (or perhaps only tax-avoiding) donors to fund lifesaving and economically stimulating research? Should we trust only donors, who typically focus on very specific medical research of specific personal interest, to fund and thus "manage" medical research? The history of eugenics research in the United States certainly provides a cautionary tale about the selection process in medical research, and this cautionary tale applies to both private and publicly funded research. Is there a need for a broader public process for supporting critical research on unpopular causes or rare "orphaned" diseases?

Conclusion

Can a decentralized philanthropy help us address such challenges? Isn't that the question both Atkinson and Dennis are asking? What is the balance among market, philanthropic, and government action in a free society? Can markets provide for all public goods without support of philanthropy? Can voluntary beneficence help us realize our social compact without financial incentives? Where the market will not fund and philanthropy does not provide, can we reach a broad public consensus about what we should support with indirect or direct government spending? What aspects of health, education, and welfare should we leave to philanthropists such as McAuley and Slaughter, motivated by God or their own human existence, and not tax policy, and where should society as a whole enforce broad funding participation, albeit in a manner that is most efficient and most necessary?

These questions are not only important philosophically, but must be considered anew in today's fiscal environment. Health care and Social Security spending, to meet the political "promises" made over the past one-hundred years, will rapidly consume U.S. federal, state, and local budgets, leaving little left over for other government functions such as infrastructure renewal, education, and national defense. We live in a world of abundance, but our resources remain limited and choices are always necessary. Honest, data-driven analysis is needed now more than ever in our public discourse. As we proceed to make hard decisions, we should not abandon our political principles, but we should bear in mind that Americans have proven time and again our mutual commitment to promote the general welfare, and that American philanthropy has always been a substantial contributor to our economic wealth, liberty, and public good, even before it was incented through tax policy. The choice before us may be to reclaim Tocqueville's republic or to prepare for European-style austerity.

NOTES

[1] U.S. federal appropriations for the Department of Health and Human Services for FY 2012 were $860 billion, out of total appropriations of $3.5 trillion. For comparison, the total for the Department of Defense was $688 billion.

[2] The Congressional Research Service assigns philanthropic subsidies to three categories classified by the recipient of the tax-deductible charitable donation: educational institutions ($5.1 billion), health care organizations ($2.5 billion), and all other charities ($29.2 billion) (CRS 2010 at 665, 759, and 785).

[3] The Kaiser Foundation estimates the federal tax expenditure was $225 billion in 2008. Levitt, "A Primer on Tax Subsidies for Health Care," Kaiser Foundation, Kaiser.edu, April 2009.

REFERENCES

Atkinson, Jr., Robert E. 2012. "Philanthropy and the Federal Income Tax: Should our Republic Subsidize Tocqueville's Democracy?" *Conversations on Philanthropy* (The Philanthropic Enterprise) IX: 9-21.

Congressional Research Service. *Tax Expenditures: Compendium of Background Material on Individual Provisions.* Committee on the Budget, United States Senate, December 2010 (Hereinafter "CRS 2010"), "Letter of Transmittal," III.

Dennis, William C. 2012. "A Radical Reform for Nonprofit Tax Exemption: A Thought Experiment." *Conversations on Philanthropy* (The Philanthropic Enterprise) IX: 1-8.

SECOND THOUGHTS ON THE TAX TREATMENT OF AMERICAN PHILANTHROPY

John E. Murray

The essays by William Dennis and Robert Atkinson suggest possible reforms of the tax treatment of American philanthropy. In this commentary I review and critique their proposals and identify some further problems these potential tax code changes would cause.

As things currently stand, nonprofit entities enjoy two kinds of tax advantages over for-profit entities. These roughly correspond to the expense and revenue sides of the nonprofit balance sheet. Nonprofit corporations need not pay income tax, need not pay property tax on the land and buildings they work in, and often need not pay sales tax. Regarding income (and donated capital) for nonprofits, donations to nonprofits enjoy tax-deductible status. These arrangements have grown up over a number of years through a variety of motivations—a classic camel as a horse put together by a committee.

Not So Different After All

One problem with this differential tax treatment is that nonprofit entities may not be quite as distinct from their for-profit counterparts in real life as they seem to be in the tax code. The distinction between nonprofits and for-profits is based on a combination of their purposes and the disposition of remaining funds after costs are paid out of revenues. Essentially, if the IRS deems the mission of a corporation to be a charitable one, broadly defined, and the residual claimant to any profits is the enterprise itself, the entity may be registered as a nonprofit. It makes little difference that some activities of a nonprofit might be more or less identical to those of a for-profit. Art museums operate small restaurants that can compete with nearby commercial restaurants. Goodwill Industries solicits donations of used cars that they refurbish and auction, much like any other used car dealer. The primary mission of such nonprofits, though, is supposed to be

Murray, John E. 2012. Second Thoughts on the Tax Treatment of American Philanthropy. *Conversations on Philanthropy* IX: 46-52. ISSN 1552-9592 ©The Philanthropic Enterprise.

something in the public interest: to display great art to the public or to provide job training to the handicapped, for example. In addition to business activities, the financial strategies of for- and nonprofit firms also bear a close resemblance. Reinvestment of non-distributed profits is a common strategy of private, for-profit firms as well as nonprofits. The nonprofit's goal is not to earn profits for its owners, but it cannot run in "the red" consistently over a long period either, so striving for income to regularly exceed expenses is a necessity.

Further muddling the picture are situations in which for-profits and nonprofits are in direct competition with each other. As Dennis notes, art, science, and history museums often operate bookstores that sell titles related to the museum's exhibits. The impact of such competition is complex. On the one hand, tax-exempt status helps nonprofits compete against other bookstores; on the other, it was not museum bookstores living on impulse purchases that killed Borders. A thornier case in the same industry, however, involves university and privately operated stores that sell expensive textbooks to students. Why the university operation should not be taxed while the private firm next door pays taxes has no clear rationale.

In some industries for-profits and nonprofits contribute to more or less the same production process, but with no clear *a priori* rationale for the profit-making status of each component. Consider the health care industry. Not only do for-profit hospitals compete directly with nonprofits, but it is unclear why nonprofit hospitals enjoy tax-exempt status while closely related pharmaceutical and equipment manufacturers, physician practices, and health insurers bear the usual tax liabilities. Whatever a hospital does to contribute to public health and well-being, it could do little of it without surgical equipment, drugs, doctors, and money.

The point of these observations is to note that whether an enterprise is by some standard primarily philanthropic or primarily profit-making is a judgment call. In our polity we have left this judgment to the IRS. The papers presented here raise the question of whether that is the best we can do. Both authors, but particularly Atkinson, emphasize that there are two kinds of charitable activity. One promotes excellence in human creative activities, a good example of which would be an art museum; the other promotes the well-being of the poor and unfortunate, such as a soup kitchen. A vigorous civil society provides for both, and as things stand in the United States, both types of enterprises receive the same tax treatment, which is to say for the most part they are exempted from payment of most taxes (through the corporate tax-exemption), and gifts reduce their donors' tax liabilities (through the personal charitable deduction). In the end, however, Dennis and Atkinson present two very different alternative reforms.

Dennis proposes that the preferential treatment of nonprofits is unneeded and that they should receive identical tax treatment as for-profits. Atkinson proposes that tax exemptions be narrowed to the types of philanthropic activities that promote "neoclassical republican" ideals. I suggest that Atkinson's proposed reforms are poorly supported in argument, unclear in intent and operation, and overall a complete nonstarter. On the other hand, Dennis' proposals seem well-grounded in argument and at least worth considering in part.

New, Uneven Burdens

Dennis proposes that both culturally creative and social welfare enterprises be taxed, and taxed in similar fashion, though at a lower corporate rate than currently prevails. I think there are hidden problems in this proposal that perhaps not even Dennis would want to see come to pass. The hidden problems concern the distinction between the two kinds of philanthropies. The charities that promote excellence tend to be rich, and those that provide social services tend not to be rich. Well-endowed foundations, hospitals, and universities, as well as nationally known charities such as the Red Cross or the USO, could probably manage the increase in their costs that taxing would represent, without dramatic consequences. On the other hand, the truly Tocquevillean efforts, such as local soup kitchens, churches, Boy Scout troops, Little Leagues, homes for the mentally challenged, and the like, would find the increased fixed costs that new tax accounting rules would impose to be more burdensome. Little tax revenue would be obtained by taxing such close-run operations, so it is questionable to saddle them with new burdens of reporting and compliance. It would be reasonable to respond that such mom-and-pop charities spend about what they receive in donations, and so are likely to face little tax exposure under Dennis' proposal. Still, arranging to pay taxes accurately must be more expensive than applying for nonprofit status, and to that extent the costs of this proposal fall disproportionately on the smaller, Tocquevillean charities. In addition, wealthier institutions are funded and managed by people who already know how to minimize their tax exposure, and that kind of human capital would make it easier to minimize the tax exposure of their philanthropies. As a result, tax treatment of nonprofits would end up looking much like the current treatment of for-profit corporations: the largest find ways to avoid paying. A better way toward tax equality might be to eliminate the corporate income tax entirely and focus on personal income taxes.

Dennis points out another potential problem with tax exemption for nonprofits: the politicization of the process by which the government designates an enterprise as tax-exempt. At present it is much more likely that a nonprofit will lose its tax-exempt status through a paperwork snafu than because it offended the government. But the sword of Damocles is there, and the state could easily identify a nonpolitical charity as having violated some political rules that would lead to the loss of its exemption. An art museum might want to sponsor an exhibit that some find obscene or blasphemous—or it might want to cancel an exhibit some find obscene or blasphemous. The Boy Scouts might want to exclude homosexuals from leadership positions. An African American church might wish to invite an ordained politician to preach at a service. The possibilities are numerous. In each case, the possibility of losing its tax exemption may make a nonprofit less likely to act according to its original purpose, and more likely to submit to the government's desires when deciding on a public course of action. If exemption were removed, the government could no longer threaten a charitable entity with dire financial consequences. Charities then could do as they pleased without concern for the state's reaction, at least in tax code terms. Uniform taxation of for- and nonprofits might actually, then, lead to a greater degree of free speech. Another rather indirect benefit would be the end of abuse of nonprofit status, as businesses such as the National Football League and various political groups were reclassified as for-profits (*Forbes* 2012). Still, as I urge above, we should hesitate to give the state one more reason to impose new kinds of taxes. Dennis' arguments for equal treatment, which I extend here to First Amendment considerations, could easily be seen by government tax authorities as an opportunity to raise additional revenue from an unexpected source. Recently, European governments have proposed taxing church properties—primarily Catholic (*Washington Post 2012*). Local 5officials note that the Church holds substantial properties in its churches, schools, hospitals, and other operations, and they argue that "costs of the crisis should be borne equally" by Church and people alike. However, it is not clear that the European fiscal crisis is a result of the churches contributing too little instead of the state spending too much. In addition, Catholic Church assets, like many of those belonging to charities, are illiquid and probably in the best hands available to manage them. Should the Vatican really sell the Sistine Chapel to Disney, so that Italian or European Union politicians can have more tax revenues to spend on their cronies?

Advantage: State

This question brings us to Atkinson's proposal, which in effect might actually accomplish just such a political takeover of cultural endowments. Atkinson proposes that the deep problem is not that nonprofits are tax-exempt but that the *wrong* nonprofits are tax-exempt. In place of the messy and very Tocquevillean diversity that characterizes the present-day nonprofit sector, he would organize tax favoring of charities according to "neoclassical republican principles." This dispensation would not favor just any old charity, but would recognize only "the most efficient provider in terms of real productive efficiency." And which organizations must surely be among those most efficient providers in terms of real productive efficiency? They would not likely be religious, as such entities are encumbered with those ridiculous "purported divine revelations." In Atkinson's view, removal of "the current system's heavy hand on the private side of the scale" would make the logical choice of manager the state (2012, 19).

The expansive array of problems inherent in this notion begins with questions regarding the standard by which nonprofits are to be judged. Apparently Atkinson is counting on the revelation of some esoteric expertise in devising a metric for efficiency in charitable service provision that has not been revealed to other mortals. Here we run squarely into the economic problem of nonprofit management: there is no robust way to determine outputs of philanthropic activity, and hence no such measure of "real productive efficiency" exists. Nonetheless Atkinson claims that private charity, by this nonexistent yardstick, falls well short of government provision of said services. This is simply argument by assertion, and Atkinson does not even offer any examples. Is Yale less productively efficient than Berkeley? Is the Cleveland Orchestra brass section less productively efficient than the Marine Corps Band? Are church-run soup kitchens less productively efficient than school lunches? Perhaps the best lesson to be drawn from Atkinson's essay is that we might expect dire consequences for the nonprofit sector if experts are put in charge of revising our tax code.

I would also caution the reader to judge with great care the few factual tidbits that Atkinson's essay does adduce in support of its thesis, which is in essence a new apologetic for the ubiquitous paradigm of "public-private partnerships." Much as President Obama recently remarked that the entrepreneur is not responsible for his own success, Atkinson proposes that government has played an important role in the development of institutions such as Yale University that was overlooked by Tocqueville. Indeed, the colony and then state of Connecticut proved to be a generous donor to the school, but to paraphrase Mickey Mantle on naming his son Mickey Jr., at that time Yale wasn't Yale yet. Yale was similar to many such collegiate institutions that hopeful towns founded as a way to draw people in, and as such was indeed a Tocquevillean venture. The early Yale College was a struggling school for prospective Congregational clergy, at a time when Congregational institutions throughout the state were subsidized. By the time Tocqueville published the first volume of *Democracy in America* both Massachusetts and Connecticut had disestablished the Congregational church. Yale's success, then, depended on the success of its early administrations in developing a workable business strategy that brought together market forces (students eager to learn, books being published, the possibility of large-scale construction, etc) and the philanthropic motivations of Congregationalist donors and others.

Atkinson also profoundly misrepresents Thomas Jefferson's approach to publicly funded education. Jefferson did not found the University of Virginia simply to have a taxpayer-supported university that he could view from his front porch. He wanted a university in Virginia that was dedicated to public service (rather than ministerial preparation) and could see no other way to provide one than to found it himself, with the aid of the state government. But Jefferson in no way believed that the purpose of public education was to "[e]nable everyone in the Republic to become a leader of the Republic," as Atkinson suggests. That is a facile reading of his intent; Jefferson was no democrat. He wanted to educate an elite. His university was to take in very few young folk from the lower sort. According to *Notes on the State of Virginia* (Query XIV; emphasis added), under Jefferson's educational plan "twenty of the best geniuses will be raked *from the rubbish* annually," after which the remainder of the rubbish presumably would return to being ground into dust (1984 [1787], 272). Jefferson's attitude toward the general populace of the Republic suggests why we need a tax policy that will enable a broadly based philanthropy to thrive, one that responds to social needs and opens real doors for opportunity by engaging as many people as possible as contributors of money and time to participate in the creation of culture and the provision of social welfare.

In the end, the broadening of opportunity will not happen by giving the state greater discretion in judging the merits of specific corporations or voluntary associations. The merit of such enterprises may not be in their economic efficiency but in the willingness of people to voluntarily participate in them. The entities that survive will be the real schools of citizenship. Whether we can realize the promises of American freedom to provide opportunity for all citizens by taxing nonprofits on the same basis as for-profits, as Dennis suggests, or if the status quo is the best we can expect, remains to be seen. This much is clear, however: to narrow the playing field by giving more power to government to determine which activities merit public preference, as Atkinson suggests, is a step in the wrong direction.

REFERENCES

Atkinson, Jr., Robert E. 2012. "Philanthropy and the Federal Income Tax: Should our Republic Subsidize Tocqueville's Democracy?" *Conversations on Philanthropy* (The Philanthropic Enterprise) IX: 9-21.

Dennis, William C. 2012. "A Radical Reform for Nonprofit Tax Exemption: A Thought Experiment." *Conversations on Philanthropy* (The Philanthropic Enterprise) IX: 1-8.

Forbes 2012. http://www.forbes.com/sites/beltway/2012/07/26charities-abuse-of-tax-exemptions-is-putting-their-special-treatment-at-risk/).

Jefferson, Thomas. 1984 [1787]. *Notes on the State of Virginia.* New York: Library of America.

Washington Post 2012. http://www.washingtonpost.com/business/economy/financially-troubled-cities-in-spain-consider-taxing-church-properties/2012/09/13/3b62c736-f842-11e1-8398-0327ab83ab91_print.html

PHILANTHROPY, LAW, AND ASSOCIATIONAL LIBERTY: A FEW REMARKS ON GIERKE'S *GENOSSENSCHAFTSRECHT*

Steven Grosby

> For only those organizations which emerge from the initiative and formative powers of their own members enhance the individual existence of their members. . . . It is as impossible to make a gift of independence in the economic sphere as it is in any other.
>
> —Otto von Gierke, *Rechtsgeschichte der deutschen Genossenschaft*[1]

Initiative and Philanthropy

The intimate and necessary relation between philanthropy and associational liberty has long been recognized. Perhaps best-known today are those numerous observations about the relation to be found in Tocqueville's *Democracy in America*. Examples include, "the most natural right of man, after that of acting on his own, is that of combining his efforts with those of his fellows and acting together," and, when he does so, the resulting "reciprocal action of one person upon another" "renews ideas, enlarges the heart, and develops understanding" such that the individuals "help one another" (1966, 193, 515, 511). The philanthropic orientation of action, expressed above as the enlarging of the heart and the developing of the understanding when one helps both oneself and another person, was seen by Tocqueville to be a corollary of the necessary, "natural" associational activity of one individual acting together with another. Key to this formulation of the relation—albeit a formulation pieced together from several extracts from *Democracy in America* but which nonetheless is faithful to Tocqueville's argument—is the recognition that the cultivation and expansion of both one's solicitude for another and one's attention to one's surroundings arise from the initiative to undertake, with others, the setting right of a perceived deficiency in a state of affairs.

Grosby, Steven. 2012. Philanthropy, Law, and Associational Liberty: A Few Remarks on Gierke's Genossenschaftsrecht. *Conversations on Philanthropy* IX: 53-73. ISSN 1552-9592 ©The Philanthropic Enterprise.

Less well-known than Tocqueville's *Democracy in America* but certainly historically and legally more illuminating about the consequences of individuals acting together as members of groups of various kinds is the work of Otto von Gierke on association or, as *Genossenschaft* is usually translated, "fellowship." In the first volume, published in 1868, of his magisterial four-volume *Das deutsche Genossenschaftsrecht*, completed in 1913, Gierke (1990, 22) provides us with a succinct formulation of the relation between philanthropy and associational liberty: the motivation for the formation of free associations is to be found in the "self-help of the people." Similar to Tocqueville's observations, Gierke argues that the philanthropic orientation of action is expressed when the attempt is made—through the initiative of either the individual or, of particular interest to Gierke, individuals as members of groups acting in concert with one another—to address a perceived deficiency in a state of affairs. For Tocqueville, the transformation of the individual that is associated with our understanding of the term "philanthropy" was evoked through phrases such as "enlarges the heart," "extension of the mental horizon," and "forcing the individual out of himself" (1966, 243-44, 511). For Gierke, that transformation was expressed through phrases like "enhance individual existence," as in the above quotation from volume one of *Das deutsche Genossenschaftsrecht*, and, more generally, through the idea (or *pace* Gierke and Frederic Maitland, the social and legal reality) of group (or corporate) personality developed throughout Gierke's work (see Maitland 1903; 1904; Pollock and Maitland 1898) and especially the arguments of his Rektor's address of 1902, *The Nature of Human Associations* (1935b). For both Tocqueville and Gierke, integral to philanthropy, *qua* philanthropy, is the freedom of the individual to act, by himself but especially in association with others—a freedom of action implied by the term "initiative." Gierke's quotation with which this essay began asserts succinctly the necessity of this relation between the initiative of the action of associational liberty and the philanthropic gift. The gift cannot bestow initiative, but philanthropically-oriented action may open space for or help elicit initiative.

Although initiative is surely key to both Tocqueville's and Gierke's understandings of philanthropic action and while we may, with very little reflection, agree with them that it is, the question remains, why is it key? Evidently there is an underlying philosophical anthropology to the relation between, on the one hand, initiative and, on the other, the "enlarging of the heart" or the "enhancement of individual existence" of philanthropic action. One assumes that this focus on the importance of initiative to the development of character must take as its point of departure an openness to the world as constitutive of human nature, *qua* human. To frustrate that openness, irrespective of however seemingly noble the goal of doing so may appear to be, is to undermine the important part of initiative in what it means to be human. Being open to the world is a beckoning to experiment, but it is a summons arising out of, or at least resonating within, the self to take initiative in forming a relation with one's surroundings. Thus, the corollary to acknowledging that openness is to recognize an anthropologically compelling engagement with—in the sense of modification of—one's environment. That is, the making of one's environment is a characteristic human activity, hence the significance of initiative. Finally, to take the initiative to modify one's environment is to take responsibility for that environment through one's action, and to take responsibility is to enhance one's existence: the enhancement of both one's self because one has taken the initiative to act, more often than not in concert with others, and the expansion of the self because of the now-established active relation with what has become, as a result, your environment. One's environment should be understood as including not merely one's modified physical surroundings but also one's modified *geistige* surroundings as a member of the emerging and sometimes consolidating association of individuals who have acted together to set right a perceived deficiency. This latter modification of one's intellectual, moral, or cultural understanding of oneself and others, and one's relation to others and the physical surroundings—expressed, once again, in Tocqueville's and Gierke's respective phrases "enlarges the heart" and "enhance the individual existence"—was of particular interest to Gierke and deserves more attention, especially in seeking a more accurate understanding of philanthropy.

The recognition of the significance of initiative for human character, expressed in the above quotation from volume one of Gierke's *Das deutsche Genossenschaftsrecht*, was also recognized by Tocqueville, when he wrote, "men must walk in freedom, responsible for their acts" (1966, 92). Thus, an alternative formulation of the evident, underlying philosophical anthropology is that the human character is enervated if responsibility for one's action is ceded to another, irrespective of the motivation for doing so. And here exists, in principle, the difference between philanthropy and charity. Both may involve help or assistance and gift-giving for a noncommercial public benefit, but the focus of philanthropy is on facilitating the conditions for the initiative of self-help to address a perceived deficiency in a state of affairs, whereas charity cannot avoid cultivating passivity by focusing on addressing the perceived deficiency itself, however noble the intention of doing so. More will have to be said about the legal frameworks that evidently correspond to this distinction between philanthropy and charity. More will also have to be said about that legal framework which, according to Gierke (and Maitland), is necessary for facilitating conditions of self-help because, by facilitating those conditions, problems arise concerning the scope or latitude of that self-help. However, before examining those legal frameworks, a brief and regrettably superficial discussion of the place of associations or fellowships in Gierke's work is required.

Associations and the State

There have, of course, always been natural or given associations, the purpose of which was largely self-help. Most notable is the family, but there are also those territorially constituted residential associations of varying sizes that Pollock and Maitland called "land communities" (1898, 510). The word "community" is generally and unfortunately used today without any precision whatsoever; it is used here to refer to those associations whose constitutive relations are perceived as being given or natural—that is, one's membership in the group is not a result of voluntary decision but rather, for example, through (the significance attributed to) birth. Furthermore, one's choices, as a member of a community—*Gemeinschaft*—are noticeably circumscribed by the traditions of the association. It is still the individual who decides and acts, but those decisions and actions largely (though of course never entirely) follow a traditional, even if occasionally conflict-ridden, pattern. (The latter is sometimes described by the term "culture.") Be that as it may, our attention is directed not to the "land community" of the township or the borough that "has come into being no one knows when, and exists no one knows why" (Pollock 1898, 510) but mostly to the free or manifestly voluntary association. I note, however, the very important, factually complicated phenomenon, acknowledged by Gierke, that these two forms of association—the natural or given and the voluntary—have often been and continue to be combined in various ways. Because insufficient attention is paid to this combination, a few observations about it are in order before turning our attention to examples of voluntary associations from different historical periods.

Examples of such a combination were the towns of the eleventh and twelfth centuries, where the "givenness" of the residential association becomes the "free union" of the city commonwealth such that individual communal fellowship is transformed into free citizenship (Gierke 1990, 19, 32). The complication of this development exists in the fact that varying aspects of the character of the relations of the earlier, given association (or, as often designated, "community") persist, are transformed, or reemerge with the later, voluntary association. To take another, geographically more extensive example, if we understand the "nation" to refer to a form of relation the referent of which is "the given," e.g. birth in the land, then we have the combination of these two forms of associations, the given or natural and the voluntary, when the nation becomes a national state through a willed compact (of one form or another) and law. In this example, the combination or intermingling of two different forms of relation would be, one, the patriotic attachment to one's own land, with two, adherence to the "rule of law," or— expressing the same combination in different terms—one, recognition of an individual as one's "fellow national," with two, the impersonality of a contractual relation with the same individual in the marketplace. Much unnecessary confusion has resulted from an unthinking adherence to a theoretically antiquated, *unequivocal* historical contrast between antique status (the given or natural) and modern contract (the voluntary).

Excursus: Gierke and Tönnies

"Voluntary" in the sense of willed or, in contrast to the natural or given, even "arbitrary," gewillkürte; or to use Ferdinand Tönnies' description of two forms of volition, Kürwille, an active volition, in contrast to the given or natural, Wesenwille. One understandably views the development of Tönnies' categories of volition and the associations that, according to Tönnies, correspond to each in his Gemeinschaft und Gesellschaft (1940) as being derived from his investigation into Hobbes and Spinoza, given the argument of Gemeinschaft und Gesellschaft. However, the influence of Gierke on Tönnies' formulation of the categories Gemeinschaft and Gesellschaft is, it seems to me, quite likely, given formulations of Gierke such as "these two forms of fellowship (the voluntary and the natural or given) must be regarded as the prototype and nursery for two groups of associations" (1990, 19). Of course, we know that Tönnies had read at least the first two volumes of Das deutsche Genossenschaftsrecht, as he quotes from volume two in Gemeinschaft und Gesellschaft. A thoughtful comparison of Gierke's and Tönnies' understandings of association, one that draws attention to Gierke's more subtle approach, would be rewarding. While, as noted above, Gierke acknowledged that these two forms of volition and their corresponding associations could be and were combined, the degree to which depended upon a particular historical period, Tönnies, at least in his influential Gemeinschaft und Gesellschaft, historically segregated the earlier Gemeinschaft, with its Wesenwille, from the later Gesellschaft, with its Kürwille. In the literature of historical jurisprudence, Tönnies' historical segregation parallels Henry Sumner Maine's (1970) historical contrast between status and contract, as argued in chapter 5 of his Ancient Law. For a recent comment on the burden of Tönnies' influential but, in my view, misguided historical segregation of these two types of association on our understanding of philanthropy, see Grosby (2009).

Having made these brief observations about the empirical combination of these two forms of associations and their corresponding relations, let us return to our discussion of voluntary associations. Examples of historically early and legally recognized voluntary associations were, according to Gierke, the ancient Roman burial associations (*collegia tenuiorum*) and the "free unions" of the early Germanic gilds, including among the latter the London peace gilds (for example, during the reign of King Athelstan, 925-40 A.D.), the *Judicia civitatis Lundoniae*, and other related developments of legal protection and pledges of peace, such as the *frithborgas* (see the Laws of Edward the Confessor).[2] Likely influenced by Gierke's research, Pollock and Maitland further observed that the early English borough was the ground upon which the voluntary associations of the early gilds flourished—for example, a borough's "knight-gild," which was constituted by men who had not grown up together as members of the community and hence presumably came together voluntarily, and which likely served as a model for the subsequent "merchant-gild" (1898, 191, 639).

These free unions or voluntary associations were, according to Gierke (1990, 26-27), acknowledged in a particular way by the State in England (and Denmark and areas north of the Frankish kingdom) that resulted in a combination of two types of legal and political order: "Fellowship" (*Genossenschaft*) and "Lordship" (*Herrschaft*). "Fellowship" refers to right-and-duty bearing associations, the capacity for which is inherent to the group—that is, an organization with an independent "legal personality." "Lordship" indicates that rights and duties come from above—that is, the legal existence of an association is conceded, granted, or even created by the Lord, Emperor, or State. (The historically modern expression and extension of *Herrschaft* is, in Gierke's categories, the *Polizeistaat*, an authoritarian moral State—authoritarian moral because the source of the rights and duties between individuals is inevitably or logically the State.)

Examples of the political expression of the legal order of Fellowship in early English history were the hundreds and the shires.[3] Later political expressions would be forms of federalism. In this regard, one recalls that it was Gierke (1939) who brought back from obscurity the work of Johannes Althusius.[4] Nevertheless, however noteworthy were such theoretical developments as Althusius' *Politica* and historical developments such as the Netherlands of the seventeenth century, it was English constitutional history that earned Gierke's (1990, 27) description of having achieved the compromise between the continued existence of the concept of Fellowship and the principle of Lordship.

To observe that the legal order of Fellowship indicates that voluntary associations, as right-and-duty bearing organizations, have, as such, independent legal personalities means that the early gilds, for example, had their own laws and courts, possessed their own capital, and, as gilds, entered into contracts (Gierke 1900, 52, 56).[5] Perhaps one gets a better idea of what Gierke was referring to by an order of independent legal personalities of free associations (*Genossenschaft*) in contrast to an order of dependency (*Herrschaft*) by considering, as examples today of free association, the Church and (increasingly less so during the last fifty years) the university as independent "juristic persons": organizations that have their own laws and courts and whose existence does not depend upon the state's concession or initiative. Another, even if modified, example of the legal order of "Fellowship" historically later than the gild, discussed by Gierke (1900, 196-204), was the joint-stock company, an organization with its own articles of association, its own capital, and capable of entering into contracts, being taxed, and being sued. The existence of the "economic fellowship" of the joint-stock company was abetted by what, for Gierke (1990, 224), were important legal developments such as the English Companies Act of 1862, where, without requiring approval by any organ of the State, "seven members can, if they observe the legal formalities, obtain the rights of corporations and protection of the law (see also Maitland 1904, 206; Maitland 1900, xxxviii, where the 1862 Act is referred to as the "Magna Carta of co-operative enterprise").

Perhaps one, once again, gets a better idea of what Gierke understood as the legal order (if not the sociological order) of "Fellowship" by considering the characteristic English protective legal screen behind which all manner of groups flourished, the trust (Maitland 1900, xxix). For our purposes here, we need not go into the likely origins of the English trust, and in any event the history of the trust and its relation to corporation was examined by Maitland (1904, 157 and following;

see also Pollock and Maitland 1898, Vol.2, 228-233 and the "Note on the phrase '*ad opus*' and the Early History of the Use," 233-39). What is relevant for our purposes here in discussing the relation between associational liberty and philanthropy is Maitland's speculation as to why numerous associations did not take advantage of the 1862 Companies Act (1904, 206-08). Maitland thought that the reason for still preferring the trust, despite its *ad hoc* character, was that "there is a widespread, though not very definite belief, that by placing itself under an incorporating *Gesetz* (law), however liberal and elastic that *Gesetz* may be (such as the Companies Act), a *Verein* (association) would forfeit some of its liberty, some of its autonomy, and would not be so completely the mistress of its own destiny as it is when it has asked nothing and obtained nothing from the State" (1904, 207). In other words, one takes it for granted that incorporation sooner or later opens the door at least to the "red tape" of regulation, and, even more to be avoided, taxation.

Now, for our purposes the significance of Maitland's speculation about why there should persist a preference for the trust comes into focus when we recall Gierke's understanding of the modern State as being authoritarian moral (a *Polizeistaat*). This characterization of the modern State is important for this brief discussion of associational liberty because the trust has been a vehicle for a number of different associations whose purpose can be loosely described as being "moral," that is, organized not to carry on a business with a view of profit—for example, and especially, the English "charities." The problem here is that the moral goals of the modern State (its assumed responsibility for the public welfare) could come into conflict with those of the "charities." The latter is to be understood as where "any goal which any reasonable person could regard as directly beneficial to the public or some large and indefinite class of men is a 'charitable' purpose" (Maitland 1904, 178). Here we see that a legal development has taken place, for the trust for a person has also now become a trust for a goal. Be that as it may, herein lies the problem: What is to be the relation, if any, between the freedom to create and maintain these presumably independent, moral vehicles of associations for pursuit of a non-commercial purpose—the charitable trust—and the modern State which views as its goal the welfare of its citizens? (Insofar as these associations are truly independent, we may refer to them not only as a "charitable trust" but also as a "philanthropic trust.") If we assume that Gierke's description of the paternalistic character of the modern State is accurate, then of course the welfare of the citizens is understood as only the State understands it.

The problem can now be formulated as follows: On what legal basis is the independence of the association to be secured or safeguarded? Here we have returned to the contrasting legal and political orders of *Genossenschaft* and *Herrschaft*, but we do so now having drawn attention to a few examples from the history of English associational liberty that further allow us to contrast two legal traditions: on the one hand, English common law, which has acknowledged the continual existence of independent associations in compromise with the principle of the sovereignty of the State; and on the other, as Tocqueville (1998, 258) described it, that tool of "absolute power," "a law of servitude," continental law—that is, Roman law and its reception (see van Caenegum 2002).

Roman Law and Common Law

According to Gierke (1990, 115), Roman law encouraged the tendency of the authoritarian State to elevate itself above the law because only private law was recognized as genuine law while public law was essentially administrative; that is, associations (the *collegia*) were, in the final analysis, considered to be a part of the State and, as such, could be eliminated by the State at any time (see Gierke 1977, 130). Thus, like Tocqueville, Gierke concluded that state absolutism found support in Roman ideas.

Contributing to that support of absolutism was, according to Gierke (1977, 128-129), "the Romans' unfamiliarity with the concept of true autonomy for associations." It may, however, have been that during the history of pre-imperial Rome *collegia* could, in fact, be freely founded.[6] In support of this possibility, he cites Gaius' reference to the Twelve Tables, in particular Table VIII, in the *Digest* (47.22.4): "by virtue of the law [the Twelve Tables] they have the power to make any agreement for themselves that they desire, provided public law is not thereby infringed."[7] Even if that were so, however, whatever latitude may have existed during the Republic to form associations was subsequently severely curtailed by the insistence that the existence of any association was dependent on the consent of the State (for example, in the Lex Julia, specifically the *Lex Municipalis*). Thus, even the above-mentioned burial guilds, as *collegia licita*, "were subject to constant supervision, [being] permitted only one monthly meeting, and were administratively suspended in the event they transcended their prescribed functions" (Gierke 1977, 128).

The problem of legally securing associational liberty now appears this way: Are or are not corporations entities with their own rights and duties? That is, are or are not corporations legally "persons"? If, on the one hand, corporations (and unincorporated associations) are legally persons, they have various rights and duties and spheres of action separate from the authority of the State. On the other hand, the insistence that corporations are not legally real means that their "reality" or "legal personality" has been artificially created (or conceded) by the State. In the latter case, it is difficult for any association to avoid having its independence called into question sooner or later. After all, if they are not real or legally persons, they do not actually bear rights and duties, and all the more so if the legal existence of any association depends on the concession (or recognition) of the State.

Now, what should be analyzed in some detail at this point in a discussion of Gierke's *Genossenschaft* is the Romanist theory of the association as a fictitious person, *persona ficta*, as clearly formulated by Sinibaldo Fieschi (1243), later Pope Innocent IV. This involves the insistence that because only individuals are legal persons, corporations must be granted or conceded a fictitious legal personality by the law of the State. Those who are familiar with the problem the legal doctrine of the *persona ficta* poses to associational autonomy will have realized that I have already suggested difficulties with its understanding of legal personality by following Gierke and Maitland in observing that associations (specifically corporations) are to some degree real because they formulate their own regulations, enforce them, enter into contracts, can sue and be sued, and so forth.[8] As Maitland put the problem (rightly, it seems to me), "If there is to be association, if there is to be group-formation, the problem of personality cannot be evaded" (1903, 230-31). Be that as it may, I wish to leave for a later time further discussion of some of the implications of the reality of corporate personality and the character or nature of human association (and in particular the argument of Gierke's 1902 Rektor's Address, "The Nature of Human Associations," 1935b). For our purposes here, it will suffice to draw attention to the more obvious threats to associational autonomy, and hence to the initiative of philanthropic action, posed by Roman law and its reception.

If, in fact, the people are understood to have conferred on the king (emperor or State) their entire sovereignty and authority (*Institutes* 1.2.6) and if what is pleasing to the king has the force of law (*Digest* 1.4.1)—for otherwise the sovereign is not sovereign—then the law conceding "personality" or legal existence to the otherwise artificial association can ultimately be only the king's (or emperor's or State's) law.[9] Furthermore, if the sovereign is to be sovereign, the king cannot, at least in principle, be bound by the laws of the realm (*Digest* 1.3.31).[10] This is how the Romanist *Lex Regia* was often understood, especially by the opponents of the reception of Roman law, the defenders of the common law. Given these propositions from Roman law, how is a true autonomy of associations possible? Now, when we also recall that, for example, in England during the fifteenth century, the king, abetted by the arguments of the legists about the *collegia illicita* of Roman law, had begun to interfere with the creation of voluntary associations or gilds by requiring a royal license, "not out of any juristic necessity, any theory of personality, but by political expedience and financial needs" (Pollock and Maitland 1898, 669-70), we realize that the foundation has been laid to eliminate the autonomy of those associations that, for the champion of an absolute State, are "like worms in the entrails of a natural man" (Hobbes 1962, 245). Will or will not corporations have liberty to dispute with the sovereign power? Once again, on what basis could the independent associations secure their existence, given these legal propositions?

One response in the tradition of common law to this threat to associational liberty posed by the reception of Roman law in the service of the increasing authority of the modern State occurs at the very end of Volume One of Pollock and Maitland's *The History of English Law Before the Time of Edward I* (1898). In a series of measured observations that rightly seek to put aside the fashionable but nonetheless heuristically unproductive contrast between an early medieval "communalism" and "individualism," Pollock and Maitland acknowledge, rightly it seems to me, the consolidation of an English national State during the thirteenth century. (At least that is how I understand their concluding remarks to Volume One.) Thus, no longer is the local community a community "because it is a self sufficient organism, but because it is a subordinate member of a greater community, of a nation. The nation is not a system of federated communities; the king is above all and has a direct hold on every individual" (688). Here we see clearly Pollock and Maitland's sober recognition of the historical, and perhaps unavoidable, fact of *Herrschaft*. However, they continue with the qualification to *Herrschaft*, so crucial to the common law, that in the English legal and political tradition the king was bound by the law of the realm: "But above the king himself . . . is the greatest of all communities, (quoting Bracton) 'the university of the realm'" (1898, 688). Thus the sovereign is not the author of the law but the guardian of the law. This tradition encompasses not only "the birth of the England of the Magna Carta and the first parliaments" (1898, 688) but also, as Gierke observed, the coexistence of the liberty of associations with the principle of sovereignty. It is a coexistence in which the king (or emperor or State) is but one estate (or association) among others, all of which are subject to the laws and, as such, where each of these estates (or associations) can have legal claim upon another. (These laws are sometimes understood as immemorial, or natural, or, *pace* Hayek's writings on the rule of law, as public opinion.)[11]

I suppose that these few remarks on Gierke's *Genossenschaftsrecht* come down to this observation: we are accustomed to acknowledging an inviolate basis for private property, based on either natural right or an immemorial public opinion, as a necessary criterion for liberty. But as liberty also requires association, above all philanthropic association, also necessary is a similar basis for the existence of associations. Considerable difficulties arise, however, and before briefly examining them in the remarks that conclude this paper, a few further comments on the relation between English common law and the reception of Roman law may be useful or at least interesting.

The acuteness of the struggle of the jurist of the common law against the reception of the Roman *Lex Regia* can be seen in John Selden's most interesting, if complicated, introductory commentary *Ad Fletam Dissertatio* (1647) to the edition of the anonymous early fourteenth century manuscript *Fleta*. The difficulty that faced Selden, as a defender (or articulator) of the tradition of common law, was how to account for those instances of the reception of Roman law found within the national legal tradition, especially when those instances involved that threat to associational liberties, the *Lex Regia*. Likely influenced by the work of his contemporary Edward Coke, Selden was well aware, as a jurist of the common law, that the significance of earlier legal judgments was not a matter of literary embellishment but rather of providing a confirmation on which the interpretation of the law may depend (1647, 6).[12] Thus, all the more important was the problem for Selden of how a defender of the tradition of English common law should understand the evident accommodation to the *Lex Regia* found in that tradition in three earlier legal treatises—Bracton's *De Legibus et Consuetudinibus Angliae* (composed around the middle of the thirteenth century, during the reign of Henry III), Thornton's *Summa* (composed during the late thirteenth century, during the reign of Edward I), and the *Fleta*. Even if Selden (1647, 157,161) was correct in observing that although frequent citations of Roman law are found during the reign of Edward II (1307-27), by the beginning of the reign of Edward III it had fallen into neglect (excluding, of course, Roman canon law; see Helmholz 1990, 1-27), the apparent putative Romanism of Bracton (and Thornton and *Fleta*), conveyed by the apparent accommodation to the *Lex Regia*, could not but be an interpretative battleground during the political and legal conflicts of the sixteenth and obviously especially seventeenth centuries. One need only recall the conflicts during that period over the scope of royal prerogative, for example, the evident suspension of common law in the *Five Knights' Case* (1627), or the legal justification of the Star Chamber.

The difficulty for Selden was that these three works interpreted the *Digest* as stating "what pleases the prince has the force of law *in accordance with* the *Lex Regia* enacted concerning his power" (my emphasis, 1647, 29). Selden thought that this apparent restatement of *Digest* 1.4.1 was in fact a peculiar interpretation, because in these three works "*cum*" is translated as a proposition, *in accordance with*, and not, as it should be, as a conjunction, *since*. The implication of this peculiar interpretative restatement for Bracton, Thornton, and the *Fleta* was that "nothing is to be determined [by the prince] of the prerogative except as allowed by the characteristic sense of the various stipulations of the *Lex Regia*," and especially so as in these works the interpretation is followed by "a passage concerning our remarkable characteristic of administering justice according to law and legislating in assemblies of Estates." Selden continued by noting that all three works omit entirely that the *Lex Regia* continues in the *Digest*, and is presented in the *Institutes*, with the clause "all their power and authority conceded by the people (to the prince)" (1647, 29). In other words, according to Selden what is remarkable about this interpretation is that it is so completely at variance with the universal understanding of the *Lex Regia*—a variation to be explained, so Selden argued, as a misguided attempt to provide a distinctly English version of the *Lex Regia*.

Selden concluded that during the thirteenth and part of the fourteenth centuries, especially during the reign of Edward II, among English lawyers there prevailed "some kind of use of imperial law" (1647, 39). Nonetheless, "in the famous question of prerogative, as debated in this country, Ulpian's opinion on the *Lex Regia* could not in itself have any weight," since it "is interpreted, or misinterpreted, by our three authors only in so far as consistent or at least not inconsistent with our immemorial customs. Indeed, the correct interpretation of that maxim, in so far as it is a part of civil law, is entirely opposed to the English constitution" (39).[13]

Rule of Law and Self-Government

Let us return to the assertion of the common law that above the king (or emperor or State) is the law of the land—a law that recognizes, either through legislation like the Companies Act of 1862 or legal vehicles like the trust, a significant degree of autonomy of right-and-duty-bearing associations. At one, clearly unsatisfactory, level, there is not much more to be said, for no one, at least explicitly, wishes for a restoration of an institution like the Star Chamber, and no one wishes, at least explicitly, to stultify an important part of human character by quashing the initiative of voluntary association. And so there exist numerous associations that, as independent and bearing legal personality, make their own regulations and enforce those regulations specific to the purpose of the association. The Church, for example, establishes criteria for who can be a priest and under what circumstances a priest would be defrocked. A university establishes the criteria for appointment of teachers and under what circumstances they can be removed. And a philanthropic trust establishes and decides on the scope and administration of a charitable purpose. Each association has its own rights and duties, and each has its own law (and court), the result being a society consisting of a pastiche of "special law." Insofar as a society consists of heterogeneous bodies of special law (sometimes referred to as "particularistic law"), the relation of philanthropy, law, and associational liberty becomes one where a number of associations are free from regulation by the State. Formulated in different terms, it is a society where philanthropy is freely undertaken and where, as a consequence, the self is enhanced with attendant responsibility for one's actions. In this situation, one has—to return to a characterization introduced above at the end of the first section—a wide scope or latitude of associational freedom.

As I, following Gierke and Maitland (and Selden), have drawn attention to the early modern recognition of the threat that the reception of Roman law posed to a society of a pastiche of special law arising from substantial associational autonomy, perhaps it is appropriate and useful to turn to a description of a few of the legal implications of how one aspect of such a society appeared in late fifteenth century England (see Strauss 1986, 122-123). The Church had jurisdiction over marriage, probate, defamation, perjury, and of course tithes (certainly so, if *iure divino*). It also had jurisdiction over those crimes considered to be spiritual: fornication, sorcery, and simony. Within these jurisdictional areas, the Church courts followed Roman canon law. Needless to say, property law, including contracts and claims of debt, fell within the jurisdiction of the common law and the State's courts (see Helmholz 1990). Now, if we indulge in a peculiar historical anachronism for the sake of pursuing a better understanding of a potential problem by overlaying this partial description of the different legal jurisdictions of the late fifteenth century on the demand today made by some in England for a jurisdictional legitimacy of *Sharî'ah*, we get a good idea of some of the complicated implications of a patchwork of distinct associations, each of which has its own, but possibly competing, special law.

The problem thus becomes a question of the scope or latitude of the special law, the relation not only between the special law of one association and that of another but especially between the special law of an association and the law of the land. Can, for example, special or particularistic law take precedence over the law of the land, or, as argued by Roman law and others, such as Hobbes, must the validity of a special law, insofar as it exists at all, be subject to the consent of the State? To formulate the problem of this relation in a dramatic fashion and putting aside for a moment the authority of the State, can a society of some degree of cultural cohesiveness (n.b., herein lies a problem) tolerate associations within its boundaries acting in a way that may be viewed as being disruptive or potentially disruptive to its existence? (Of course, how one understands "disruptive" is often the rub.)

The acuity of the problem may be lessened in several different ways. One is by not approaching the relation between special law and the law of the land theoretically but instead by insisting that it be understood historically. That is, as the relation has achieved approximate formulation and stability through the gradual development of a consensus—for example, how federalism has evolved in the United States. However, to proceed even this way is still to turn one's back on the merit of Gierke's assessment of the moral authoritarianism of the modern, supervisory State which, as such, declares not only that there is a "public welfare" but also that there can be only one understanding of what that public welfare is— its own. It is a declaration that is based on what Gierke (1990, 72-91) described as the legal development of a "law of the land," where the land, having become the "territory" of a national state (see Grosby 1995), has achieved an "invisible unity" such that it now has its own political and legal-moral personality.[14] Thus, one now speaks of the "public good" of the (national) territory. However, if sovereignty can only be understood as having absolute power, then this "public welfare" of the territory has to be expressed as the State's "monopolized care of the common good" (Gierke 1990, 98)—a solicitude that, as such, must, at a minimum, look askance at any independent philanthropic initiative.

Conclusion

For Gierke (1900, 39), this development of a monopolized conception of the public good was not only modern, for the "act of alienation performed by the people in the *Lex Regia* was for Positive Law the basis of the modern, as well as of the ancient, Empire." With Gierke one does not have anything like a perspective of "ancients versus moderns"; for in antiquity, political thought asserts that the end of man is that virtue only made possible in and through the State, and today political thought asserts that the public good is only made possible in and through the State. This is why in Gierke's work we find the category "antique-modern thought." Thus, for Gierke both ancient and modern political thought stand opposed to the freedom of the autonomous association.

The principle of sovereignty strives toward the realization of not only the absolute State but also, as the articulator of and guardian for the common good, the supervisory State. Moreover, if in fact *salus publica lex suprema est* (supported by the assertion that the public good requires the priority of the State's claim, so *Digest* 49.14.46),[15] then the sovereign's breach of the law becomes possible if he or she judges the public good to be at stake (Gierke 1990, 110).

Nevertheless, Gierke was well aware that the development of this state of affairs so distressing to associational liberty paralleled "one of the greatest deeds of history": the political emancipation of the individual. One part of this political emancipation was legal equality of all, and both were "the beneficial consequence(s) of the destruction of the medieval corporations" (113). Here is where we come upon a most vexing paradox. We know that opposition to tyranny requires the predictable "rule of law" in contrast to the capricious rule of men. We further know that the three classic requirements of the rule of law are that the laws must be general, equal, and certain (see, for example, Hayek 1955, 34-36). So, how is the criterion of equality of the law—the law must be the same for all—to be reconciled with the special law of an independent association? Is it the case that the rule of law must require a strong prejudice against any and all bodies of special law? Here is our paradox: liberty requires the rule of law, but it also requires the independence of associations; and the latter achieve significance when those associations have in fact their own legal personality, including their own special law. The paradox deserves to be formulated as angularly as possible, for otherwise "the quest for community" is not much of a quest, having lost its legal and political significance.

An angular formulation also forces one not to view Roman law as simply an alien, albeit orderly, incursion against the associational liberty of the native, common law, for the idea of sovereignty contains within itself the expectation that all should be subject to the same authority, same law, and same courts. Thus, as Gierke acknowledged, one consequence of the reception of Roman law was to sweep away the discriminatory privileges of the Middle Ages. This expectation bears with it a procedural and seemingly unavoidable, substantive rationality in legal development. Of course, the realization of that rational expectation of the rule of law has also resulted in the individual remaining a minor to the end of his days because the State both defines what his welfare consists of and provides for it, and because his political freedom and legal equality is, for the most part, as a passive subject, the latter only aggravated by the centralization of government. And now we come upon another paradox. Must the rigorous, logical extension of the rule of law undermine self-government because that extension must sooner or later sweep aside the freely constituted, philanthropic association of self-help?

It may be possible, as Gierke thought, to formulate in response to this paradox a basic law that would make handling in a productive way this relation between special law and the rule of law's equality before the law, or, put in different terms, the relation between associational autonomy (*Genossenschaft*) and sovereignty (*Herrschaft*). This is a second way of lessening the acuity of the problem of this relation. In fact, Gierke's *Genossenschaftsrecht* and associational liberty rest upon the formulation of such a law—for example, a Bill of Rights. The rub here is the subsequent interpretation of the relation of those rights of the individual to any substantial expression of associational autonomy. Regardless of whether one is hopeful about realizing this possibility, I think it is clear that Gierke was more right than not about the character of the modern State. He was also correct when he observed that "the vigorous, unfettered building of associations is not only useful but indispensible if the individual and the collectivity are to have their lives shaped into a harmonious whole. For the individual, it counteracts the danger of isolation and fragmentation; at the same time, it [the unfettered building of associations] is a powerful confederate and effective balance [that is, a corrective] for a free state" (Gierke 1990, 170).

NOTES

[1] See page 216, volume 1 of *Das deutsche Genossenschaftsrecht,* much of which appears in English (Gierke 1990). English translations of sections of the other volumes of *Das deutsche Genossenschaftsrecht* appear in Gierke 1900, 1935a, 1958, 1977. For other works by Gierke translated into English, see 1935b, 1939. Of the secondary literature on Gierke, I cite here only Runciman (1997) because of its discussion of Maitland and its analysis of the challenge of Gierke and Maitland to Hobbes.

[2] Note, however, the still valid comments of qualification about the Laws of Edward the Confessor in Pollock and Maitland (1898, 103-04). See also Plucknett (2010, 256).

[3] For a discussion, influenced by Gierke's work, of the juristic personality of the corporation in early English history, see Pollock and Maitland (1898, 486-510).

[4] In fact only the first three of the nine chapters of Gierke (1939) deal directly with the politics and jurisprudence of Althusius. The later chapters—for example, on "the idea of federalism," "the idea of the legal state," "the doctrine of popular sovereignty," and "religious elements in the theory of the State"—are quite important in themselves.

[5] Or as Max Weber (1978, 711) formulated it, "the problem of juristic personality has usually appeared in legal history in close association with the problem of the capacity of organizations, especially public ones, to sue and be sued." If sued, the question arises as to the scope of liability, that is, the property of each individual member or only that of the corporation? Pollock and Maitland (1898, 488) put the question of the personality of the corporation this way: "The core of the matter seems to be that for more or less numerous purposes some organized group of men is treated as a unit which has rights and duties *other than* the rights and duties of all or any of its members" (my emphasis).

[6] So Mommsen's view; see note 181 (Gierke 1977, 129). I note here only one among a number of possibilities to account for such apparent discrepancies— so the argument of François Hotman in *Antitribonianus* (1567)—that the *Corpus Iuris* was a distortion of earlier Roman law, having been an imperial product crafted by Greeks and Byzantines. To pursue this possibility, overstated it seems to me, would take us too far afield.

[7] *his autem potestatem facit lex pactionem quam velint sibe ferre, dum ne quid ex publica lege corrumpant.*

[8] For the bearing of this observation on the early English borough, see Pollock and Maitland (1898, 676-88).

[9] As widely observed and as part of another political tradition, *Institutes* 1.2.6 can be understood to imply that the *princeps* is only a representative of the people. *Digest* 1.4.1, *"Quod principi placuit, legis habet vigorem."* For this alternative political tradition, see Gierke (1939) and Kantorowicz (1965, 158-59).

[10] Digest 1.3.31, *"Princeps legibus solutus est."* Whatever Ulpian may have intended by *"princeps legibus solutus est"*—for example, perhaps only that the state could in certain circumstances put aside private or police laws—the early modern tradition of common law took the statement to be an argument for absolutism, and so it was intended by its proponents at that time.

[11] Each of these understandings of the law is not without difficulties. For example, regarding the immemorial character of the law, see note 2 above.

[12] *"Atque ita certe tam autoritatem e qua juris interpretatio pendeat eos habere manifesto in disputationibus forensibus scholasticisque est agnoscendum quam ornamento esse."* This recognized significance contributed to forgeries, the most famous of which was the Donation of Constantine. Thus the evaluation of sources (both philological and historical contexts) achieves paramount importance, contributing to the development of a historical outlook. For a good, brief summary of the significance of Coke's work, see Plucknett (2010, 282-83).

[13] At this point it is worth examining the possible reasons for the English attachment to the common law, although doing so here would lead us astray from the problems at hand. Nevertheless and briefly, Selden's (1647, 164) explanation for the faithfulness to the common law centered on *qua gentis hujus genio*; while Maitland's (1901, 23-26) account for the resistance to the reception focused on a more institutional reason, the Inns of Court, i.e. although civil law was taught in university, "medieval England had schools of national law."

[14] For this development, see, for example, Kantorowicz's (1957, 232-72) discussion of "pro patria mori." There is a long history of authoritarian absolutism in the name of the public good. For one early example, that of Bavaria during the 15th and 16th centuries, see Strauss (1986, 259-62).

[15] *Fiscus semper habet ius pignoris.*

REFERENCES

Gierke, Otto von. 1900 [1881]. *Political Theories of the Middle Ages* (from volume 3 of *Das deutsche Genossenschaftsrecht*). Translated and edited by Frederic William Maitland. Cambridge: Cambridge University Press.

______. 1935a [1868]. "Introduction to Volume 1 of *Das deutsche Genossenschaftsrecht*." In John D. Lewis, *The Genossenschaft-Theory of Otto von Gierke*. Madison: University of Wisconsin.

______. 1935b. "The Nature of Human Associations" (1902) and "The Basic Concepts of State Law and the Most Recent State-Law Theories" (1874). In John D. Lewis, *The Genossenschaft-Theory of Otto von Gierke*. Madison: University of Wisconsin.

______. 1939 [1878]. *The Development of Political Theory* (*Johannes Althusius und die Entwicklung der naturrechtlichen Staatstheorien*). Translated and edited by Bernard Freyd. New York: W.W. Norton.

______. 1958 [1913]. *Natural Law and the Theory of Society 1500 to 1800* (from volume 4 of *Das deutsche Genossenschaftsrecht*). Translated and edited by Ernest Barker. Cambridge: Cambridge University Press.

______. 1977 [1881]. *Associations and Law: The Classical and Early Christian Stages* (from volume 3 of *Das deutsche Genossenschaftsrecht*). Translated and edited by George Heiman. Toronto: University of Toronto.

______. 1990 [1868]. *Community in Historical Perspective* (from volume 1 of *Das deutsche Genossenschaftsrecht*). Translated and edited by Antony Black. Cambridge: Cambridge University Press.

Grosby, Steven. 1995. "Territoriality." *Nations and Nationalism*, 1(2): 143-62, reprinted in *Biblical Ideas of Nationality: Ancient and Modern*. Winona Lake, Eisenbrauns, 2002.

______. 2009. "Philanthropy and Human Action." *Conversations on Philanthropy*, VI: 1-14. ©2009 DonorsTrust.

Hayek, F.A. 1955. *The Political Ideal of the Rule of Law*. Cairo: National Bank of Egypt.

Helmholz, R. H. 1990. *Roman Canon Law in Reformation England*. Cambridge: Cambridge University Press.

Hobbes, Thomas. 1962 [1651]. *Leviathan*. New York: Macmillan.

Kantorowicz, Ernst H. 1957. *The King's Two Bodies: A Study in Mediaeval Political Theory*. Princeton: Princeton University Press.

______. 1965. *Selected Studies*. Locust Valley, NY: J. J. Augustin.

Maine, Henry Sumner. 1970 [1861]. *Ancient Law*. Gloucester, MA: Peter Smith.

Maitland, Frederic William. 1900. "Introduction." In Otto Gierke, *Political Theories of the Middle Ages*. Cambridge: Cambridge University Press.

______. 1901. *English Law and the Renaissance*. Cambridge: Cambridge University Press.

______. 1903. "Moral Personality and Legal Personality." In *Maitland: Selected Essays*, eds. H. D. Hazeltine, G. Lapsley, and P. H. Winfield. Cambridge: Cambridge University Press, 1936.

______. 1904. "Trust and Corporation," In *Maitland: Selected Essays*, eds. H. D. Hazeltine, G. Lapsley, and P. H. Winfield. Cambridge: Cambridge University Press, 1936.

Plucknett, Theodore F. T. 2010 [1956]. *A Concise History of the Common Law*. Indianapolis: Liberty Fund.

Pollock, Frederick and Maitland, Frederic William. 1898. *The History of English Law Before the Time of Edward I*, 2nd ed. Cambridge: Cambridge University Press.

Runciman, David. 1997. *Pluralism and the Personality of the State*. Cambridge: Cambridge University Press.

Selden, John. 1647 [1925]. *Ad Fletam Dissertatio*. Edited and translated by David Ogg. Cambridge: Cambridge University Press.

Strauss, Gerald. 1986. *Law, Resistance, and the State: The Opposition to Roman Law in Reformation Germany*. Princeton: Princeton University Press.

Tocqueville, Alexis de. 1966. *Democracy in America*. Edited by J.P. Mayer and translated by George Lawrence. New York: Harper and Row.

______. 1998. *The Old Regime and the Revolution*. Edited by François Furet and Françoise Mélonio and translated by Alan S. Kahan. Chicago: University of Chicago Press.

Tönnies, Ferdinand. 1940 [1887]. *Gemeinschaft and Gesellschaft*. New York: American Book.

Van Caenegum, R. C. 2002. *European Law in the Past and the Future: Unity and Diversity over Two Millennia*. Cambridge: Cambridge University Press.

Weber, Max. 1978. *Economy and Society*. Berkeley: University of California.

CHARITY AND RELIGION:
HISTORICAL CONNECTIONS IN OUR LAW

Richard H. Helmholz

Introduction

Charities hold a privileged position in our law. They enjoy a freedom from most forms of taxation, and they still hold at least a partial immunity against tort and contractual liability that is fastened upon for-profit enterprises. Charities can also take advantage of legal privileges, procedural and substantive, that are not granted to other private organizations. The doctrine of *cy près* is perhaps the best-known example, but there are many others. It is often said in legal textbooks that gifts or trusts established for charitable purposes are favorites of the law, and this is no idle statement. Its veracity and consequences are manifested in many corners of our jurisprudence. Almost always it is to the advantage of donors to be able to claim that their gifts were made with a charitable purpose, and the charitable organizations themselves support these claims—no cause for wonder.

But what constitutes a charity, and what is a charitable purpose? What does it take to qualify for these advantages? Sometimes the answer seems obvious. A gift to one's friends or to the members of one's family may have a benevolent motive, but it is not charitable in nature. It is a private gift. This is common ground among commentators. A donation to a school, by contrast, even the one a donor attended as a youth, counts as a charitable gift. It promotes an educational purpose, and this is so even if the donor's motives have a hint of self-interest— they may stand a little taller, for example, if their school is highly ranked in *U.S. News and World Report*. Still, the alum's predominant motive is to benefit education. So we count the gift as charitable. What about a gift to the school one's children attend? That has been a more contentious question in the law, since it lies somewhere between the two. It can help keep the (nondeductible) costs of tuition a little lower for the parents. It gives them more than bragging rights; it saves them money they would otherwise be obliged to spend on their child's education, at least if other parents do the same. Purposes and circumstances sometimes matter.

Helmholz, Richard H. 2012. Charity and Religion: Historical Connections in our Law. *Conversations on Philanthropy* IX: 74-83. ISSN 1552-9592 ©The Philanthropic Enterprise.

Hard cases thus exist, but the standard that has been widely adopted in modern law for drawing a distinction between purposes that are charitable and those that are not has come to be whether the gift promotes what can be called "a substantial public interest." The gift to one's children promotes a private interest; the gift to the school promotes a public interest in the furtherance of the education of the country's citizens. Thus only the latter qualifies for the various benefits conferred on charities under today's law. This is why the gift to the school attended by one's children is a difficult case. It does a little of both. However, there is general agreement that certain purposes are presumed to be charitable no matter the motivation: the relief of poverty, the furtherance of education, the preservation of public health, and the fulfillment of governmental purposes. They obviously qualify as charitable. And with the expansion of modern government into many spheres of life once counted as private—the provision of health services being the most immediately topical today—the scope of charitable purposes has expanded naturally, until it can now be said with some veracity that charitable organizations merit special treatment under the law precisely because they perform functions that would otherwise be left to the government. Charities deserve a tax break, it is said, because they take a financial burden off the taxpayer.

If this is so, gifts to religious organizations present a problem. In what sense can religion be said to fit the definition of a charity as something that provides a public benefit or takes a financial burden off the government? That is a little hard to see. In American life today, religion is widely regarded as a private matter. Indeed, a tide of secularism is sweeping over our constitutional law. In this climate of opinion, it seems natural that the promotion of any specifically religious purpose should be treated with suspicion. To some, granting a privileged status to religious organizations seems contrary to the Establishment Clause of the First Amendment to the Constitution of the United States. That clause bars the establishment of any religion by Congress, and this has made it particularly difficult to fit religion into the current definition of a charity. Religious organizations are established to promote private interests. In fact they do many things the government is constitutionally prohibited from doing. How, then, can they be relieving the government of a financial responsibility that belongs to it?

So far, at least, this apparent inconsistency in logic has caused problems only around the edges of our law. Gifts to churches are treated as charitable despite it. Atheist activists grumble about "tax subsidies," but so far they have not made much headway in Congress or the courts. It has been interesting, all the same, to see the answers that have been given to their arguments. One answer, certainly the most common, has been to say that religion is simply "an exception" to the requirement that a charity be organized for a public purpose. However anomalous it seems, it is too well established to be overturned. Another response has been to discern a connection between religious and public purposes. This has been a recurring theme. A bequest in trust for masses to be said for the soul of the donor, for instance, is held by the *Restatement of Trusts* to be charitable because "according to the doctrines of the Roman Catholic Church [the benefit] is not confined to the particular souls but extends to the other members of the church and to the rest of the world" (American Law Institute 1959, 371g). Explanations like these are beginning to sound a little hollow, however, at least when one starts from the language in recent U. S. Supreme Court cases on religion. Who knows? Things may change. Some wish it.

The purpose of this essay is not to enter directly into the debate on this difficult and contentious subject. Its purpose is historical—to consider the nature of European laws of charity as they developed from the Middle Ages to the time of the founding of the American republic in the eighteenth century. It was this law upon which our own was built. It was upon the definition of charity inherited from the past that our own law long depended, and this old law looked very different in its assumptions from that of recent decades. Although our ancestors would have been familiar with the favor accorded bequests for public purposes, they would have regarded the exact equation of governmental and charitable purposes with incomprehension. On this score, we have taken a quite dramatic turn away from the law with which we began.

The European Law of Charity, ca. 1600

On first sight, the similarities between the law of charity in 1600 and today's law seem great. Continuities stand out. Then as now, charities were favorites of the law. Gifts and legacies devoted to charitable purposes enjoyed many privileges. Substantial treatises called "On the Privileges of Pious Donations" (or some variant of that title) were written to discuss and analyze these privileges. A standard bibliography lists eleven of them compiled between 1550 and 1750, and of course the subject was also covered in most general treatments of European law. English law did not differ markedly from that of the Continent on this score, except that it was complicated by the passage of several detailed statutes of charitable uses and by the condemnation of superstitious uses that followed from the English Reformation. I have been able to consult several from among these treatises, one by Andreas Tiraquellus (d. 1558), a French jurist active in the courts of Paris, the second by Francisco a Mostazo (17th century), a Spanish commentator of the following century, and compare them with the treatment found in two English works written around the same time, the first by Henry Swinburne (d. 1624), the other by Sir Francis Moore (d. 1621). I have also made use of two more general works on testamentary law in the *ius commune*, both of which contain substantial treatments of the subject. One is that of Franciscus Camarella (17th century), and the other of Franciscus Mantica (d. 1614). All of them mentioned the importance of religion in defining and implementing the law of charity. Mostazo, for example, began his treatment by assuming that "Free rein is to be granted in favor of gifts to churches and to other pious purposes, which the laws encourage by both divine and natural law." Gifts are to be counted as charitable, he added, whenever they are made for the honor of God, "to whom we must show ourselves most grateful" (1698, Lib. I, c. 3).

Privileges Accorded to Charitable Gifts

The privileges accorded to charities under the *ancien régime* turn out to have been numerous and valuable, just as in modern law. Tiraquellus provided a long list of 167 of them (1582, 460-85), although one must say that a modern observer would count some of them as slight variations on a theme. The compilation of ever-longer lists of fine distinctions was always a temptation for the European jurists— it could become something like a contest to see who could provide the longest lists, and Tiraquellus seems to have been an eager contestant. In his defense, he did provide a separate legal reference for each privilege, usually a text from the Roman or canon law, supported by at least one learned commentary on the text. It might also be said that all the privileges were distinct from one another. Separating them did no harm. We ought to recognize that advantage. Even making allowance for the disconcerting consequences of prolixity, the list would have been useful in practice. It showed that the privileges of charitable gifts and legacies were many, and it allowed lawyers easy access to authorities supporting each of them.

Even more striking today than their utility or their large number, however, is the overlap in substance with a great many of the early privileges and those still recognized today. Many would be entirely familiar to modern lawyers. Indeed they are the same as those that still exist. It is impossible not to regard them as ancestors, even progenitors, of our modern list of the special privileges accorded to charitable bequests. Here are four representative examples.

One is that a charitable trust will not be held invalid because it lacks an ascertained beneficiary. An essential element of a normal private trust is the existence of a designated, certain and identifiable person or persons to whom the trustee owes a duty to administer the trust property. Furthermore, the identity of this beneficiary must be ascertainable within the period allowed by the Rule against Perpetuities. Without such a beneficiary, one essential element of any obligation—someone with standing to enforce it—is missing. Hence a trust "for the benefit of such persons as the trustee shall select" is invalid from the start, even if the trustee wishes to act under it. With a charitable trust, however, the reverse is true. The lack of any named person to enforce it does not render it invalid, and thus it does not fail. The law allows a public official, typically the attorney general, to bring suit against a negligent or dishonest trustee. Hence a trust "for the benefit of such paupers as the trustee shall select" is valid, simply because its purpose is charitable. On this distinction, Tiraqellus (1582, 41-42) and Swinburne (1590, Pt. I §16, nos. 5-6) were at one.

A second privilege, both modern and medieval, accorded to charitable bequests is the possibility of perpetual existence. The Rule against Perpetuities, even in its weakened modern form, prevents property from being held forever inalienable. A family settlement must eventually come to an end. A charity, however, need not. We see monuments to that generous treatment all around us: charitable institutions that have lasted over the years, some of them still subsisting in part on grants of money and property made long ago. Churches and universities are the most obvious examples. This too was a medieval rule. Gifts to the church were to last (Tiraquellus 1582, 575-76). Indeed, under the canon law the circumstances in which property granted to a church could ever be alienated were subject to strict requirements of need and consent from above. The strictness of these requirements resulted in what was called the "dead hand" control of the church. It resulted in the adoption of mortmain statutes in many European lands; they prohibited unlicensed alienations to the church (Mostazo 1698, Lib. I, c. 3, no. 12). The privilege of perpetuity accorded to charitable bequests thus made a difference in practice, and it has not been altogether abandoned in modern law.

A third illustrative privilege, already mentioned, was the doctrine of *cy près*. It was connected with, and perhaps even required by, the second privilege. Charitable purposes could become obsolete over the course of time. A trust established to find a cure for a specific disease becomes useless when that cure is found. A fund set up to aid the students of one educational institution will be useless if that school ceases to exist. In such circumstances the doctrine of *cy près* allows the fund to be redirected to a charitable purpose which is "as near as possible" to the donor's original intention. Modern lawyers are sometimes surprised to learn how old this doctrine is, but in fact it is a product of the European *ius commune*. Tiraquellus put it as number 135 on his list, stating: "Gifts for a certain pious use can be converted to another pious use" (1582, 618-619). A legacy to build a church in one location could be used to build a church elsewhere if the first location was impossible or even inconvenient. As an English civilian stated circa 1600, "[I]f it bee not possible to observe the saide use, then the ordinarie may convert the same to some other use" (Civilian's Notebook, Worcester Record Office, MS). Deviations from a donor's original intention—much in the news in the United States in recent years because of the (successful) attempt to move the Barnes Collection of Impressionist art from Merion into the city of Philadelphia—in fact have had a long history.

A fourth is what was called the interpretative privilege, probably as important and valuable in the law of charity as any of the others, even though it has always rested on a presumption rather than a clear rule of law. Presumptions can be rebutted. This was something like a rule of lenity, one with exceptions. Ambiguous or insufficient language in a will or deed would be treated as charitable if possible, particularly where the gift would otherwise fail. "In dubious cases, it was to be presumed that legacies should be interpreted and enforced in a way that promotes charitable purposes" (Tiraquellus 1582, 488-89). Swinburne seemingly had this in mind when he approved wills *ad pias causas* even though they were lacking in certainty of statement (Moore 1676, Ch. VII § 2, no. 9). Similarly, in modern U.S. law it sometimes happens that a donor or testator uses ambiguous language in a conveyance or a will; if so, courts will presume the existence of a charitable purpose where it is compatible with the language used. The early jurists put this preference in a dramatic way. They said that testators should be presumed to have wished to favor their souls over the interests of their kin (Mantica 1735, Lib. V, tit. 14, no 34). It is doubtful that such a rationale would be invoked in modern law, but the presumption lives on.

In all this there is a striking resemblance between the old law and the modern law. The favor accorded to charitable purposes has been a characteristic of our law for many centuries. It continues to appear in legal rules and presumptions in our legal system. They have been remarkably durable over the centuries. Not everything is unchanged, of course. We have a system of taxation today that differs greatly from that found in the Middle Ages. No "privilege" to take an income tax deduction for charitable gifts could then have existed because there was no income tax. The tithe—the closest equivalent to an income tax—was regarded as being owed to God and to his servants, the clergy, as of right. No privilege not to pay other taxes or meet other societal obligations ensued from its payment. The circumstances of modern life have dictated changes in the law of charity. What seems most noticeable in the lists of legal privileges, however, is how many of them have remained the same.

The Centrality of Religion in the Law of Charity

As has happened in modern law, the existence of so many charitable privileges in early European law required a working definition of exactly what made a gift charitable. Put in medieval form, what was a gift *ad pias causas?* It mattered then, as it does now. An affirmative answer was required before any one of the privileges could be invoked. Here again, there are some remarkable similarities between the old law and our law. The underlying reason given for them has, however, changed to match changes in thought in our own day—principally the secularization of society and the rise in the role accorded to government in our lives.

If one examines the purposes counted as charitable in modern law, comparing them with a similar list from 1600, it quickly becomes obvious that the main categories have remained quite similar. Gifts to hospitals, gifts for the relief of the poor, gifts to promote educational institutions, gifts for the construction and maintenance of public works, and gifts for religious purposes all qualified then, as they do now. True, there have been additions. A trust for the prevention of cruelty to animals is considered charitable today; nothing of the sort appears in the early manuals. There have also been subtractions. A trust for the payment of marriage portions for poor maidens figures in the list Tiraquellus compiled (1582, 449-51), as it did in that of the Englishman Sir Francis Moore (1676, Ch. 7 § 1, no. 5). Such a bequest might not qualify as charitable today unless it could be read as intended solely for the relief of the poor. So the parallels are not exact. Changes in sentiment have made a difference. But most of the medieval categories have remained intact—a wonderful example of a lawyerly habit. It retains the substance of a legal rule but changes the reason given for it.

That change has been in the theory underlying these categories. Today, "public interest" provides the touchstone. Although the promotion of religious values continues to qualify, it is an exception to the ordinary rule. In earlier centuries, it was the other way around. The basic assumption upon which the various charitable purposes were founded was the promotion of religious values. In this the canon law played an obvious and pivotal role. Its texts were used to show that specific purposes were charitable because they grew out of the dictates of the Christian religion. Far from being an exception, religion, not the needs of government, furnished the starting point for analysis. Mostazo, for example, defined a charitable gift as "whatever is granted for the love of God for divine purposes or other works of mercy for the good of [the donor's] soul" (1698, Lib. I, c. 1). Tiraquellus had begun with a simpler but similar definition: "Whatever is given for the love of God," but Mostazo rejected it as so wide that it might include a gift made to a rich man if the gift were inspired by the love of God. In this he seems to have been "scoring a point" in scholastic fashion, but the similarity between the two is more important than the difference. Both began with religion. Swinburne more succinctly stated the same point. Charitable gifts were those "made for good and godly uses" (1590, Pt. 1 § 13, no. 3). Camarella went even further, holding that, strictly speaking, it was wrong to accord charitable status to a gift made for public purposes; in truth, he said, only a gift made for one's soul qualified (1681, Lib. VII, quaest. 1, no. 2). All of these authors, with varying degrees of intensity, used religion as the main reference point in defining and implementing the law of charity.

This approach made a difference in practice. In England, for example, the ecclesiastical law moved away from its Roman law roots by dispensing with many of the formal requirements once imposed in the law of last wills and testaments. The classical law's requirement of seven witnesses to a formal testament became a dead letter in later practice. Only two were ever required, and this step was justified by the biblical admonition that the testimony of two or three sufficed to prove the truth. The Gospels so stated (Matthew 18:16). In testamentary law, as the English civilian Swinburne put it, "The lawe of God requireth no more" (1590, Pt. I § 9, n. 3). Courts should follow this religious admonition, he thought, and so they did in English practice.

Some of these uses of religion underlying the law of charity now seem to have been exercises characteristic of the medieval Schools. For instance, Tiraquellus held that a gift to support study at a university might qualify as privileged only if it were limited to the study of theology (1582, 452-53). Study of a different subject would not qualify. Mostazo argued that the permissible area might be expanded to include the study of grammar, if this course was "preparatory" to entrance into the theological faculty (1698, Lib. I, c. 2, no. 25). They both concluded, however, that a gift for scholarships might be classed as charitable if use of the gift was limited to poor students. The poor held a special place in the law of the church. It was said that "the poor were a special treasure of Christ" (Tiraquellus 1582, 441-42). To help with the burden of the expenses of the poor would therefore fulfill a religious duty.

Tiraquellus took a similar position in dealing with gifts to fraternal organizations. In themselves, fraternities did not seem to be charitable in nature. Their primary purpose was human fellowship, not the worship of God. However, if it could be shown that members of the fraternity were in fact devoting their attention to worship or engaging in works of mercy, such as aiding the poor, then he considered that a gift or bequest to the organization would qualify for charitable status (440-41).

The importance of religion for the jurists was particularly evident in the hard cases, situations where a religious purpose was harder to discern. An example was the gift for the repair and maintenance of bridges and roads. Today, such a gift would easily pass muster; it benefits the public. In early centuries, however, it was not so easy. What had bridge repair to do with God? The jurists were up to this challenge, however. Public interest was mentioned as a possible justification. So were several texts from the Roman and canon laws. Some jurists argued for a close connection between municipal purposes and divine purposes. But more was needed. Tiraquellus cemented the argument in favor of this category by finding a connection. Churches were themselves bound to repair bridges and roads, he noted, citing texts from both the canon and Roman laws that so stated. If this was so, bridge and road repair must qualify as a religious obligation in some sense. Perhaps not satisfied with this chain of reasoning, he added that widows and orphans would most especially be benefitted by adequate provisions for their comfort and safety in travelling (1582, 455-56). The poor, widows, and orphans were a special responsibility of the church (Deuteronomy 10:18; James 1:27), so the purposes of the church would be benefitted—indirectly but inevitably—by bequests for road repairs which would permit safer travel for them. The argument here requires a stretch, no doubt. It would be fair to characterize it as asserting that these purposes must have been charitable because they took the financial burden off the church. This is very like the argument we hear today, except that we substitute the word "government" for "church." The connection between religion and charity lay at the foundation of the law's approach.

Conclusion

As a matter of power, modern legislatures have the ability to rewrite virtually any legal rule. The law of charity is no exception. Legislators, perhaps even judges, can fashion a new definition of a charitable purpose if they desire. They should, however, be honest about what they are doing. They should not pretend that the long-accepted definition of charity requires the exclusion of religion. It does just the opposite. American law began with the law of charity just described, one that put religion in the center. It has long been difficult to define a charitable purpose exactly, but defining charity as a substitute form of governmental action is to embrace an assumption that is as false to the history of the subject as it is to the motives of most philanthropists. In fact, religion has been a legitimating force, both in defining and in encouraging charitable acts, from the time our law began to take definitive shape in the twelfth century to the day before yesterday.

REFERENCES

American Law Institute. 1959. *Restatement* 2d § 371g.

Camarella, Franciscus. 1681. *De legatis et singulis rebus per fideicommissum relictis opus.* Venice.

Civilian's Notebook, Worcester Record Office, MS. 794.093 BA 2470, f. 170v.

Mantica, Franciscus. 1735. *Tractatus de conjecturis ultimarum voluntatum.* Cologne.

Moore, Franciscus. 1676. *Reading of Sir Francis Moore upon the Statute of 43 Eliz. Concerning Charitable Uses.* London.

Mostazo, Franciscus a. 1698. *Tractatus de causis piis in genere et in specie libri VIII.* Venice.

Swinburne, Henry. 1590. *Briefe Treatise of Testaments and Last Willes.* London.

Tiraquellus, Andreas. 1582. *Tractatus de privilegiis piae causae.* Cologne.

TOWARDS A MODERN IDEA OF CHARITY

Joseph Isaac Lifshitz

Introduction

When studying the philosophy of property ownership in Jewish law (*halacha*), the issue of distributive justice arises. Even those who refrain from associating Judaism with socialist ideals explicitly use Jewish law's approach to the roots of ownership to determine the principles behind the relationship between society and the individual in Judaism (Falk 1980, 117, 119).[1] The more moderate scholars point to Jewish law's commitment to principles of social justice, which allow the individual liberties up to a certain point while obligating him to be socially responsible and to engage in give-and-take with others.

Such claims about the imperative of social justice are often based on the limitations placed by Jewish law on personal ownership, the land-connected commandments of aid to the poor, and the custom of Jewish communities to enforce charity-giving. The prohibition against working the land in the Land of Israel during the Sabbatical Year, and the obligation to return land to its original owners during the Jubilee Year, point to the fact that in Judaism the individual is not considered to be master over his possessions (Tamari 1998, 37-38).[2] A similar claim has been heard concerning distributive justice, based on the explanation of the rule of *kofin al middat Sodom* (literally: coercing over the trait of Sodom), according to which an owner's unwillingness to help another person is overridden by a court of law, if he himself will not lose anything by complying (Lichtenstein 1972, 362-382; Dagan 1999, 179).

Claims in favor of distributive justice are not generated from concern for legal sources. Many of the prophets' preachings were focused on charity. Perhaps Isaiah is the most explicit in regarding charity as the utmost value, even more than faith in God:

> "What need have I of all your sacrifices?" says the Lord. "I am sated with burnt offerings of rams, and suet of fatlings, and blood of bulls; and I have no delight in lambs and he-goats."... Wash yourselves clean; Put your evil doings away from My sight. Cease to do evil; Learn to do good. Devote yourselves to justice; Aid the wronged. Uphold the rights of the orphan; Defend the cause of the widow (Isaiah 1:11-17).

Lifshitz, Joseph Isaac. 2012. Towards a Modern Idea of Charity. *Conversations on Philanthropy* IX: 84-104. ISSN 1552-9592
©The Philanthropic Enterprise.

To be sure, they ask Me daily, eager to learn My ways. Like a nation that does what is right, that has not abandoned the laws of its God, they ask Me for the right way, they are eager for the nearness of God: Why, when we fasted, did You not see? When we starved our bodies, did You pay no heed? Because on your fast day you see to your business and oppress all your laborers! Because you fast in strife and contention, and you strike with a wicked fist!... No, this is the fast I desire: To unlock fetters of wickedness, and untie the cords of the yoke, to let the oppressed go free; to break off every yoke. It is to share your bread with the hungry, and to take the wretched poor into your home; when you see the naked, to clothe him, and not to ignore your own kin (Isaiah 58:2-7).

The number of scriptures which are concerned with charity and found their ways into liturgy as well had always a strong effect on the priority of values. It is indeed no wonder that many give the value of charity an upper hand over a right for private property, and that is why this discussion has led to the conclusion that the Jewish concept of ownership, since it limits the right to private property when a social cause is involved, rejects the classical liberal approach that sees people as absolute masters of their possessions. Both the claim and the conclusion are expressed in the following quote from Rabbi Aharon Lichtenstein:

Coercion over the trait of Sodom completely contradicts the widespread idea that man is the supreme ruler over his possessions, that his property is his to do with it as he pleases; as long as he is not causing direct damage to another person, no one can hinder him. Jewish law has a different spirit to it.... In Jewish Law there is almost none of the aversion to private property that the Church Fathers expressed.... But Jewish Law never idolized this concept, and other moral necessities may occasion its limitation. Though Jewish Law is extremely removed from Proudhon's statement that "Property is theft," on the other hand, it refuses even to agree with the popular expression that "An Englishman's home is his castle."... We must differentiate between ownership for the sake of usage and ownership for the sake of sovereignty; we must agree with the first statement, and condemn the latter (1972, 380-381).

On the other hand, radical scholars more inclined to socialism claim that the injunctions to charity, the commandments relating to the Land, and the matter of forcing a person to help his fellow if he himself is not inconvenienced by it—all evince Jewish law's social agenda. According to these radicals, Jewish law is not satisfied with placing general limitations on the right to private ownership, but rather demands its implementation in a distributive policy applicable to the possessions in society, the goal being to decrease poverty or even do away with it altogether (Federbush 1952, 126-127). In this context, charity has been seen as one of the expressions of a social plan for balancing class gaps. It seems that all property belongs to God, and man is entrusted with it for his own use, and for sharing it with the needy. A claim repeated time and again is that the words *tzedaka* (charity) and *tzedek* (justice) are one and the same (Kister 1968, 168-169). It must be noted that this claim is not completely accurate, for the word *tzedaka* in the Bible is merely a different form of the word *tzedek,* and is not the same as the term *tzedaka* in the language of the Talmudic sages and in Modern Hebrew (Frisch 1924, 77).[3]

According to one of these opinions, the dynamics of the commandment to give charity bring about the transfer of the individual's personal obligation to the society as a whole, and then the society is permitted to collect funds from its members beyond the sum they are obligated to give as individuals—and not only as a moral obligation but rather with the goal of establishing social justice (Tamari 1998, 52).[4] According to yet another opinion, charity is proof of Jewish law's social policy, which is binding on the social organization and obligates it to engage in distributive policies according to equal basic needs determined by the society's culture and resources (Walzer 1983, 3-6, 75-78, 92).

The attempts of radical social commentators to prove the value of Jewish law as a relevant social message would have been praiseworthy if only they had not taken such an extreme stance regarding distributive justice, which has led them to misrepresent Jewish law's approach, namely, the overall picture of commandments and rulings that deal with the definition of ownership and the moral nature of charity. Their conclusions are based on a selection of sources which are presented as the social manifest of Jewish law, but they ignore other sources from which other conclusions arise.

As I have shown elsewhere (Lifshitz 2004, 34-66), Jewish law does not present in any way the limitations on the right to private property and the individual's obligation to be considerate of others as two sides of the same coin. In other words, Jewish law does not put charity to the test of adversary relationship. Jewish law does sometimes limit the individual's mastery over his possessions, but it does not do so from a stance of distributive justice and does not place these limitations within its judicial system. The wealthy man's moral conscience does not translate into a judicial right of the needy person, and the needy person—and society in his name—may not demand anything from the wealthy man. Moreover, the effort to find distributive justice misrepresents the Talmudic approach to social welfare and the process of development of the concept of welfare as expressed in Jewish communities in the Middle Ages.

Where, then, do the limitations on property rights come from, and how can they be reconciled with the legal definition of ownership as sovereignty over property? Jewish law's complex attitude toward property rights is connected to the complex relationship between man and God. Limiting man's freedom in the face of the Divine reflects the unequal relationship between them. Curtailing man's mastery over his possessions is derived solely from man's religious obligation, and not from his status vis-à-vis other human beings. His rights over his property are limited by the religious obligation to leave the land fallow on the Sabbatical Year and to return land to its owner during the Jubilee. Similarly, acting in accordance to the trait of Sodom is considered a defiance of a religious value, since it is construed as a tendency to identify with the values of the city of Sodom, the moral antithesis of Jewish law.[5] So too, giving charity is a religious norm, one which channels the natural God-given tendency to be merciful into personal responsibility and generosity; this in no way lessens a person's mastery over his possessions.

All the limitations placed by Jewish religious law on property rights are of a moral nature—they provide for no legal standing or enjoin no monetary obligation, and there is nothing in them that changes the legal definition of property rights. Therefore, any interpretation that claims the existence of distributive justice in Jewish law as separate from the individual's religious identity, and defines individual obligations in legal terms and not in moral ones, must be merely a reduction of Jewish law's theological principles to an anachronistic political manifesto; and this reduction distorts the judicial principle as well.

Public responsibility regarding charity-giving arises from viewing the Jewish People as a religious body whose existence as a collective group has intrinsic meaning. The Jewish People has a covenant with God and is committed—as a people—to Torah values; it is also obligated to force the individuals within the collective to perform those commandments that apply to them as individuals.

Thus, the collective has obligations of its own. The obligations of each individual are translated into collective obligations as well, owing to the collective's obligation to force individuals to observe the commandments. This is how Maimonides defined the obligation to perform the commandment of giving charity, seeing one's belonging to a religious collective as the root of this commandment: "All of Israel and those who join them are like brothers, for it says, 'you are children of the Lord, your God.' If a brother will not have mercy on his own brother, who will have mercy on him? And to whom do the poor of Israel look to? To the non-Jews who hate them and persecute them? Obviously, they look only to their brethren" (10:2; see also 10:1).

The fulfilling of a moral obligation expresses the Jewish spiritual ethos, and the mutual help enables the continued physical existence of the Jewish People. And so, the existence of the political entity is demanded by the religious entity and nourishes it.

The Concept of Welfare in the Talmud

The concept of welfare in the Talmud leans, to a great extent, on the agricultural-social commandments as they appear in the Bible. There are almost no commandments to give charity that are not connected to agricultural produce. That being said, the Torah does specifically command to give charity to the poor and forbids ignoring their distress: "If there shall be a destitute person among you, any of your brethren in any of your cities, in your land that the Lord, your God, gives you, you shall not harden your heart or close your hand against your destitute brother. Rather, you shall open your hand to him; you shall lend him his requirement, whatever is lacking to him" (Deuteronomy 15:7-8).

But besides this commandment and others that demand that one be considerate of the poor when it comes to legal actions and collecting loans, the Torah does not mention the commandment to donate money to the poor many times. On the other hand, the Torah does mention many agricultural-social commandments. It commands to leave a *pe'ah*—a corner—of the field for the poor, to leave them also *leket* (stray wheat stalks that fall from the hand of the harvester) and *shichechah* (stray bushels left behind in the field); a further commandment is to leave the poor the small bunches of grapes as well. The Torah also commands to set aside one tenth of the crops for the poor in the third and sixth years of the Sabbatical Year cycle.

It is possible that until the time of the Mishnah, the Jewish society being a basically agricultural one, these measures were sufficient for supporting the destitute. But the changes wrought by the Hellenistic period, specifically the creation of an urban society, caused the poor to lose their sources of livelihood, and this brought the sages to fill in what was missing by expanding the commandment to give charity; it became not only a matter of providing food for the needy but also giving money and other means of subsistence.

The changing of the commandment to give charity from one that has a connection to rural life to one connected to urban living is apparently what added a public and monetary aspect to it, as opposed to the personal and agricultural aspect that this commandment had until then. This was the background to the appearance of the institution of charity collectors (*gabba'ei tzedaka*) and the right of the community to force individuals to give charity in the Mishnah and the Talmud. The term "*gabbai tzedakah*"—charity collector—appears already in the Mishnah[6] and the Tosefta[7] as a known entity, and there are even rules laid down regarding ethics and transparency. Talmudic law even mandates the establishment of a charity organization in every town: "Any town that does not have the following ten things, no Torah scholar is permitted to live in it: the court flogs and punishes, and charity is collected by two and distributed by three, and a synagogue, and a public bath, and a lavatory, a doctor, and craftsman, and scribe (and cook), and a teacher for the young children" (BT Sanhedrin 17b).[8]

This law recommends aboveboard distribution of charity and determines the number of people required for it. On the other hand, one can also note the authority given to these collectors, placing their role within the context of the public's obligation to care for the needy. The collectors are given a certain degree of authority to enforce their collecting, and the Talmud even calls them *ba'alei serarah*—bearers of authority, for they have the authority to take collateral from those who refuse to give to the poor "even on the Sabbath eve (= Friday)" (BT Bava Batra 8b). The role of the collector was to encourage the individuals to give charity, and then to collect it and to distribute it. This task was dealt with by a number of authority-bearing people, as stipulated by Jewish law when describing the establishment of a special court of justice that was placed in charge of the collection and distribution of charity: "The [charity] fund is collected only by two, for one may not invest [people] with the power to collect funds unless there are two ... and it is distributed only by three, because it is like monetary cases, for they give each one his needs for the Sabbath. Food for the soup kitchen is collected by three, for it is not a set thing, and is distributed by three" (Maimonides 9:5). Many Jewish laws in the Talmud guide the appointment and behavior of charity collectors: they must have a good name and lineage, and they are commanded to conduct themselves particularly honestly, in a way that raises no suspicion of their having embezzled any of the money intended for charity (Mishnah, Kiddushin 4:5; BT Bava Batra 8a-9b). Two charitable institutions were established in the cities: the charity fund and the soup kitchen. Money was donated to the fund, and food to the soup kitchen. In this way, basic subsistence was guaranteed to every needy person.

The commandment to give charity is described as an obligation that is binding on any person, regardless of his social status and economic situation. Even a poor person who himself is supported by the charity fund is obligated to give to others. The pain and distress of the needy should touch everyone's heart and cause them to give of their money to him. The establishment's work for the poor people's welfare does not exempt the individual from his moral obligation to care for the needy.

There is one commandment, though, that seems to command distribution: the commandment of the Jubilee year. According to this commandment, every fiftieth year, all lands that were sold before should be redistributed to their original owner so every citizen should have land. But my claim is that this commandment as well should be understood within the rural context. That is why it was never used to extract from it any law but always stayed as a secluded commandment. It wasn't even practiced during the second temple period. The first reason for that is that the Jubilee year is not a social commandment but a religious one. Its purpose is not to enhance justice but sanctity. The second reason is that the Jubilee year is a typical rural commandment. In a rural society, selling land was usually connected to slavery. To own land was not only a matter of rights but a matter of lordship— of being a master over whoever works in the land. The commandment of the Jubilee year came to correct it. If land can't be completely sold, the same should be true of slaves. That is why we may deduce from such a commandment that it is slavery that should be eliminated, not poverty.

The Custom of a Monetary Tithe

In the Middle Ages, the "urban" welfare institutions were an inseparable part of Jewish communities. As Maimonides testifies, "We have never seen nor heard of a community of Jews that does not have a charity fund" (*Hilchot Matnon Aniyim* 9:3). One of the notable examples is the acceptance of the custom to give one-tenth of all profits to the poor, modeled upon the mitzvah of *ma'aser ani* (the obligation to give the poor one-tenth of the agricultural produce in the third and sixth years of every Sabbatical cycle). This obligation set a minimal standard for charity, and allowed anyone who wished to do more, to give up to one-fifth of his profits. This institutional form of redistribution did not, however, uproot the role of private charity. The community collected a welfare tax from its members, and at the same time recognized the right of every individual to give charity to his family members and to other needy people according to his own wishes. Therefore, the community did not collect the full sum that it was entitled to from every individual, so that he would be able to fulfill his obligation by giving to his relatives as well.

The connection between the custom of a tithe taken from money and the land-based commandments arises from the custom of devoting to charity one-tenth of any profits, which was apparently common in the Middle Ages. An example is a Tosafot that quotes a *midrash* extrapolating from the verse that contains the commandment to tithe the crops the obligation to set aside one-tenth even from non-agricultural profits: "It says in the *midrash* in the Sifrei: 'You shall surely tithe the entire crop of your planting, the produce of the field, year by year.'—I have only the crop of your planting that is obligated in a tithe. How do we know that interest and trade and all other types of profits [are also included in this obligation]? It says 'the entire [crop]'; it would have been enough to say 'the crop'. Why does it say 'the entire'? To include interest and trade and anything else that profits a person" (Ta'anit 9a, "*Aser Te'aser*").

The Tosafot attribute this *midrash* to the Sifrei. In the Sifrei that is extant today, this *midrash* does not appear. But in the Peskita Derav Kahana similar things are said: "'You shall surely tithe' (Deuteronomy 14:22), so that you will not be caused loss. Tithe so that you will get rich. The Holy One, Blessed be He, said: Tithe what is mine, and I will tithe what is yours. 'The entire'—R. Abba bar Kahana said: this hints to the traders and the seafarers, that they should separate a tenth for those who labor in Torah" (1952, 172).

The custom of a monetary tithe was apparently common in Western Europe even before the thirteenth century—the Sefer Chasidim mentions it (1957, 144), as does R. Isaac of Vienna. R. Isaac offers as a source for this the *midrash* that promises blessing to he who is careful to tithe his produce:

In the first chapter of [tractate] Ta'anit [it says]: R. Yochanan says: aser te'aser? Tithe so that you should be rich (a play on words— te'aser—titasher). R. Yochanan saw the young son of R. Shimon ben Lakish. He said to him: "Tell me what verse you learned in school." He said to him: "You shall surely tithe." He said to him "Tithe so that you will be rich." He said to him: "Is it permitted to test the Holy One,

Blessed be He? Doesn't it say 'You should not test the L-rd, your God'?" He said to him: "That is what R. Oshaya said: Except for this, for it says, 'Test me with this, said the L-rd of Hosts, [and see if] I will not open for you the Heavens and rain down on you blessing ad bli dai'. What is ad bli dai? Rami bar Chama said that Rav said 'Until your lips will be tired (yiblu) from saying "enough!" (dai).' We learn that a person is commanded to tithe his money, and the more he gives [as part of the] tithes, the richer he gets. And whoever gives charity more than the tithes, the better, as long as he does not spend more than a fifth... (1852, Pt. 1, 13).

Like R. Isaac of Vienna, his student the Maharam of Rothenburg related to the monetary tithe as a widespread custom:

It would seem that after the tithe-monies were set aside for the poor, they should not be used for fulfilling a different commandment, for it looks like he is stealing from the poor, for even though it (the money tithe) is not from the Torah, but rather a custom, we have a standing principle that things that are permitted, and others consider them forbidden, you are not permitted to allow them in their presence, for it says "He should not profane his words". And that is a Rabbinical law, as it says in [Nedarim] 15a. And it is not like the case brought at the beginning of the first chapter of Arachin (6b): a Jew who committed himself to donate a candle and a lamp to a synagogue, it is permitted to use it for fulfilling a different commandment; for that case is different, for in both cases it is a deed done for the High (for God), but the poor have already merited the tithe money by custom, for the entire exile has this custom, and one may not change [the usage] from [charity for] the poor to a different commandment for which the poor have no need, as it says in the second chapter of Shekalim (mishnah 5)—the remnants of the poor go to the poor (74).[9]

The Maharam relates to the custom of giving the tithe of the profits to charity as a custom and not as a commandment whose source is in the Torah or in the Rabbinical tradition. The custom creates an inferred stipulation, for the assumption is that anyone who sets aside money for a tithe intended it for charity alone. This assumption obligates the collectors to relate to this money as money intended only for charity.

The tension between this personal commandment and the public one can be explained by two Talmudic principles. According to one, charity is a personal commandment—one's obligation to care for the needs of one's relatives first. This principle is learned from the commandment regarding lending money, where it says, "Your poor and your town's poor—your poor come first. The poor of your town and the poor of another town—the poor of your town come first" (BT Bava Metzia, 72a).[10] This obligation does not negate, of course, the individual obligation toward the poor of one's own town, but by placing the position of a person's close relatives above that of other needy people it weakens the ability to raise enough money for the town's poor who have no relatives.

And indeed, against this principle of "your poor come first" we have R. Abba bar Zevda's saying in the Talmud: "Whoever gives his gifts to one priest, brings famine to the world" (BT Eiruvin 63a). This saying expresses the sages' fear of denying the distant poor person his part, and recommends balancing the principle of "your poor come first" by giving part of the charity to more distant poor people—those of the town at large. But in the Talmud itself, I did not find an opinion that provides a balance between these two principles.

The existence of two obligations toward the poor—the individual's and the community's—raises a problem, for the individual strives to fulfill his obligation to others out of a feeling of personal involvement and prefers his relatives, while the collectors, who bear the public responsibility toward all of the town's needy, prefer an objective, fair distribution.

This problem is not limited to the question of charity. The relationship between the individual's freedom and the desire for centralized action is one of those problems that arise from the dynamic character of the public organism—a changing and developing entity—and from the awareness of its individual components. In spite of the value attributed to the community, Jewish law accepts the freedom of the individual as a value that must be preserved, and guides us to restrain ourselves when coming to the activation of community values. It grants an individual freedom of action whenever this will not bring about a collapse in the public arena.

A balance between the poor who is a close relative and the other needy people does appear in the works of the codifiers of the Middle Ages. Maimonides, for instance, related to this issue when dealing with the question of the tithes, and ruled that when giving *ma'aser ani*—the tithe intended for the poor—one must divide it into two equal parts. Half should go to one's poor relatives, and the other half "to any poor person going by" (6:11).[11]

The Rabbis' awareness of the tension between individual and community generally led to matters being settled within the community. The laws of charity, like many of the laws relating to the community, were worked out through an inter-communal discussion between the individuals and the community at large, determined by the customs, the needs of the public, and the individuals' consent, as the Re'em (Constantinople, 1450-1526) wrote: "Since vows and pledges are dependent only on the will of the entire community or its majority, then vows and pledges have also become one of those things that belong to the community, such as city laws, enactments and decrees. And therefore, just like in matters of city laws and enactments we go by the majority opinion in the community, so it is right that in matters of vows and pledges we should follow the majority opinion in the community" (Mizrachi 1938, 53).[12]

The responsa of the Rabbis in the Middle Ages who ruled on questions in this matter reflect the various patterns of solutions used by the communities. Some ruled from a position that supported the idea of protecting the public, and some ruled from a position of concern for the liberty of the individuals. Those that supported the public's interests did so because of a pessimistic approach, fearing that too much freedom of the individual will endanger the public. Those that advocated protecting the individuals' right to donate as they saw fit were more optimistic. It seems that the pessimistic approach expressed a relatively extreme stance, whereas the optimistic approach became the mainstream in Jewish law. But both maintained the legal framework which protects the basic rights of both the individual and the community.

The discussion among the Rabbis in the Middle Ages was based on the interpretation of a law brought in the Tosefta, and, to a certain degree, on its various versions. The Tosefta deals with the way of distributing money for charity, and the collectors' authority in this distribution. The Tosefta discusses a case in which someone pledged money for charity but did not specify which charity. The Tosefta's assumption is that the individual prefers giving to the poor of his own town, over giving to the poor of another town, and similarly, the collectors prefer to give to the poor of their own town. Therefore, in the case of an unspecific pledge, the assumption is that the donator wished to donate to the local poor. At the end of the section, the Tosefta declares that in the case where the money has already been handed over to the collectors, the authority lies with the collectors, and not with the donator:

> An individual, who pledged money to charity in his town, gives it to
> the poor of his town. In another town—he gives it to the poor of the

other town. The collectors that pledged charity in their town give it to the poor of that town. In a different town, they give it to the poor of the other town. Someone who pledged money to charity, and the collectors have not taken it yet, is permitted to change it (its usage) to another cause. Once the collectors have it, he is not permitted to change it to another cause, unless they agree (Megilla, 2:15).13

There is disagreement among the Rabbis regarding the ruling in the Tosefta that the individual has the authority to determine where the money will go as long as he still has it in his own hands—a disagreement arising from different versions of the text. It turns out that there is another version of the Tosefta, according to which the last section grants full authority to the collectors, from the minute the individual has made his pledge verbally: "Someone who pledged money to charity, and the collectors have not taken it yet, is not permitted to change [its use] to another cause, unless they agree" (Megillah 2:15).[14]

Anyone who has made a verbal pledge to give of his money to the poor, has thereby relinquished his right to determine the cause toward which it will go, and the authority is placed in the hands of the collectors.

This difference between two extant versions was apparently the basis of the disagreement between the authorities of the Middle Ages. Among the Western European authorities were the Ritzva, R. Isaac son of R. Abraham of Dampier (d.1210) (Auerbach 1976, 270 note 47)[15] and R. Isaac of Vienna (1180-1250). The Ritzva thought that the authority is in the hands of the collectors. As a general rule, he tended to side with the public against the individual and thought that usually it was permitted to force a person to give charity.[16] In a *responsum* to the heads of a community who demanded that they be authorized to distribute all donations for charity, he accepted their stance. He based his decision on a passage in the Talmud that grants the leadership of a central community the authority to collect from adjacent communities (BT Megillah 27a-b). He thought that this outstanding authority given to collectors over people not from their community indicates that the collectors have sole authority in the community itself, and therefore any donation to charity, of any individual in the town, should be given over to the collectors (R. Isaac son of R. Moshe of Vienna 1852, 23).[17]

The obligation to give charity monies to the collectors of the community depends, according to the Ritzva, on the assumption that they will act in accordance with Jewish law, and will give some of the money to the donator's relatives as well, according to their judgment. The right of the donator to set aside money for his relatives must be preserved: "But an individual who donated charity on his own initiative, may give it to anyone he wants to," but this is only as an addition to the sum that he has given the collectors. The Ritzva adds that the limitation placed on the freedom of the individual to decide where his donations are going to go arises from a municipal decision, in which the individual participated and which he agreed to: "But only if he decided upon charity with the townspeople."[18] The Ritzva's opinion that power must be given to the collectors continues Rashi's approach, according to which the collectors may use charity donations to buy even mats for the synagogue (see BT Bava Batra, 8b and Rashi ibid.).

Other halachic authorities held that as long as the money pledged for charity has not reached the hands of the town leaders, the decision regarding the destination of the monies remains in the hands of the donator, and he may do with his money as he wishes. R. Isaac of Vienna, for instance, held that in general the community institutions do not have the authority to take over all the fundraising for charity in the community, and giving money to charity should remain in the hands of the individual. According to him, the ruling to give the poor-tithe primarily to relatives should be teaching us the law about the commandment of giving charity in general (1852, Part I, 22).[19] R. Isaac of Vienna is of the opinion that the relative receives the charity by default, and therefore in any case of a donation to charity where the receiving cause was not stipulated, we can assume that the giver intended to give to his relatives and not to the town poor. Even if the giver stated explicitly that he wishes the donation to be given to the town poor, the collectors must distribute the monies according to the accepted compromises—half-and-half, or one-third vs. two-thirds.

When settling the disagreements, the responsa range from recognizing the greater power of the public to recognizing the individuals' demands, but it seems that as a matter of course R. Isaac's ruling was the one that was accepted as law in later times (Shulchan Aruch and the Rema, Yoreh Deah, 251:5).[20] In another place, his opinion is offered in similar words:

> And from this I learn that a person who made a vow to give charity may give it to his poor relatives, up to half of all that he vowed to give, and according the other opinion even two parts he may give to his relatives from the tithe (even two parts...). And this is a a-fortiori assumption: If even the poor-tithe that the Torah said to give to poor people he can give it to his relatives, up to half or two parts, all the more so charity, that he gives on his own initiative; this is true if he set aside money for charity and said it was for the general poor but if

he pledged charity without specifying at the time of the pledge whom he wishes to distribute it to, he may give it to all to his poor relatives; and more, since he is wealthy, and the responsibility for the livelihood of his poor relatives is placed on him and not on the local collectors, as it says in chapter R. Eliezer in Nedarim. So the charity is his relatives', and therefore they take it. So it seems to me, Isaac the son of Moshe (R. Mordecai son of R. Hillel Hacohen, Bava Batra, 659).

This discussion of the compromise—half or one- and two-thirds, is also discussed in the Mishnah and the Tosefta, and later on in the Jerusalem Talmud: "This measure is stipulated for the Priests, Levites and Israelites alike. Should he desire to save aught, he can only retain half and give the other half away. If he has only a very small quantity, then he must place it before them and then divide it among themselves" (Mishnah, Peah, 8:6).

According to this Mishnah, any person—whether a Priest, a Levite, or an Israelite—is permitted to give half of the Maaser to a needy relative and the other half to a stranger. The Tosefta quotes this possibility as well but adds another opinion—to give to the relative two-thirds (Peah 4:2; see JT Peah 8:6).

The various approaches of the authorities all recognized the social pact as a factor that lies at the base of the public decision, just like they recognized the obligation of the individual to be personally involved. The only limitations of the public decision are the limitations placed on it by Jewish law, and these determine that the total sum given to charity may not exceed one-tenth of a person's possessions and profits (or one-fifth of them, for those who wish to give more than is necessary). It is from this sum only that every person is obligated to help his relatives. The public decision will have to apply, therefore to a compromise within the framework of that 10 percent, so that the individual will be able to fulfill his obligation to his relatives and the public will fulfill its obligations to the town poor. The form of compromise achieved in each society gives its public welfare institutions their particular character. But in any community, whatever compromise was made should be perceived as a tax-deductible system. Accepting the wishes of the individual to devote some of the money he was asked to give to charity to his relative was perceived as meaning a deduction from the whole sum. Can we deduce from that a Halachik acceptance of the modern idea of tax deductibility? That question should only be answered in the context of an account of the transition which was made in the creation of the modern state, which I shall discuss in the next section.

Charity in a Modern State

As we saw so far, the social obligations in the Jewish tradition went through a transition, due to changes in the market, from completely privatized charity in antiquity to a collective or public charity in the Middle Ages. Should we assume now, when the political sphere developed the modern state, that a change should be formed towards a welfare state? Should we accept policies of the sort we find in socialist countries? Should we accept social goals such as the elimination of poverty or more equal distribution? Should we accept the idea of distributive justice? In a nutshell—should we replace charity with justice? My claim in seeking answers to these questions is not that the state should abdicate responsibility and refuse to help the needy but rather that we must consider the nature of the responsibility the state assumes. A state does represent a collective responsibility of its members—but this responsibility is not different in its essence from the responsibility that falls upon the individual. It is a responsibility which is bottom-up and not top-down. The many never have a responsibility that the individuals don't have. They just take it upon themselves collectively.

In order to make any deduction from Jewish sources of antiquity to the Middle Ages to modernity, we must note that political thought underwent a massive transformation during the Enlightenment, and hence economic thought as well, abandoning its descriptive posture for a prescriptive one. If Aristotle, Augustine, and Aquinas focused upon describing the workings of the economy, Bernard Mandeville and Adam Smith directed attention to prescribing how the economy ought to run. This change in approach could arise only once the market had come to be perceived as a discrete entity. Prior to the modern state's historical emergence, the market was not conceived as an autonomous system susceptible of manipulation. Only when the modern state arose in the 17th and 18th centuries did particular Enlightenment ideas about the nature of liberty and equality combine with other concepts to give rise to our present notions of the polity and of the market economy. It was the idea of the state as a *political project*, as a creation of the many rather than simply something that is given, which enabled man to contemplate parallel ways of developing the market. The market came to be understood as a human project that should be directed and shaped by man. The idea that an entity as spontaneous as a market could be developed, improved, or regulated by man did not exist previously. Thus it is not surprising that neither the Talmudic Sages nor the Rabbinic authorities proposed these ideas before they rose to prominence in early modernity. To argue otherwise would be anachronistic.

However, the changes that the polity and the market have undergone are not moral but conceptual. They don't demand a new constitution of values, such as a quest to alleviate poverty, but can lead us instead to new applications of the old values, such as our ongoing individual responsibility to care for the poor. What should be deduced from the development of the modern state is a better and more sophisticated idea of how to provide for the welfare of the poor, not a moral change challenging us to eliminate poverty or equalize incomes. For some, the modern state came to replace the kings of the past; that is why they expect the state to have a total welfare responsibility. They neglect the fact that this responsibility should always be estimated to be the sort of responsibility that falls upon the individual, as was demanded in the past. This responsibility can be discharged through collective means, whether governmental or through charitable organizations, but there is no foundation in Jewish law to rationalize the expansive demands of social justice. The same principles of the Torah which don't include any responsibility to eliminate poverty are still standing.

Why does politics in modern times indulge a pretension to eliminate poverty? Where did ideas of economic equality and social justice come from? The source for such attempts is secularity. Modern man not only "killed" God but also wants to be his heir. Many responsibilities that used to be attributed to God came to be seen as man's responsibility, and the alleviation of poverty is one of them. I contend that such an undertaking is not only super-pretentious but also very unhealthy for individuals and for our political communities. Man should try to help his fellow man but should not expect the state to resolve all miseries. Every person is different, and as long as societies exist, all people will never be economically equal, and poverty will not be extinguished. Stewardship, compassion, charity, generosity—those are the values that fall upon man. Let's leave complete responsibility for justice to God.

NOTES

[1] Falk 1980, 117, 119; Dagan 1999, 178-190; Federbush 1952, 23-25, 126-128, 138-140; Rabbi Lichtenstein 1972, 380-381; Tamari 1998, 36-38, 52-56, 210-211, 240, 242-243, 248-249, 277; Frisch 1924, 77, 80; Walzer 1983, 3-6, 75-78, 92.

[2] Tamari 1998, 37-38; Ben Shalom 1998, 52-53.

[3] Frisch was the first to point out the etymological connection between *tzedaka* (charity) and *tzadikut* (righteousness); according to him, it arises from the changing meanings between Biblical and Talmudic language. In the Bible,

tzedaka means *tzadikut*, in other words, the characteristic of a righteous person, whereas in the language of the Talmudic sages, it means giving money to the needy. See also Meir Tamari: "The Divine origin of wealth is the central principle of Jewish economic philosophy. All wealth belongs to God, who has given it temporarily to man, on the basis of stewardship, for his physical wellbeing" (1998, 36); and: "The 'haves' in Judaism have an obligation to share their property with the 'have nots,' since it was given to them by God partly for that purpose"(52).

[4] Tamari 1998, 52: "Charity is not simply an act of kindness but rather the fulfillment of a legal obligation"; p. 240: "The community has a responsibility for the welfare of its members and a corresponding right to finance those needs through taxation over and above the individual's duty to contribute to charity." See also p. 277. Public responsibility does not allow the public to collect more than the amount that an individual is obligated for, since this is not a legal obligation. The community is allowed to oversee only the distribution (see more on this below). See also Dagan 1999, 179: "The giving of charity in Jewish tradition is not a matter of mercy, kindness, generosity or personal conscience, but rather a matter of justice (thus explaining the linguistic affinity between *tzedakah* and *tzedek*). Giving charity is a fulfillment of a legal obligation: the realization of the community's rights and the rights of the unfortunates in the community, by way of the possessions of those who have." Dagan's main claim is based on a Talmudic discussion regarding a person who benefits from another's resources, while not depleting them in any way; in his opinion, this principle is a result of the ruling that a person is forced to give if it does not harm him ("coercion over the trait of Sodom"). The problem with this claim is that according to most medieval scholars—and their opinion was accepted as the common ruling—there is no connection between benefit without any obligation attached and the coercion over the trait of Sodom. Therefore, his assumption that it is justifiable to force a rich person to give of his possessions to the poor person is mistaken. According to Dagan, only some loss that the poor person causes the rich one can absolve the rich man from the legal obligation of benefitting the poor. But according to Jewish Law, the virtual interactions that take place between the receiver and the giver who does not lose anything in the process are contractual, and based on the benefit. The minute the benefit causes loss, the virtual

contract translates into a legal claim against the one who has benefitted. Only a benefit that does not cause loss does not create a contractual obligation and does not entail any claim for payment.

5 Mishnah, Avot, 5:1: "There are four character types among people. He who says what is mine is mine and what is yours is yours is an average character; some say it is the character of Sodom (*middat Sodom*)."

6 Mishnah Demai 3:1; Mishnah Kiddushin 4:5; Mishnah Bava Kamma 10:1.

7 Tosefta Peah 4:15; Tosefta Demai 3:16-17; Tosefta Bava Kamma 11:6; Tosefta Bava Metzia 3:9.

8 The community records of Jewish communities in Europe indicate the wide prevalence of the charity collectors in Jewish communities. See, for example, *Pinkas Kahal Tiktin 5301-5566*, 1997, section 242, p. 152.

9 Responsa of the Maharam of Rothenburg (1608), 74: "The money of the tithe, it seems that if they were intended to be given to the poor, they should not be used for [fulfilling] a different commandment." Also, see Rema, Shulchan Aruch Yoreh Deah 349:1, and the Shach there, 3.

10 This rule was stated originally in reference to lending money to a poor person.

11 Maimonides, *Mishneh Torah, Hilchot Matnot Aniyim* 6:11. R. Isaac son of R. Moshe of Vienna, *Or Zarua*, Part I, Laws of Charity, 22; see also Mishnah Peah 8:6. On the other hand, see Tosefta (Liberman Edition), Peah 4:2: "Abba Yoseh son of Dustai said in the name of R. Liezer: If he wants, he places a third before them, and leaves two parts to his relatives." This is the ruling that was later accepted. See, for instance, Schulcan Aruch Yoreh Deah 251:5: "The man who makes a living like an important person, who eats well— bread and meat and cooked foods—and is dressed and covered properly, certainly is obligated to give charity—one tenth or one fifth of his livelihood [for if he does not have a sufficient livelihood he should not be obligated even this sum] and a great part of the charity he should give to his relatives and the town poor, and a small amount he is obligated to give to far away people and to the poor of another town, for otherwise [in] a town of poor people they will starve to death, God forbid...."

12 See Shach, Shulchan Aruch Yoreh Deah 251:9.

13 Tosefta Megilla (Lieberman) 2:15. And in a similar version of that, in the London Manuscript: "An individual who pledged money for charity in his town, gives it to the people of his town. Elders who pledged in their city give it to the poor of that city. One who pledges money for charity, as long

as the elders have not taken it, they are allowed to change [its use] to something else. Once the elders have taken it, he may not change [its use] to something else, unless they agree." Also in the JT, Megillah, 3:2, and Nachmanides in his *chiddushim*, Bava Batra, 8b.

[14] Tosefta (Liberman), Megillah 2:15, according to the Erfurt manuscript. This same version appears in the Responsa of the Rashba, Jerusalem, 1997, Part I, 604.

[15] The Ritzva was French, but for the purpose of this discussion one should consider northern France and Germany as one unit. See, for instance, Chaim Soloveitchik 2003, 17-18.

[16] *Sefer Or Zarua*, Part I, Laws of Charity, 4. Tosafot, Bava Batra 8b, D"H Akfe.

[17] See also Mordechai, Bava Batra, 502, and the Beit Yosef on Tur Yoreh Deah, 251.

[18] The Maharam of Rothenberg presented a similar claim in his Responsa, Part IV (Prague), 918: "About Reuven who is separating himself from the community by not donating to the charity fund and not to pay taxes with them, if the townspeople had this custom from long ago [not] to give together but each one gives on his own, they cannot coerce him and change their custom if he does not agree, but if they had the custom of giving together, he cannot separate himself from them."

[19] See also the Mordechai, Bava Batra, 500. In saying "It seems to me" the Or Zarua means to point to the fact that he does not agree with the Ritzva. In the Mordechai, on the other hand, he does not make a point that his opinion is different from the quote. He quotes Ritzva as though he expresses his own opinion as well.

[20] See also the Beit Yosef, Tur Yoreh Deah 251:5; R. Eliezer of Metz, the Shita Mekubetzet Nedarim 65b; the Kol Bo 82; and the Tashbetz Hakatan 405, in the name of the Maharam of Rothenburg. The Ritzva's responsum was quoted with the addition of the words "he who separates money for charity," and that is the way it is mentioned in the context of trying to determine the intentions of someone who pledged money for charity but did not specify his intentions. See the Mordechai: "He who pledges money for charity and has a relative in town is not permitted to give it only to his relative, but rather should give it to the town charity collectors and they will distribute it properly to each and every one." Also see the quote in the Beit Yosef mentioned above.

REFERENCES

Classical Judaic Sources:

Mishnah, Avot.

Mishnah Bava Kamma.

Mishnah Demai.

Mishnah Kiddushin.

Mishnah, Peah.

Tosefta Bava Kamma.

Tosefta Bava Metzia.

Tosefta Demai.

Tosefta Megilla.

Tosefta Peah.

JT Megillah.

BT Bava Metzia.

BT Bava Batra.

BT Eiruvin.

BT Megillah.

BT Sanhedrin.

Pesikta Derav Kahana 1952. Dov, son of Yaakov Yisrael Mandelbaum, ed. New York.

Tasafot, Ta'anit.

Rashi, *Responsa.*

Maimonides, *Mishneh Torah, Hilchot Matnot Aniyim.*

Sefer Chassidim (Bologne Manuscript).

Maharam of Rothenberg, *Responsa* (Prague, 1608).

Rema, Shulchan Aruch Yoreh Deah.

R. Eliyahu Mizrachi, Responsa (the Re'em), (Jerusalem, 1938).

R. Shabtai HaKohen, Shach, Shulchan Aruch Yoreh Deah (Kraka 1647).

Nachmanides *chiddushei HaRamban*, Bava Batra,

Rashba, *Responsa* (Jerusalem, 1997).

R. Isaac son of R. Moshe of Vienna, *Sefer Or Zarua*, Zhitomir, 1852, Jerusalem 2006.

Beit Yosef, Tur Yoreh Deah.

R. Eliezer of Metz, the Shita Mekubetzet Nedarim.

R. Shimshon B"R Tzadok, Tashbetz Hakatan, Jerusalem 2005.

R. Mordechai son of R. Hillel Hacohen, *Sefer Hamordechai*, Bava Batra.

Pinkas Kahal Tiktin 5301- 5566, Mordechai Nadav (ed.), Jerusalem, 1997.

Kol Bo.

Secondary Sources

Auerbach, Efraim A. 1976. *Ba'alei Hatosafot*. Jerusalem.

Ben Shalom, Menachem. 1998. *Hasids and hasidism in the periods of the Second Temple and the Mishna*. Tel Aviv (Hebrew).

Dagan, Chanoch. 1999. "Dinei Asiyat Osher: Bein yahadut leliberalism." *Mishpat Vehistoria*. Daniel Gottwin and Menachem Mautner, eds. Jerusalem (Hebrew).

Falk, Zeev. 1980. *Erchei Mishpat Veyahadut: Likrat philosophia shel hahalacha*. Jerusalem.

Federbush, Shimon. 1952. *Mishpat Hamelucha Beyisrael*. Jerusalem (Hebrew).

Frisch, Ephraim. 1924. *An Historical Survey of Jewish Philanthropy*. New York.

Kister, Isaac. 1968. "Dinei Tzedakah Beshimusham Bamishpat BeYisrael." *Hapraklit*. Vol. 24, 168-169 (Hebrew).

Lichtenstein, Rabbi Aharon. 1972. "Leveirur 'Cofin al Midat Sedom.'" *Hagut Ivrit BeAmerica*. Menachem, Zohari, Aryeh Tartakover and Chaim Ormian, eds. Tel Aviv (Hebrew).

Lifshitz, Yosef Yitzhak (Joseph Isaac). 2004. "Foundations of a Jewish Economic Theory." *Azure* 18: 34-66.

Soloveitchik, Chaim. 2003. *Yeinam*. Tel Aviv.

Tamari, Meir. 1998. *With All Your Possessions*. Jerusalem.

Walzer, Michel. 1983. *Spheres of Justice: A Defense of Pluralism and Equality*. New York.

PHILANTHROPY AND RESEARCH BIOBANKS:
THE MODEL OF BIOTRUST

Ilaria Anna Colussi

Biobanks: Definition, Birth, Typology

The necessity of cataloguing information is apparent in different fields of human activity. In the healthcare sector and the medical field, the need to assemble data on a population appears historically at the beginning of the modern state (ca. the nineteenth century) not merely for statistical reasons but also for the state's need to control resources which could be found in the surrounding territory (Hacking 1982).

In the twentieth century, the human body has been studied more deeply in terms of each of its components (molecules, cells, tissues, blood, etc.). This has stimulated the establishment of "biobanks" (Loft and Poulsen 1996) that represent a new way "of organizing life, of collecting, storing, and assembling life in the form of human materials" (Gottweis 2008, 24).

There are many typologies of biobanks (Sallée and Knoppers 2005), and the different terms used to describe them "reflect not only their diversity, but also demonstrate a lack of consensus on what exactly is a biobank" (Bovenberg 2006, 23).

On the basis of the *contents*, biobanks can be classified into DNA banks, tissue banks, cells banks, blood banks, stem cell banks, egg and sperm banks, etc. Classified according to the *aim*, they are distinguished into research biobanks, pathology biobanks (having diagnostic or therapeutic purposes), forensic banks used in crime prevention and detection, and biobanks for transplants. Taking as criterion the *target of reference*, biobanks can collect data belonging to small groups of people, or they can be useful for studies of entire populations (for example, in the case of population genetics).

This paper focuses on biobanks that store human tissues and are established for research purposes, the value of which has gained them the appellation of "encyclopaedia of tomorrow" (Lyotard 1984). Our specific focus is on the role of

Colussi, Ilaria Anna. 2012. Philanthropy and Research Biobanks: The Model of Biotrust. *Conversations on Philanthropy* IX: 105-117. ISSN 1552-9592 © The Philanthropic Enterprise.

philanthropy in building a reasonable model of research biobank and the complex legal issues entailed in donative activity involving human tissue.

Legal and Ethical Status of Body Parts

In order to know how best to establish and maintain research biobanks, we must understand the *status* of body parts and, as a consequence, who should be allowed to handle them.

According to international legal and ethical instruments, human beings and their bodies are not reducible to objects of experimentation without the subject's permission: the Nuremberg Code of Ethics, Oviedo Convention, and Helsinki Declaration all stress the importance of informed consent as a fundamental requirement for every kind of medical activity upon humankind. Also accorded wide acceptance around the world are the respect for human dignity and a disdain for the commodification of the human body, which cannot be sold freely on the market (see Radin 1987).

If this is the view about bodies as a whole, what about body parts? Are we owners of our own body components? What legal relationship do we have with them?

Questioning whether the individual is the owner of his or her body means asking whether one can exercise property rights over it and its components. A clarification of the concept of "property rights" is useful. When we make reference to "owning" the body, we adopt a clear property pattern. The notion of property here considered is the one that starts from the Roman Law tradition, the right *utendi et abutendi*[1] (of use and abuse), and ultimately arrives at modern property law, understood as "a bundle of rights with four key attributes: use, possession, exclusion, and disposition" (see Feldman 2011, 8). In modern framework, which includes attention to disposition, the concept of property has a close link with commercialization.

The human body is presently a highly contested area in the evolution of the laws of property. Whereas the commodification of the whole body is internationally recognized as wrong and prohibited, about the body's components there are at present at least two different positions commonly held. According to some scholars (e.g., Andrews and Nelkin 2001), body parts are nothing different from other chattels, and thus can be objects of trade and assigned at the owner's will. It is a matter of "self-dominion," "self-determination," and "autonomy" to be able to manage and handle our body parts in line with our own interests and preferences (see Morgan 2001). Others, by contrast, think that body parts must not be considered as property in this way in any case, because to do so would be to reduce human beings to commodities (see Kant 1963; Munzer 1993). There is a moral repugnance at the idea of people selling their body parts, and it is viewed as a violation of human dignity. In addition, it is believed that the consequent commercialization of body parts could bring on inequalities of protection and result in exploitation of poor people.

Questions about the application of property rights to parts of the human body necessitate further typological distinctions. Trying to categorize body parts, we can suggest the following classification: (a) inert, renewable parts; (b) parts having independent functionality, and (c) stored human tissues.

Inert, renewable parts: In determining whether property rights could apply or not, it is important to distinguish among different types of body parts. Inert, renewable body parts are those—such as hair or mammal milk—that can be reproduced by the body and the loss of which does not affect the body's physical integrity in a permanent way. When we consider such parts, it does not seem problematic to adopt a proprietary model. Indeed, it is commonly accepted that such parts, or products, after leaving a person, do not belong to him or her anymore and can be treated according to property rights.

Parts having independent functionality: A second category of body parts comprises those that have autonomous functionality (such as blood or bone marrow), which are commonly objects of transplant. In this case the preferred logic governing rights of dispensation has been the one of "gift" or "donation," based on the principle of gratuity: once a donor has given consent to donation, he or she loses the control over that blood or bone marrow, which goes to "enrich" another person and becomes part of the other's body. In this case, the property right over blood or bone marrow is transferred by the gratuity; profit is excluded, and the individual has the "management" of that part of his or her body until he or she transfers the right to it according to a spirit of gift. This is the application of a "weak" principle of gratuity which allows the exercise of a property right upon a good (from which the power of giving blood or bone marrow derives) but doesn't permit a profitable gain from the transfer.[2] This perspective, based on Titmuss' view of blood donation (1970), finds a confirmation within the Oviedo Convention, where the ban on obtaining profit by the sale of the body or its parts is mentioned (art. 21). We should note here, however, that legal regime governing blood and plasma transactions differs among the countries. The main adopted framework is the one of donation, according to Titmuss' view (for solidarity and moral reasons), but the notion of property seems not to be excluded in particular with reference to plasma. For example, in the United States the purchase of plasma is admitted, while in Europe the regime of donation is preferred for the whole blood components (see, for example, the Recommendation (95) 15 of the Council of Europe).

Stored human tissues: A third category of body parts comprises human tissues assembled in research biobanks. They do not have independent functionality, cannot be reproduced by the body, and have three facets: the *material* one (the physical structure); the *informational* facet, as those goods carry information about the individual, his/her family and biological group, his/her identity, diseases, and state of health; and the *ethical* dimension, as they could be considered inherently part of the personhood which is the carrier of human dignity (in a Kantian meaning of having an intrinsic value and not being reducible to "chattel").

With these delineations of different categories of body parts in mind, we can now turn to consider more in depth the applicability of property rights in the case of human tissues.

Property Rights and Human Tissues

If property rights could be exercised over human tissues, who would be the hypothetical owners? We will examine three possibilities.

Does the person who provided the tissue retain property rights over it?

The most common and "natural" idea is to confer such a right to each individual for his or her samples, but some relevant judicial cases indicate weaknesses in this position.

The plaintiff in *Moore vs. Regents of University of California*, John Moore, was an American citizen who was diagnosed with a rare form of leukemia and whose spleen was removed for therapeutic purposes. When doctors discovered the unique potential his spleen possessed, they asked for a patent on his spleen's cells. After obtaining the patent, they granted the license for commercial exploitation of it to two different pharmaceutical companies. When he found out about this, Moore filed a lawsuit against the hospital where the doctors worked, claiming ownership of his biological samples and the right to participate in the gains achieved by the hospital and university.

The California Supreme Court did not find conclusively that Moore either did or did not possess property rights over all of his body and its parts, demonstrating "the confusion in the various philosophical principles operating in this area"

(George 2001, 25). It did find that whatever rights Moore might have had, he could not have claims upon his samples after donation. The court ruled that the doctors and researchers could exploit Moore's body parts because through their labor they had transformed them into their own property.

A similar situation occurred in *Greenberg v. Miami Child Research Institute*, regarding a claim of ownership of biological material from a single donor. The United States District Court for the Southern District of Florida ruled that individuals do not possess property rights over biological material gifted for research purposes, and that participants in research projects do not have a right to benefits arising from the commercialization of such discoveries.

Do researchers have property rights over human tissues?

Important to the discussion of whether researchers have property rights over human tissues they collect is the ruling in *Washington University v. William J. Catalona* which deals with the conflict between a researcher at Washington University (who had collected and catalogued more than 250,000 tissue samples, removed from 3,600 patients) and the university which employed him (considered as the repository owner of those biological materials) (see Andrews 2006).

After some disagreements with the university, Catalona decided to leave the research center and move to Northwestern University near Chicago. Before leaving, he asked patients to sign a statement in which they said that the samples had been entrusted by them to Dr. Catalona for his research purposes. Washington University did not accept these statements, and it claimed to be the sole owner of those donated human tissues. The clash between patients, a university researcher, and the custodian of the samples (the Washington University biobank) was resolved by the U.S. Supreme Court, which recognized Washington University as the owner of any biological material. The Court stressed that medical research can progress only if the scientific community's access to biological materials is unhindered by the interference (and whims) of private individuals. Declaring these materials as an individual's property, the Court stated, would render them— as the District Court had earlier affirmed—mere "chattels going to the highest bidder" (*Washington University v. Catalona (Catalona I)*, 437 F. Supp. 2d 985 (E.D. Mo. 2006), at 1002).

In sum, American courts have generally ruled against individuals claiming property rights over biological materials, tending instead to assign contested rights to research institutions.

Allowing researchers to assert property rights over human tissues taken from other people raises logical problems. In particular it would seem strange to refuse property rights to the person who provided the tissue but then allow another individual to assert the very rights that were ruled not to have existed in the first place. Another thorny issue is how to ensure that the needs of research are met without allowing researchers to use samples for their own purposes or economic exploitation. A grant of property rights to researchers would put the matter on a slippery slope into a pure business model potentially ruled by greedy people more interested in gain and in what is economically advantageous than what is ethically and scientifically justifiable and useful for society. As Dickenson has stated, if body parts are gifted but then exploited by researchers, could not this be considered ultimately as commodification of the body (2002, 55-63)?

Do property rights work for human tissues?

The above-noted flaws in recognizing property rights over human tissues for individuals who donated them or to researchers who received them show the limits of property rights in this field. In either case, problems arise. In addition, such a proprietary model could lead to the well-known "tragedy of the Anti-Commons" (Heller 1998),[3] the overutilization of privatization and exclusive property rights (with limited access to data), thus blocking innovation and research.

In conclusion, the examples given here strongly suggest that the proprietary model does not work for human tissues.

Can the "commons" model apply?

Because of the difficulties associated with delineating clear property rights to body parts, some scholars have suggested considering human tissues as "common goods" (see Knoppers and Fecteau 2003; Widdows 2009).

The main instrument supporting this view is "anonymization": if human tissues are rendered anonymous—by deleting each reference to personal data that might identify the donor—they may be considered as goods to be freely used by anybody without prejudice and exempted from prior property rights as a result of consent from the person to whom they originally belonged.[4] But if the quality of "commons" were really attributed to the goods (and thus they were the community's common estate), there still would remain the problem of deciding who controls and manages the data. There would remain the danger of falling into the "Tragedy of the Commons" (Hardin 1968, 1243-1248), the situation that occurs where different people use the same resource, which is commonly accessible, for their private interests, and thus risk overexploiting the resource in such a way that fails to realize the optimal use and can result in depletion of the resource. It is likely that such problems would arise with reference to body parts, if they were considered as "commons." Consequently, the model of commons cannot work, and another perspective is needed (see Macilotti 2008).

Philanthropy in the Context of Research Biobanks

In the search for a new, justifiable foundation for research biobanks, the role of philanthropy appears significant.

Etymologically, "philanthropy" is intended to signify "love toward human beings, as an attitude of the soul and an operative individual's and social groups' effort to promote the others' happiness and wealth" (translated from *Treccani.it Enciclopedia Italiana*).

A notion of philanthropy that is clearly relevant to biobanks is Richard Gunderman's definition of "liberal philanthropy," in which the aim "is not merely, or even primarily, to reduce, prevent, or eliminate need. The ultimate goal of philanthropy is to promote sharing," transforming receivers into givers and developing people's full potential (Gunderman 2005, 5).

In considerations of "property" or "ownership," the "core conception is the notion of absolute control; ownership is the ability to do what you like with your own, without having to account to anyone else for your actions" (Singer 2000, 29). In contrast, the concept of philanthropy "connotes a form of cooperative human relations with respect to shared conditions and aims" (Winickoff 2007, 443). Philanthropy, in other words, shifts attention from property rights and the extraction of gains therefrom to "partnerships" in which there is shared participation in creating broader social value.

Applied to biobanks, a philanthropic conceptual framework may help us (a) better define the legal status of human tissues, (b) shape the relationship between the participants in research projects (whose biomaterials are placed in the biobank) and the community, (c) more clearly establish the role and responsibilities of scientists; and (d) indicate the appropriate structure of biobanks.

Philanthropy and the Status of Human Tissues

A philanthropic perspective can help us overcome both the proprietary view of body parts and the model of commons. In the awareness of belonging to a global community and sharing a common genetic heritage (declared in international acts such as the UNESCO Universal Declaration on the human genome and human rights, 1997),[5] philanthropy pushes us to conceive of each participant in biological research as a "settlor," a custodian or steward, not an owner of his or her biological samples. Seen from this perspective, voluntarily donated human tissues become a philanthropic endowment to others, an object of "trust" managed by the settlor for the benefit both of him- or herself and the community.

Philanthropy and the Position of Research Participants

Philanthropy already shapes the role of many research participants. It reminds them of one aspect of medical research that is often underappreciated: their membership in humanity and the solidarity of their links with other human beings. In fact, in a medical field dominated by the individualistic dimension, philanthropy can contribute by drawing attention to those invisible ties that connect the individual to the rest of the community (Williams 2005) without forgetting the self. The object of individuals' philanthropy in donating to biobanks thus becomes elastic: it could be intended as an openness to narrow groups of people (carriers of a specific disease to study), to all the people of a particular country (as in the case of genomic population repositories), or to humanity as a whole.

Furthermore, a philanthropic perspective shifts donors away from personal profit speculation, and may incentivize them to examine the profit model of the biobank to which they donate, in the belief that commercialization of their tissues would have adverse effects on the integrity of scientific research. This negation of market exploitation is counterbalanced by participants' recognition of a right to know or not to know the results of analysis that concerns their body parts and to have access to discoveries resulting from the biobanks' data at a reasonable cost. In a nutshell, philanthropy can be the foundation of a new participatory approach to research, founded on a renewed sense of shared participation in the human community in space and time (Knoppers and Chadwick 2005).

Philanthropy and the Role of Scientists

The temptation to engage in economic and financial speculations on bio-specimens touches scientists, too. Philanthropy, however, draws attention back to the principles of beneficence and justice that should guide scientists' activities. Philanthropy redefines research as a means of pursuing the public and common good (according to Aristotle's vision) and encourages researchers to look for the improvement of people's health conditions and the benefit of future generations. Indeed, philanthropy might prevent the sort of rights claims of individual scientists such as Catalona by stressing the very nature of scientific research as a means to pursue *"external justice in avoiding a bias of interest in diseases affecting the rich rather than the poor,"* as well as *"internal justice, [in the sense that] no party involved in the biobank research process should be exploited by another"* (Oystein Ursin, 2010). Therefore, scientists are incented to mold their research for the good of human beings, to put aside any kind of profit purposes, and not to consider biomaterials as commercial goods to be valued through money.

Philanthropy and the Structure of a Research Biobank

Philanthropy can permeate the structure of research biobank by rendering it a "charitable trust" (Charo 2006; see also Macilotti et al. 2008) or "biotrust" (Winickoff and Winickoff 2003; see also Yassin et al. 2010; Winickoff and Neumann 2005). Just as the relationship of the individual settlor to the donated human tissues is one of trust (from the participants' point of view), so too can the biobank be conceived as a form of trust. As the depository of the samples, the biobank should operate as a trustee or steward which acts as a third party—impartial and equally distant—between the researcher, who signs a special agreement with the biobank, giving him access to samples for study, and the individual donor, seen as a settlor of body parts.

In this paradigm, the donor would give his or her tissues or other data (along with the right to control the use of that material) with a benefit-sharing and philanthropic intent. The researcher would be allowed access only within the limits of the license, and in the case of the production of new knowledge, the results should re-enter the scientific community, thus increasing the sum of knowledge and promoting further research. The biobank would be a system operator, called to decide among the claims of various researchers, ensure application of the principles of the trust, and spread the results of research into the community.

Most of all, the biobanks, as a philanthropic intermediary among participants and researchers, behaves as a re-distributor, promoting a culture of philanthropy within society by advancing our understanding of "what it is to be human" (McCully 2010).

Conclusion

The importance of bio-repositories of human tissues has grown progressively through the years, making "the design of an appropriate regulatory regime and institutional structure for genomic biobanks a novel challenge" (Winickoff and Neumann 2005, 9). In such a context, philanthropy can be very meaningful. It can shape a new relationship between the person and his or her body parts; remind us of the altruistic dimension that should connote participation in research; help prevent abuses of scientific research; recall scientists to their duties to humanity in conducting their research; and give sanction to the structure of the biobank as independent from different actors, impartial and able to balance diverse interests at stake.

NOTES

[1] This expression is found in Hotman, a sixteenth century jurist (in *Commentarius de verbis iuris antiquitatum*).

[2] Opposite to the "weak" notion of gratuity is the "strong" version which implies that no property right over the human body can be exercised.

[3] The expression was used for the first time by Michael Heller, formulated as a consequence of the U.S.A. Bayh-Dole Act or University and Small Business Patent Procedures Act (Pub. L. No. 96-517, 94 Stat. 3015, 1980, codified as amended at 35 U.S.C.§§ 200-212, 2000), which dealt with the privatization of academic science and commercialization of inventions.

[4] About anonymization, see Recommendation (2006) 4 by the Committee of Ministers of the Council of Europe on research using biological materials of human origin (https://wcd.coe.int/wcd/ViewDoc.jsp?id = 977859).

[5] See also Statement on Benefit-Sharing (2000) and the Statement on Human Genomic Databases (2002), enacted by HUGO Ethics Committee.

REFERENCES

Andrews, Lori. 2006. "Two Perspectives: Rights of Donors: Who Owns Your Body? A Patient's Perspective on *Washington University vs. Catalona*." *Journal of Law, Medicine & Ethics* 34: 398-407.

Andrews, Lori and Dorothy Nelkin. 2001. *The Body Bazaar: The Market for Human Tissue in the Biotechnology Age*. New York: Crown Publishers.

Bovenberg, Jasper A. 2006. "DNA as Personal Property." *Property Rights in Blood, Genes and Data. Naturally Yours?* Leiden: M. Nijhoff Publishers.

Charo, R. Alta. 2006. "Body of Research—Ownership and Use of Human Tissue." *The New England Journal of Medicine* 355 (15): 1517-1519.

Dickenson, Donna. 2002. "Commodification of human tissue: implications for feminist and development ethics." *Developing World Bioethics* 2 (1): 55-63.

Feldman, Robin C. 2011. "Whose Body Is It Anyway? Human Cells and the Strange Effects of Property and Intellectual Property Law." *Stanford Law Review* 63: 1377. https://www.law.stanford.edu/sites/default/files/event/265105/media/slspublic/Whose%20Body%20Is%20It% 20Anyway.pdf.

George, Alexandra. 2001. "Property in the Human Body and Its Parts. Reflections on Self-determination in Liberal Society." *EUI Working Papers, Law* (August 2001), Badia Fiesolana (FI).

Gottweis, Herbert. 2008. "Biobanks in Action. New Strategies in the Governance of Life." *Biobanks: Governance in Comparative Perspective.* Herbert Gottweis and Alan Petersen, eds. London: Routledge.

Greenberg v. Miami Child Research Institute, 264 F Supp. 2d 1064-76 (2003).

Gunderman, Richard. 2005. "Giving and Human Excellence: The Paradigm of Liberal Philanthropy." *Conversations on Philanthropy II*: 1-10. ©2005 DonorsTrust.

Hacking, Ian. 1982. "Biopower and the Avalanche of Printed Numbers." *Humanities and Society* 5:279-95.

Hardin, Garrett. 1968. "The Tragedy of the Commons." *Science* 162, no. 3859: 1243-1248.

Heller, Michael A. 1998. "The Tragedy of the Anticommons: Property in the Transition from Marx to Markets." *Harvard Law Review* 111 (3) (January): 621-688.

Helsinki Declaration: Ethical Principles for the medical research involving human beings, adopted by World Medical Association in 1964 and amended most recently in 2008 (http://www.wma.net/en/30publications/10policies/b3/index.html).

Kant, Immanuel. 1963. [1775-1801]. *Lectures on Ethics*. Indianapolis: Hackett.

Knoppers, Bartha M. and Ruth Chadwick. 2005. "Human Genetic Research: Emerging Trends in Ethics." *Nature Reviews Genetics* 6 (January): 75-79.

Knoppers, Bartha M. and Claudine Fecteau. 2003. "Human Genomic Databases: a Global Public Good?" *European Journal of Health Law* 10 (27).

Loft, Steffen and Henrik E. Poulsen. 1996. "Cancer Risk and Oxidative DNA Damage in Man." *Journal of Molecular Medicine* 74: 297-312.

Lyotard, Jean-François. 1984. *The Postmodern Condition: A Report on Knowledge*. Minneapolis: University of Minnesota Press.

Macilotti, Matteo. 2008. "Property, Information and Interests in the Regulation of Biobanks for Research Purposes." *The New Civil Case Commentary* 7-8: 222-235.

Macilotti, Matteo, Umberto Izzo, Giovanni Pascuzzi, and Mattia Barbareschi. 2008. "La disciplina giuridica delle biobanche." *Pathologica* 100: 86-101.

McCully, George. 2010. "Philanthropy and Humanity." *Conversations on Philanthropy VII*: 43-48. ©2010 DonorsTrust.

Moore vs. Regents of University of California, 51 Cal. 3d 120 (June 9, 1990).

Morgan, Derek. 2001. "Where Do I Own My Body and How?" *Issues in Medical Law and Ethics*. London: Cavendish.

Munzer, Stephen R. 1993. "Kant and Property Rights in Body Parts." *Canadian Journal of Law and Jurisprudence* 6: 319-341.

Nuremberg Code of Ethics on Medical Research, 1946, in http://ohsr.od.nih.gov/guidelines/nuremberg.html.

Oviedo Convention for the protection of human rights and human dignity in reference to the applications of biology and medicine, Convention about human rights and biomedicine, signed on April 4, 1997, and made legally binding on December 1, 1999 (http://www.conventions.coe.int/Treaty/en/Treaties/Html/164.htm).

Oystein Ursin, Lars. 2010. "Privacy and Property in the Biobank Context." *HEC Forum* 22 (3): 211–224.

Radin, Margaret J. 1987. "Market-Inalienability." *Harvard Law Review* 100: 1849-1937.

Sallée, Clémentine and Bartha M. Knoppers. 2005. *Existing Human Genetic Research Databases*, Organisation for Economic Co-operation and Development (OECD), Directorate for Science, Technology and Industry, Report on Human Genetic Databases, DSTI/STP/BIO, 14.

Singer, Joseph W. 2000. *Entitlement: The Paradoxes of Property*. New Haven: Yale University Press.

Titmuss, Richard M. 1970. *The Gift Relationship: From Human Blood to Social Policy*. New York: The New Press.

Treccani.it Enciclopedia Italiana Online, s.v. "Philanthropy,"
    http://www.treccani.it/enciclopedia/filantropia/ (accessed March 6, 2013).

UNESCO, Universal Declaration on the human genome and human rights. 1997.
    http://www.unesco.org/new/en/social-and-human-
    sciences/themes/bioethics/human-genome-and-human-rights/.

Washington University v. William J. Catalona et al., U.S. Dist. LEXIS 22969,
    2006 and *Washington University v. Catalona (Catalona I)*, 437 F. Supp. 2d
    985 (E.D. Mo. 2006) at 1002.

Widdows, Heather. 2009. "Between the Individual and the Community: The
    Impact of Genetics on Ethical Models." *New Genetics and Society* 28 (2).

Williams, Garrath. 2005. "Bioethics and Large-Scale Biobanking: Individualistic
    Ethics and Collective Projects." *Genomics, Society and Policy* 1: 50–66.

Winickoff, David E. 2007. "Partnership in U.K. Biobank: A Third Way for
    Genomic Property?" *The Journal of Law, Medicine & Ethics*: 440-456.

Winickoff, David E. and Larissa B. Neumann. 2005. "Towards a Social Contract
    for Genomics: Property and the Public in The 'Biotrust' Model." *Genomics,
    Society and Policy* 1 (3): 8-21.

Winickoff, David E. and Richard N. Winickoff. 2003. "The Charitable Trust as a
    Model for Genomic Biobanks." *New England Journal of Medicine* 349:
    1180-1184.

Yassin, Rihab, Nicole Lockhart, Mariana González del Riego, Karen Pitt, Jeffrey
    W. Thomas, Linda Weiss, and Carolyn Compton. 2010. "Custodianship as
    an Ethical Framework for Biospecimen-based Research." *Cancer
    Epidemiology, Biomarkers & Prevention*. 19: 1012-1015.

PHILANTHROPIC INSTITUTIONAL DESIGN AND THE WELFARE STATE

David F. Hardwick and Leslie Marsh

Introduction

The topic of philanthropy has a great deal of philosophical interest because it exists at the nexus of issues surrounding distributive, remedial, and commutative justice, perennial issues in political philosophy (Ealy 2010, vi). It is perhaps because of this that, conceptually speaking, philanthropy seems to have a twilight existence, typically laboring under one of the most prevalent confusions—the synonymous usage of the terms "nonprofit" and "philanthropy" (McCully 2010). Yet, discussion of the philosophy of philanthropy is surprisingly neglected. The present discussion examines the relationship between private philanthropy and the welfare-oriented state: Is it possible for the philanthropic sphere and/or indeed the philanthropic impulse to coexist in an expansive governmental environment that sees health care as a natural part of its administrative monopoly? We answer with a qualified "yes." Our paper, however, is not concerned with an appraisal of welfarism in its many guises nor with recommendations for reform, but with the *pragmatics* of operating within such an environment. As such we: (a) assess the philosophical presuppositions that animate recent discussion of the "Big Society" and the role philanthropy is accorded within it; and (b) offer practical guidance about protecting and encouraging the philanthropic impulse when a climate of welfarism prevails.

Our discussion will begin with a look at two of the great theorists of liberty, whose works have often informed contributions to this journal: Adam Smith and Friedrich Hayek. This examination of conceptual intersections between liberty and philanthropy sets the stage for a case study—an examination of the British Columbia Children's Hospital Foundation (BCCHF), a highly successful Canadian philanthropic enterprise. In the penultimate section we critically examine the presuppositions of the recent discussion of the so-called "Big Society" and "Third Party Government," a literature that has shone new light on philanthropy as part and parcel of public policy. In the final section we offer some concluding observations.

Hardwick, David F. and Leslie Marsh. 2012. Philanthropic Institutional Design and the Welfare State. *Conversations on Philanthropy* IX: 118-137. ISSN 1552-9592 ©The Philanthropic Enterprise.

Smith, Hayek, and Sympathy

Adam Smith and Friedrich Hayek are frequently sequestered into the service of "invisible hand" and "spontaneous order" explanations, respectively. Discussions of the two thinkers is skewed by overemphasis on these concepts to the detriment of other concepts they talk about. In this section we examine Smith's concept of sympathy, the touchstone of his moral philosophy and, of course, a key philosophical idea informing the philanthropic impulse.[1] After all, let us not forget that Smith was Professor of *Moral* Philosophy. We then turn to Hayek, who, as we have argued elsewhere, is *not* the *laissez-faire* hard-liner many theorists take him to be (Hardwick and Marsh 2012a, b; Marsh 2012).

We think it worth quoting an elegant summary from the great Smith scholar and classicist Glenn Morrow:[2]

> His [Smith's] purpose here is to set forth the stages by which the moral consciousness develops and the individual passes beyond himself and his individual concerns. The guiding thread in the discussion is the principle that personal contact is the basis of the social consciousness. There is no mysterious affinity between human beings from the mere fact of their humanity, no love for humanity in general. The individual is brought out of himself by his sympathetic participation in the sentiments and affections of other individuals with whom he associates, . . . The social consciousness thus begun in the family group grows as his sympathies spread out in widening circles, first to his clan or neighborhood, then to his nation, and finally to the whole system of the universe. Hence the individual belongs to many groups by which his own sentiments are formed, and toward which his loyalties are directed. . . . But the state itself is a group of societies, each possessing a life of its own and an instinct for self-maintenance; and the mutual adjustment of these orders and societies gives the state its constitution. Each individual endeavors to secure the aggrandizement of his own group, and to help it resist the encroachments of others. None of these groups is self-sufficient, however, and the interplay of them all with one another is necessary in the harmonious ordering of the state (1923, 74-75).

Four points are worth noting. First, the concept of sympathy in Smith's meaning of the term roughly connotes the relatively recent sense (Titchener 1909) attached to empathy. Smith uses sympathy in a much broader way to include "fellow-feeling with any passion whatever" (Smith 1984, I.i.1.5). Second, sympathy, in Smith's account, is *not* merely a benevolent impulse in the individual; sympathy is not the object but the *basis* of moral approbation. This accounts for his rejection of utility as an explanation of moral approbation. Third, Smith's idea that moral judgment is the result of empathy, whereby we place ourselves in the position of the individual judged, and feel to some extent as our own the sentiments and passions he feels, has a deep resonance with recent work on mirror neurons in the field of social cognition (Jabbia et al. 2007).[3] Fourth, *society* as a mirror reflects ourselves: virtue and vice have an immediate reference to the sentiments of others. Like most other moral theorists, Smith takes the view that an isolated individual cannot have a moral consciousness.

Turning to the Smith of *The Wealth of Nations* provides cold comfort for those who see the text as a libertarian economic tract and as such give it priority over *The Theory of Moral Sentiments*. *The Wealth of Nations* specifies three roles for the state: (a) protecting society from external threats, (b) protecting each individual of society from injustices perpetrated by others of the society, and (c) the duty of "erecting and maintaining" certain public works and certain institutions, which can never be in the interest of any one individual or small group of individuals. Though current libertarianism looks to Smith's idea of negative freedom (or "natural liberty") for conceptual validation, it is far from obvious that adherence to Smith's three roles would reduce the level of state activity in current conditions.

Now to Smith's great intellectual descendant—Hayek. As Hayekians our thoughts naturally turned to what, if anything, Hayek might have to say on the topic of philanthropy. We were pleased to come across Robert Garnett's discussion (2008, 2010) and the surprising discovery of Hayek's apparent exclusion of philanthropy from his vision of the Great Society. Garnett notes that Aristotle's ethics and theory of social order were among Hayek's chief targets. Garnett continues: "Carrying his argument one step further, Hayek classifies philanthropy as a species of Aristotelian socialism. Like socialism, philanthropy enjoins us 'to restrict our actions to the deliberate pursuit of known and observable beneficial ends'" (Hayek cited in Garnett 2008, 3). From Hayek's perspective, the preference for known others diminishes, rather than enhances, each individual's capacity to assist others. In a memorable turn of phrase, he claims that a social order in which "everyone treated his neighbor as himself would be one where comparatively few could be fruitful and multiply" (3).

It must be conceded that Hayek's critique of philanthropy is a rather strange affair. We think (along with Ealy 2008, 58-59 and Garnett 2010, 56) that the motivating thought behind Hayek's ambivalence toward philanthropy must lie in his famous conception of the incoherence of the notion of "social justice." There are three conundra in Hayek's treatment.

First, why in the world Hayek selected Aristotle for special criticism, or special representativeness, is beyond us. Hayek needed only to refer to the face-to-face world of the city-state, the *polis,* or the Roman *urbs.* Furthermore, "Aristotelian socialism" is a screaming nonsense. There's no implication that any of the three types of justice Aristotle distinguishes in *Nicomachean Ethics* V (1969, §1130b-1132b) concerns collective justice or "social justice," as Hayek usually calls it.

Second, at one level Hayek knows this all too well, of course. The references to Aristotle and to Aristotelian socialism reflect Hayek's disregard for the niceties of intellectual history. For his purposes it's perfectly acceptable to take a bit from Aristotle, and a bit from socialism, and put them together as "Aristotelian socialism." It's the way Hayek's mind worked: he rushed in where historians feared to tread.

Third, Hayek's idea seems to be that the market capitalism he visualized but never realized, produces the optimum allocation of resources. So the best thing we can do is to join the system; leave it to the system to allocate by its invisible hand, and all will be for the best. Get a job, pay your taxes, produce, buy and sell: this is the best rule of thumb. When you step outside the system and give money to a beggar, you don't know what the consequences will be. By contrast, you do know that a supporting system will produce an optimum outcome, because Hayek has proved the point.

Let us be clear about it: Hayek's view is *not an absurd* view, but it does run counter to some intuitive cases which are merely abused by being called "atavistic."[4] If one sees a starving old woman in the street, is one to walk over her emaciated body and do it, moreover, with cheer in one's heart because one is serving the best system and indeed indirectly promoting her own best interests? Even with that sort of emotive example aside (important though it is), Hayek is too extreme. All his argument shows, at most, is that we should not engage in charity that is damaging to the system, charity which encourages people not to work and so on. Of course, not all charity or philanthropy is of this kind. It simply isn't. How is a foundation (or an individual) undermining market capitalism if it pays for a new laboratory at some university? Thus we are in accord with Garnett when he concludes, " Hayek's dogged efforts to defend market processes against their socialist critics seem to have placed severe limits on his ability to integrate philanthropy into his baseline conception of the Great Society" (Garnett 2008, 4; see also Garnett 2008, 11; Garnett 2010, 56; cf. Ealy 2008, 58).

Boettke and Prychitko, economists who draw heavily on Hayek's works, do see a role for philanthropy, but they put a somewhat different spin on it by encouraging philanthropy or the "third sector" as a wedge against state expansionism:

> In a genuinely free society, the voluntary sector should play a critical role in reinforcing the constitutional constraints that limit government to those activities. . . . [A] robust interconnected system of nonprofits and other civil-society associations can—as an unintended consequence—function to reinforce constitutional constraints (2004, 27).

Although there is no logical incompatibility between the relationship of the voluntary sector and the state thus conceived, this seems to be a stance at odds with the more standard view that suggests the "proper relationship between philanthropy and government is *partnership*, in their *mutual* efforts to enhance quality of life in this democracy. Government needs philanthropy as society's sensory system, the first-alert to emerging public issues and problems. Philanthropy is far more creative than government . . . and has greater sensitivity and creativity to . . . the philanthropic sector needs to operate freely and without stifling government regulation. Philanthropy helps improve government and public policy, not just as a partner, but often as a leading partner" (McCully 2008, 104-105, our emphasis).

Protection of Donor Intent

In this section we shed light on the tensions of constitutional political economy by looking at the way real charities navigate in an arena. On offer is an analysis of British Columbia Children's Hospital Foundation's (BCCHCF) "bespoke" institutional design, a case study that should go some way in assuaging the understandable concerns liberals of all stripes share, notably a wariness of state expansiveness. Conspicuous by its absence in the philanthropic literature is discussion of institutional design and the understanding of the actual decision-making process in a given environment—in other words there seems to be a gap between the philosophical and the practical aspects of nonprofit management. To this end we offer some pointers for developing a toolbox for private philanthropic initiatives that operate in similar situations. As we said at the outset, our approach is pragmatic—our concern is with the *de facto* operating environment and not with a philosophical appraisal of welfarism.

Despite operating within the more expansive welfarist culture characteristic of Canada, the British Columbia Children's Hospital Foundation is one of North America's most highly successful fundraising foundations. Given the supposed tensions between welfarism and philanthropy (a tension reflected in various debates over crowding out of charitable donations by government welfare), it's fair to ask how the hospital has managed to successfully raise philanthropic contributions. Our examination has demonstrated not only the feasibility of designing institutions but moreover that donor intent is both *protected* and *promoted.* Of course, understanding the dynamics of institutional life, the practices and rules embedded in different types of institutions, the context of reasoning, and an institution's values and worldviews, are vital to achieving this task. Needless to say, constitutive rules specify agencies and agents, and their proper jurisdictions, responsibilities and relations, a cluster of issues relevant to all institutions within a liberal-democratic society (Olsen 1997, 213). Any analysis of a given institution should reveal the level of procedural reliability and predictability and proscribe the limits of power and jurisdiction.

Independent individuals associate with each other for a wide variety of reasons. One powerful force for such coherence is the focus on improving the well-being and enhancement of individuals within society. Indeed, there are many manifestations of this phenomenon in civil society, some of which have political ramifications, such as those seen in welfare states. Indeed, the welfare state is seen by some as directional in prescribing philanthropic or aggregate behaviors. In the extreme, the *absolutist* welfare state is dictatorial and prescriptive. However, survival of absolutist welfare states such as the USSR is limited in the West, where societies are typified by democratic civil processes and pressures to accommodate the wishes of the broader population.

Institutional design for philanthropic organizations is similar in all civil societies, whether liberal or "welfare" oriented. The required design focuses on individual behaviors that are similar in both and that are designed to protect the philanthropic initiatives from predation and enhance fulfillment of the overall initiatives described in the original objectives of the philanthropic institution.

The scenario described below derives from the conceptualization of the BC Children's Hospital Foundation—one of Canada's most successful philanthropic institutions. In the late 1970s, a group of philanthropic-oriented individuals—

members and former Board of Directors members of the BC Children's Hospital—agreed that the then-nascent Children's Hospital required a suitable support base. The provincial government, with a friendly, often personal relationship with the Board of Directors, had approved construction funding for a new hospital and an adjacent Women's Hospital which would provide a major facility with suitable, but basic, operation funding.

Propelling a newly created nascent hospital to an operational level that would attract a suitable cadre of innovative and expert health practitioners required the support of the broader community and a philanthropic institution to facilitate the process. Creation of a desirable health "destination" required more than a suitable facility. A strategy to attract the brightest and the best practitioners involved offering the "opportunity" to pursue their research interests, the freedom of "choice" as to how to effect this, the "security" of a position—all this in addition to the "comfort" of providing suitable academic health center facilities (Hardwick 1989).

A small group of key individuals—which would conceptualize the institution—decided to assess the institutional design of other successful children's hospital foundations and thus over a brief period in 1978 visited the following: the Hospital for Sick Children Foundation in Toronto, the Los Angeles Children's Hospital Foundation, the Boston Children's Hospital Foundation, and the Cincinnati Children's Hospital Foundation.

The essence of the findings that ultimately led to the design of the British Columbia Children's Hospital Foundation was basic but clear. The Foundation needed to be an independent, incorporated institution that did not report its financial status directly to the incorporated hospital. In Canada, where public hospitals are funded by government, the financial status of the institution is overseen by a hospital board, but it is legally open to systematic review and alteration by the provincial government where the hospital is located. In general, this system operates well but is subject to financial pressures during economic recessions or political pressures during elections.

It was clear that hospital administrative pressures might similarly compromise the philanthropic intent. This later became evident in U.S.-located institutions as well. To ensure the integrity of the philanthropic intent, an institutional design was created that incorporated the BC Children's Hospital Foundation as a separate entity with no requirement to report its financial status to the hospital or indirectly to the government. Foundations, of course, are legally obliged to report to the federal government regarding taxes—income and expenses and received donations and tax receipts. Reports are made to the provincial government about meeting the percentage of donated funding allocated to the charitable acts, but the two levels of government do not appear to share data. The intent of the BCCHF founders was to design a structure that was not a subsidiary of the Children's Hospital and in which funding allocations are not subordinated to bureaucrats who might wish to channel funding away from the initial intent of the Foundation—that is, a structure that avoids conflicts of interest.

Let us summarize the design objectives:

(1)   The specific institutional design is to ensure that donor intent is maintained and philanthropic donations are used as intended.

(2)   The design is to ensure that monies are not redirected by those who have a conflict of interest (e.g., furnishing offices as opposed to patient care).

(3)   The design ensures that the Foundation has the authority to direct monies as indicated by donors.

(4)   The design ensures that the level of government control over hospitals does not have fiscal knowledge or leverage capacity over funds. It is worth noting that the *bête noir* of monolithic government (in liberal democracies) tends to be overstated. Government is not a monolith—the central government has functions that Canadian provinces and American states and cities don't have. There has often been little if any sharing of information between levels of government. (Of course, each level of government may want donated funds to serve its purposes.)

This "firewall" design of BCCHF has served well. The BCCHF is seen by donors as serving its institutional philanthropic objectives. Donors do not need to concern themselves about "hidden agendas" or "fund diversions" to support political or other agendas. The philanthropic agenda to support the creation of an innovative institution that attracts a sophisticated health-care staff has been extremely successful. The volume of competitive research grant funding received by the hospital staff increased logarithmically over the past thirty years. The funding of the B.C. Research Institute for Child and Family Health with both capital costs for facilities and operating costs has led to the attraction of a remarkable team of innovators and as a consequence medical research innovations.

The board of the Foundation initiated a capital fundraising project for $200 million which will lead to the reconstruction of the hospital and has almost completed this fundraising objective. The board has also confirmed that it will maintain and as necessary enhance the discretionary funding to ensure maintenance and expansion of the sophisticated health-care team.[5]

This "firewall" design has not been popular with all involved. A senior hospital administrator was dismayed at not having the ability to direct foundation funding to what was a personal opinion of need and wondered why the board would not comply with these proposed wishes. Apparently, access was available to foundation funds in some other children's hospitals where no such institutional design existed to protect the philanthropic initiatives of the Foundation.

In our case study, there was the luxury of implementing institutional design from the outset, guided by a small caucus of principals alert to the perfectly rational machinations of the bureaucratic phenomena that can be found within nongovernmental organizations and beyond. As any management consultant worth their salt can tell you, barging into an environment will quickly reveal institutional rigidity and resistance if one doesn't come to terms with the institution's identity (Olsen 1997, 214).

In conclusion, separate institutional incorporation and governance of philanthropic institutions are important in ensuring the integrity of the philanthropic objectives and protecting the foundation from any distorting predatory initiatives of government, hospital-funding agencies, or staff-focused initiatives.

The Big Society and Third Party Government

In this section we examine the conceptual continuities and/or discontinuities between the trans-Atlantic notions of "The Big Society" (UK) and "Third Party Government" (US). In a generic sense both notions are concerned with conceptual space between governmental apparatus and civil society at large, philanthropy being a major participant.

According to The Big Society Network website the initiative "exists to support and develop talent, innovation and enterprise to deliver social impact. By working with business, philanthropists, charities, and social ventures we believe we can unleash the social energy that exists in the UK to help build a better, healthier society" (http://www.thebigsociety.co.uk). This rather bland quote shows just how conceptually murky invocations of "The Big Society" are. In what sense is this any different from liberal (civil) society? Though there are resonances to this phrase from the past in the eminent Fabian Graham Wallas' *The Great Society* (1914) and Lyndon B. Johnson's use of the same phrase in the 1960s (University of Michigan, May 22, 1964), they are not useful in shedding much light on the current invocation. (This is not, of course to dismiss their ideas. For a historical account see Harris 2012.) Though discussion of the Big Society in its current guise emanates from the UK, the philosophical issues remain salient to other liberal democracies: Canada, for one, is very cognizant of this discussion (Curry 2011). In effect, Big Society discussion is a species of theorizing that concerns the demarcation between state and civil society (or as Cornuelle 2011 puts it, the "independent sector") and as such seeks to shift public expectations regarding the role of government in assisting social causes in this post-subprime-meltdown economic climate. Putting it in a somewhat flippant way, Fraser Nelson writes, "'The Big Society' is a silly name for a good idea: that lots of companies, charities, etc. will help provide government services" (http://blogs.spectator.co.uk/coffeehouse/2012/02/the-dark-side-of-the-big-society/).

Having been out of power for thirteen years, the UK Conservative Party felt the need to rethink its philosophical commitments. This could be taken as a genuine and substantive intellectual realignment and clarification or, in a more jaundiced view, merely a rebranding exercise. We will be charitable and assume the former.[6] The lead theorist behind the party's philosophical discussion is Jesse Norman (2010).[7] There is much to commend Norman in a broadly impressionistic sense, but there is a conspicuous lack of philosophical detail in his work which needs to be fleshed out.[8] In an earlier work Norman put forward five central tenets that inform the Big Society, foundational to the rebranding of the Conservative Party (2006):

(1) a large-scale program of decentralization;

(2) greater empowerment for intermediary institutions;

(3) greater emphasis on sharing (British) culture;

(4) celebration of individual freedom; and

(5) an audit of government.

Jointly and severally, acceptance of these tenets would ostensibly create the conditions necessary to ameliorate poverty, inequality, and class division. The Big Society, in Norman's account, emphasizes *institutions, competition, and entrepreneurship*. Norman very briefly addresses five criticisms leveled against the aforementioned list:

(1) The notion that the idea of the Big Society is at best vague, at worst empty.[9]

(2) That the idea is too ideologically "thin" to be aligned with party politics, specifically the Conservative Party.

(3) That the Big Society is in essence about the transfer of public services into the "third sector."

(4) The idea is merely reheated Thatcherism.

(5) Greater economic equality can only be achieved through social redresses
     covering the complex of crime, education, and health.

A few points are in order here. Audit of government surely belongs on a
different logical level from the other tenets. It's like having an independent central
bank. It's not up there with major concepts defining a view of society. Yes, we're
sure that the Big Society does celebrate individual freedom, freedom as a part and
parcel of British culture. (So here's another join-up of supposedly distinct tenets.)
But British Prime Minister David Cameron, it seems, also stresses cooperation, a
sense of shared communal interests working together to solve our own problems.
This is partly what motivates the program of decentralization. We think there's
something slightly different here from the bare idea of sharing British culture. It
requires a *reworking* of British culture. Sharing British culture is about making sure
that everyone understands English, that a shared system of justice is respected
(and Sharia courts have no legal status), that kind of thing. More than this is
involved in Cameron's idea that an ethos of self-help and cooperation should
prevail. That ethos could be and is missing from people who are as "British-
cultured" as anyone could wish.

Norman suggests that the more fundamental concerns of the Big Society
concept involve the "rediscovery" of politics. Specifically, he says that one has to
overcome three pernicious and mistaken ideas: that politics solely concerns the
relationship between the state and the individual; that individuals are
fundamentally economic automata; and that any derogation from perfect
competition is a cause of inefficiency and makes some people worse off. Though
we are in full accord with Norman on these three points, we cannot detect
anything distinctive about any of his tenets. Is there anything distinctive even
about this *combination* of tenets? How do the tenets relate to one another with
respect to independence, entailment/implication, and contradiction? We can't find
much of interest here on any of these scores. We fully accept that ideas don't have
to be new and original to be of interest and importance, but they do have to be
developed to a level of intellectual sophistication, and that is not the case here.

To be fair to Norman, UK governments do from time to time come under the
influences of bodies of ideas, even if they've not always applied them discerningly.
The Liberal government of 1905 was influenced by the "New Liberalism" of T. H.
Green and L. T. Hobhouse; the Labour government of 1945 bore the imprint of the
Beveridge Report, a cornerstone of the welfare state; and the Thatcher government
was supposedly influenced by Hayek.[10] Norman's parallels are more with the

architects of the "Social Contract" in the dying days of the 1970s Labour government and Will Hutton's book from the mid 1990s, *The State We're In* (1995). So far as we can make out, the Big Society stresses a few simple ideas.

First is the vital role of a thriving civil society. This is standard liberal thinking.

Next is a presumption, like the EU idea of "subsidiarity," that collective decisions should be made as far as practicable by those affected by them. If a decision affects Level 3, then it should be made at Level 3 unless there are overriding reasons to make it at a higher level.

Third, in policy terms this means that state-run services and institutions should be taken down a level. The two biggest examples are (a) general practitioners and not higher-level area health authorities should run the National Health Service, and (b) parents and not the local educational authority should run schools if they have the competence. While not explicitly endorsed by Norman, at least in the realm of healthcare, it is very much part of government policy (http://services.parliament.uk/bills/2010-11/healthandsocialcare.html).

The fourth idea is the rejection of an atomistic model of society in which people follow self-interest at the cost of community-mindedness—*homo reciprocans* rather than *homo economicus*. Bernard Bosanquet, for one, hated the atomistic view and derided it as a model of society composed of "reciprocally exclusive atoms" (2001, 79).

One might think that communitarianism is the elephant in the room. It hasn't been mentioned because we don't think that it has much to do with the Big Society philosophically. Communitarianism as you find it in Michael Sandel (1998) and Charles Taylor (1989) is a theory of the self—of how the self acquires its identity through the institutions and practices of a society. Clearly Sandel and Taylor would reject the atomistic view of the self, and thus would endorse the fourth idea above. But we don't think the idea of the Big Society goes deep enough philosophically to have much to say about the theory of the self.

As indicated at the outset of this section, in what sense is "The Big Society" any different from liberal (civil) society? Apparently none—according to one of the idea's major promoters: "You can call it liberalism. You can call it empowerment. You can call it freedom. You can call it responsibility. I call it the Big Society," said David Cameron (McSmith 2010).[11] Szreter and Ishkanian make the point that the "very name is contested (civil society, third sector, voluntary sector, non-profit sector etc.), there dwell many species and genera" (2012, 4).

Prima facie, invocations of "The Big Society" seem no different from

Salamon's so-called "third-party government," discussion predating "The Big Society" by some twenty-five years (Salamon 1981). Indeed, on Salamon's view these days the *welfare state* itself is a not dissimilar partnership between government and the nonprofit sector (Salamon et al. 2004). He makes the point that conceptually speaking third-party government is *not* coextensive with "privatization," which amounts to a simplistic offloading of governmental functions onto private hands. Third-party government, by contrast, emphasizes the *collaborative* nature of public problem solving. Salamon is also keen to distance third-party government from "new public management" a notion that (a) focuses on the direct operations of the public sector and recommends the introduction of business-type incentives and metrics into the operation of government agencies, and (b) recommends the outsourcing of governmental functions as a solution to government's problems, "conveniently overlooking the enormous extent to which third-party government is already in place around the world" within inherent issues of accountability and legitimacy (Salamon 2009). Salamon is of the view that third-party government is more about learning how to *comprehend* and to *manage* the de facto dispersion of power, a state of affairs that carries substantial discretionary authority.

Unlike "The Big Society" theorists, Salamon is far more sensitive to organizational design and behavioral considerations, understanding that each third-party entity enters into relationship with governmental authorities on its own terms and expectations. Furthermore, traditional hierarchic control is corroded leaving agency administrators and elected officials who lean on them, ill-equipped to ensure the outcomes they want. Salamon's discussion is more finessed and in accordance with the practicalities which we earlier set out in the discussion of the British Columbia Children's Hospital Foundation and philosophically more in tune with McCully and our pragmatic "partnership" conception of philanthropy than with Boettke and Prychitko's "wedge" conception of philanthropy. This is echoed by Szreter and Ishkanian when they write that the Great Society is about "Collaboration, cooperation and complementarity" and not a stark relationship of alternatives (2012, 92).

Conclusion

Given our declared interest in institutional design, one theorist has been conspicuous by his absence—Herbert Simon. Simon's early work in administrative behavior found voice in the eponymously titled *Administrative Behavior* (1947), a work whose themes would inform his celebrated notion of "bounded rationality."

Simon's targets were the progenitor of modern organizational theory—Frederick Winslow Taylor (1911)—and the later generation of influential theorists led by Luther Gulick and Lyndall Urwick (1937). Taylor's "scientific management theory" (Taylorism) gained a great deal of traction in both capitalist and socialist economies in the early part of the 20th century. Gulick and Urwick developed "administrative management theory" or more familiarly, modern management consultancy. For Taylor, since work is supposedly routinized, humans are, in essence, cogs in a machine, automatons if you will. This is not surprising since Taylor was a mechanical engineer by training: all that was needed was a blueprint and accordingly mere implementation. Gulick and Urwick's hyper-rationalism assumed that all the activities that need to be performed within an organization's department could be specified in advance. For Simon, the unremitting rationalism inherent in Taylor, Gulick, and Urwick's approach was that they crucially overlooked the rich inner life (mental processes) of agents, agents who of course had wants, desires, beliefs and goals shaped by a myriad of socio-cultural contexts. Agents' rationality is necessarily bounded not only by a conceptual context but by structural cognitive limitations, most notably limited informational processing capacity. There are those in healthcare that are oblivious to these ideas, still proffering a top-down rationalistic worldview (Frenk and Moon, 2013).

These are the insights that we believe are vital to any organizational design and which are embodied in the case of the British Columbia Children's Hospital.

There was a failed attempt at sustaining a socialist commune based on cooperation, with the socialists in this experiment seeking their own salvation within the confines of the existing system with the state playing no central role. We are of course referring to "New Harmony," a utopian venture funded by Robert Owen (1771-1858). This strand of socialism should be contrasted with the reformist and welfarist drivers animating state socialism and the current style of socialism that has been termed market socialism. What is significant is the idea of self-responsibility emphasized by Cameron's Big Society. Whatever the philosophical and practical failures of socialism, the *bêtes noires* of poverty, inequality, and class division present perennial challenges to all ideological positions, us liberals being no exception. It is therefore not at all helpful to begin to see socialism everywhere as Alexander Gray once did (1946) as do many current anti-statists.

North-American and European politics are in practice a messy mix between civil association and enterprise association, to use Oakeshott's famous distinction (1975).

Civil association connotes the idea that substantive theories of the good, if there are any, refer to voluntary activities of citizens and not to collective decision-making. Enterprise association, by contrast, is a view of politics that posits a common good to which collective decision-making should be directed. The philanthropic impulse has to operate in a sociopolitical climate that ebbs and flows between these two poles or ideal types of association. In any event, ideologies are far more fluid than is normally conceded in public discourse (Freeden 1994). It is conceptually disingenuous crudely to equate welfarism with absolutism when, for example, socialism shares with liberalism a rationalistic tendency and with conservatism a communitarian strand. Welfare states vary in governance from absolutist on behalf of the state or on behalf of the proletariat. Some are patrimonial, while others are theocratic or doctrinaire. Some civil societies adopt a "welfare" orientation that is kept tightly in check through liberal democracy—for example, Canada. Others worry about social democratic regulation—for example, the United States.

As George McCully and others have noted, perhaps the fundamental motivating impulse behind philanthropy has been obscured, and whatever the sociopolitical landscape, the philanthropic impulse should be conceived as an intrinsic good. Once again we invoke Adam Smith, from his famous opening to *The Theory of Moral Sentiments*: "[P]ity or compassion [is] the emotion we feel for the misery of others, when we either see it, or are made to conceive it in a very lively manner," and these "interest [man] in the fortune of others, and render their happiness necessary to him, though he derives nothing from it except the pleasure of seeing it" (Smith, 1984 [1853], I, 1, i).

This view is also promoted by recent philosophy of philanthropy theorists such as Richard Gunderman (2005, 1, 5; 2008a, 49-55; 2008b). Smith (2011), Gunderman, and others take issue with the prevailing, instrumental view of philanthropy as a problem-solving exercise or, in other words, a proxy for social reform or political activism (Lynn & Wisely 2002). The current identification of philanthropy with the "nonprofit" indicates the degree to which economism has encroached upon or corrupted the meaning of philanthropy and thereby undervalued the greater part of the philanthropic impulse—the countless volunteers' hours, the unquantifiable sweat equity that underpins philanthropic activity, the very things the theorists of the Big Society seem so eager to promote.[12] Finally, careful design of the philanthropic instrumental organization is required to ensure protection of donor intent.

We like to end with a couple of rhetorical questions posed by Simon, the dean of organizational design:

> Why, in a modern society do we have markets, and why do we have organizations, and what determines the boundary between these two mechanisms for social organization? These questions go to the heart of the roles of our diverse political and administrative institutions, public and private, in contemporary society (Simon 2000, 751).[13]

NOTES

[1] This is not the place to discuss the so-called Adam Smith problem, the supposed tension between Smith's two major works. See Garnett (2010), Göçmen (2007) and Marsh (2014). The similar ascription of inconsistency has been leveled at Hume between the *Enquiry* and the *Treatise*.

[2] For information on Morrow, see http://www.richard-t-hull.com/publications/GlennRaymondMorrow.pdf.

[3] There is already a vast philosophical and empirical literature on mirror neurons.

[4] In a discussion at the Law of Charity Colloquium (Indianapolis, November 2011), Isaac Lifshitz made the good point that surely philanthropy could qualify as a spontaneous order in its own right, thereby not contravening Hayek's antirationalist sensibility. Cornuelle (2011) makes a similar point.

[5] Forty-seven percent of donated funds are earmarked for research, 43 percent for the construction of a new hospital (2010/2011 BC Children's Hospital Foundation Annual Report, 25).

[6] Apparently Steve Hilton, Cameron's director of strategy, has claimed credit for the Big Society idea.

[7] Norman was elected to parliament in the 2010 elections as a Conservative member, but he also has a long and successful commitment to the philanthropic world. Last, but by no means least, Norman is a very good technical philosopher, noted for his work on C. S. Peirce, deeply influenced by Michael Oakeshott and possessing some appreciation of Hayek. Michael Ignatieff, the former leader of the Liberal Party of Canada and sometime academic, is the closest approximation to Norman in Canada.

[8] The most comprehensive academic discussion of the "Big Society" can be found in Stott 2011.

[9] A sampling of UK press coverage from both the Right and the Left on the Big Society seems to validate this claim.

[10] Though Hayek was admired by Thatcher and Reagan, it is unlikely that they read much beyond *The Road to Serfdom* and other highly selective readings refracted through others (in Thatcher's case, Keith Joseph; in Reagan's case, Martin Anderson and Paul Craig Roberts).

[11] For an analytic, annotated analysis of Cameron's speech explaining the Big Society, see "The Big Society: a genuine vision for Britain's future—or just empty rhetoric?" *The Independent*, July 20, 2010, http://www.independent.co.uk/news/uk/politics/the-big-society-a-genuine-vision-for-britains-future-ndash-or-just-empty-rhetoric-2030330.html.

[12] This tendency is marked by Olsen (1997, 214) who writes, "This is an aspect of democratic governance that may be of special relevance in periods, like the current one, characterized by rapid economic and technological modernization and a tendency to make economics the *new prima philosophia*, that is, the type of reasoning used as a measuring stick for all aspects of human life." In Hardwick and Marsh (2012a), Hardwick and Marsh (2012b), and Marsh (2012) we make the same point and have argued that to make one order answerable to (or reducible to) another order's teleology or metric is both rationalistic and indeed anti-liberal.

[13] We are grateful to Lenore Ealy, Steven Grosby, and Isaac Lifshitz for their pointed comments and to the other discussants at The Law of Charity Colloquium in November 2011. The usual disclaimers apply.

REFERENCES

Aristotle. 1969. *Nicomachean Ethics V*. Trans. W.D. Ross. Oxford: Oxford University Press.

Boettke, Peter J. and David L. Prychitko. 2004. "Is an Independent Nonprofit Sector Prone to Failure? Toward an Austrian School Interpretation of Nonprofit and Voluntary Action." *Conversations on Philanthropy I*: 1-40. ©2004 DonorsTrust.

Bosanquet, Bernard. 2001. *The Philosophical Theory of the State and Related Essays*. Eds. G. F. Gauss and William Sweet. South Bend, IN: St. Augustine's Press.

Cornuelle, Richard. 2011 [1993]. *Reclaiming the American Dream: The Role of Private Individuals and Voluntary Associations*. Piscataway, NJ: Transaction.

Curry, Bill. 2011. "Ottawa Looks at Rewriting Rules on Charitable Giving." *The Globe and Mail.* (Oct. 28, 2011). http://www.theglobeandmail.com/life/giving/giving-news/ottawa-looks-at-rewriting-rules-on-charitable-giving/article2216738/.

Ealy, Lenore T. 2010. "Introduction." *Conversations on Philanthropy VII:* v-vii. ©2010 DonorsTrust.

Ealy, Steven D. 2008. "On Happiness—Personal and Political." *Conversations on Philanthropy V:* 57-70. ©2008 DonorsTrust.

Freeden, Michael. 1994. "Political Concepts and Ideological Morphology." *Journal of Political Philosophy* 2, no. 2: 140-64.

Frenk, Julio and Suerie Moon. 2013. Governance Challenges in Global Health. *The New England Journal of Medicine* 368, no. 10: 936-942.

Garnett, Robert F. 2008. "Positive Psychology and Philanthropy: Reclaiming the Virtues of Classical Liberalism." *Conversations on Philanthropy V:* 1-16. ©2008 DonorsTrust.

______. 2010. "Commercial Society after Modernism." *Conversations on Philanthropy VII:* 49-64. ©2010 DonorsTrust.

Göçmen, Dogan. 2007. "Adam Smith Problem: Human Nature and Society in 'The Theory of Moral Sentiments' and 'The Wealth of Nations'." *International Library of Economics* 1.

Gray, Alexander. 1946. *The Socialist Tradition: Moses to Lenin.* London: Longmans.

Gulick, Luther and Lyndall Urwick, eds. 1937. *Papers on the Science of Administration.* New York: Institute of Public Administration, Columbia University.

Gunderman, Richard B. 2005. "Giving and Human Excellence: The Paradigm of Liberal Philanthropy." *Conversations on Philanthropy II:* 1-10. ©2005 DonorsTrust.

______. 2008a. "Authentic Flourishing." *Conversations on Philanthropy V:* 49-56. ©2008 DonorsTrust.

______. 2008b. *We Make a Life by What We Give.* Bloomington, IN: Indiana University Press.

Hardwick, David. F. 1989. Editorial: "Destinations in Pathology." *Modern Pathology* (Nov. 26): 551-552.

Hardwick, David F. and Leslie Marsh. 2012a. "Clash of the Titans: When the Market and Science Collide." In R. Koppl, S. Horwitz and L. Dobuzinskis, eds. *Experts and Epistemic Monopolies. Advances in Austrian Economics* 17: 37-60.

_____. 2012b. Science, the Market and Iterative Knowledge. *Studies in Emergent Order* 5: 26-44.

Harris, Josh. 2012. "'Big Society' and 'Great Society': A Problem in the History of Ideas." In Simon Szreter and Armine Ishkanian, eds. *The Big Society Debate: A New Agenda for Social Welfare?* Cheltenham: Edward Elgar.

Hutton, Will. 1995. *The State We're In: Why Britain Is in Crisis and How to Overcome It.* London: Vintage.

Jabbia, Mbemba, Marte Swarta, and Christian Keysers. 2007. "Empathy for Positive and Negative Emotions in the Gustatory Cortex." *NeuroImage* 34, no. 4: 1744-1753.

Lynn, Elizabeth and Susan Wisely. 2002. "Toward a Fourth Philanthropic Response: American Philanthropy and its Public." In Amy Cass, ed., *The Perfect Gift: The Philanthropic Imagination in Poetry and Prose.* Bloomington, IN: Indiana University Press.

Marsh, Leslie. 2012. "Hayek and Oakeshott: Situating the Mind." In Paul Franco and Leslie Marsh, eds., *A Companion to Michael Oakeshott.* University Park: Penn State University Press.

Marsh, Leslie, ed. 2014. *Propriety and Prosperity New Studies on the Philosophy of Adam Smith.* Basingstoke: Palgrave-Macmillan.

McCully, George. 2008. *Philanthropy Reconsidered: Private Initiatives—Public Good—Quality of Life.* Bloomington, IN: AuthorHouse.

_____. 2010. "Philanthropy and Humanity." *Conversations on Philanthropy VII:* 43-48. ©2010 DonorsTrust.

McSmith, Andy. 2010. "The Big Society: A Genuine Vision for Britain's Future—or Just Empty Rhetoric?" *The Independent* (July 20, 2010).

Morrow, Glenn R. 1923. "The Significance of the Doctrine of Sympathy in Hume and Adam Smith." *The Philosophical Review* 32, no. 1: 60-78.

Norman, Jesse. 2006. *Compassionate Conservatism.* London: Policy Exchange.

_____. 2010. *The Big Society: The Anatomy of the New Politics.* Buckingham: University of Buckingham Press.

Oakeshott, Michael. 1975. *On Human Conduct.* Oxford: Clarendon Press.

Olsen, Johan. P. 1997. "Institutional Design in Democratic Contexts." *The Journal of Political Philosophy* 5, no. 3: 203-229.

Salamon, Lester. 1981. "Rethinking Public Management: Third-party Government and the Tools of Government Action." *Public Policy* 29: 255–275.

_____. 2009. "Third-Party Government." In *International Encyclopedia of Civil Society*. Eds. Helmut K. Anheier, Stefan Toepler, Regina List. 1546-1550. New York: Springer.

Salamon, Lester and S. Wojciech Sokolowski. 2004. *Global Civil Society: Dimensions of the Nonprofit Sector*. Greenwood, CT: Kumarian Press.

Sandel, Michael. 1998. *Liberalism and the Limits of Justice*. Cambridge: Cambridge University Press.

Simon, Herbert A. 1947. *Administrative Behavior: A Study of Decision-Making Processes in Administrative Organization*. New York: The Macmillan Company.

_____. 2000. "Public Administration in Today's World of Organizations and Markets." *Political Science and Politics* 33, no. 4: 749-756.

Smith, Adam. 1984 [1853]. *The Theory of Moral Sentiments*. Indianapolis: Liberty Press.

Smith, Mark J. 2011. "The Intellectual Roots of Big Society." In *The Big Society Challenge*. Ed. M. Stott. Cardiff: Keystone. http://www.keystonetrust.org.uk/documents/128.pdf.

Stott, Marina, ed. 2011. *The Big Society Challenge*. Cardiff: Keystone. http://www.keystonetrust.org.uk/documents/128.pdf.

Szreter, Simon and Armine Ishkanian, eds. 2012. Introduction: What is Big Society? Contemporary Social Policy in a Historical and Comparative Perspective. In: *The Big Society Debate: A New Agenda for Social Welfare?* Cheltenham: Edward Elgar.

Taylor, Charles. 1989. *Sources of the Self: The Making of Modern Identity*. Cambridge, MA: Harvard University Press.

Taylor, Frederick Winslow. 1911. *The Principles of Scientific Management*. New York: Harper and Brothers.

Titchener, Edward Bradford. 1909. *Lectures on the Experimental Psychology of the Thought-Processes*. New York: Macmillan.

Wallas, Graham. 1914. *The Great Society: A Psychological Analysis*. New York: Macmillan.

CHARITY, RECIPROCITY, AND THE MORAL LAW

Todd Breyfogle

In her classic novel *Death Comes for the Archbishop*, Willa Cather provides a short but rich scene which helps crystallize the tensions underlying the relationship among charity, reciprocity, and the moral law (1990). The setting is the New Mexico territory in the middle of the 19th century. Father Joseph arrives at a remote *rancho* riding his broken-down mare. He's greeted by the patron, Manuel Lujon, who affords him all the hospitality due a stranger and, indeed, the hospitality due a priest visiting a faithful clan of believers. On the day before Father Joseph's departure, after an evening of marriages and feasting, Manuel takes Father Joseph for a tour of his corral, where he displays his two prize, cream-colored mules, Contento and Angelico. Father Joseph swings up on Contento's back and parades around, lamenting that his own lame mare will never see him through the miles to his final destination. Thoughtfully and, we are led to believe, somewhat reluctantly, Manuel offers the mule to the priest as a gift. "You have made my house right with Heaven," he tells Father Joseph, "and you charge me very little. I will do something very nice for you; I will give you Contento for a present, and I hope to be particularly remembered in your prayers" (61).

We have the picture here of an apparently simple gift, but one whose contours prove to be complex. Father Joseph has, in some sense, cleverly asked for the mule. Manuel, for his part, cares genuinely for the well-being of Joseph, who has performed his sacramental duties with joy and generosity of spirit. Both men have acted in the spirit of charity—*caritas*, self-giving love. Neither sees the gift in the spirit of reciprocity—Manuel is not responding to a sense of being in debt, and Joseph makes no moral claim in his playful yet serious intimation that the mule might make a suitable substitute for his nag. And yet the gift might be seen to

AUTHOR'S NOTE: I am grateful for the stimulating comments on an earlier version of this essay made by participants at The Law of Charity: History, Theory, and Social Practice colloquium sponsored by The Philanthropic Enterprise. I am also grateful to Jay Marshall for his characteristically careful reading and thoughtful suggestions, and to Lavinia Ochea for her insistence on moderation in certain parts of the text.

Breyfogle, Todd. 2012. Charity, Reciprocity, and the Moral Law. *Conversations on Philanthropy* IX: 138-152. ISSN 1552-9592
©The Philanthropic Enterprise.

contain a hint of duress and exchange—Manuel parts with the mare with circumspect happiness, but asks to be remembered in the priest's prayers. Cather continues: "Springing to the ground, Father [Joseph] threw his arms about his host. 'Manuelito!' he cried, 'for this darling mule I think I could almost pray you into Heaven!' The Mexican laughed, too, and warmly returned the embrace. Arm-in-arm they went in to begin the baptisms" (61).

The scene ends with friends on equal footing embracing each other in the spirit of freedom—a gift has been freely offered and freely accepted. Any reservations on Manuel's part are eclipsed by the joy of his new friend's pleasure and well-being. The mule is not a payment for past or future prayers; Joseph's prayers are not recompense for the mule. In this, both he who gives and he who receives would seem to stand outside a logic of gift-giving which often has unspoken within it a legal notion of proportional justice.

The Logic of Reciprocity

There is—for perhaps every gift—an unspoken expectation of reciprocity, a sense that a gift (if only a gift of thanks) must be given in return, proportionate to the original gift (von Mises 1962, 75-77; see also Mauss 1967; Godbout and Caille 1998).[1] This expectation obtains sometimes on the part of the giver, sometimes on the part of the recipient; very often it is an expectation shared (if not explicitly acknowledged) by both parties. My aim is to consider this underlying juridical notion of proportionality, not concerning the legal code of charitable giving but rather the moral law and logic of reciprocity and the nature of the gift itself. These issues relate significantly, if indirectly, to the possibilities of a culture of philanthropy in a free market, and specifically to the beliefs most conducive to a truly philanthropic society. Does the logic of the gift permit the giving of a gift without the expectation of something in return, or does every gift ultimately reduce itself to the logic of exchange? That is, can there ever be a wholly free gift, or are all human relations inescapably implicated in what Marx called the "naked cash nexus"? How do we separate, both psychologically and morally, a gift for the good of another from the possibility that we are really giving for selfish (or primarily self-interested) motives?[2]

Let us return to our New Mexican *rancho*. All is well between Joseph and Manuel until the following morning, the morning of Joseph's departure. Manuel finds Joseph in the barnyard, "leading the two mules about and smoothing their fawn-coloured flanks, but his face was not the cheerful countenance of yesterday"

(Cather 1990, 61). Joseph insists that he cannot accept the gift of such a beautiful mule while his bishop rides a common hack. A troubled Manuel offers Joseph the pick of his horses, but Joseph declines, saying that he will work hard to buy the pair. Manuel looks around the barnyard for an avenue of escape, but he sees his position clearly. Reluctantly, he gives both the mules to Father Joseph, who cries, "You will be all the happier for that, Manuelito.… Every time you think of these mules, you will feel pride in your good deed" (63). Manuel watches "disconsolately" as Joseph departs with the mules. "He felt he had been worried out of his mules, and yet he bore no resentment. He did not doubt Father Joseph's devotedness, nor his singleness of purpose.… He believed he would be proud of the fact that they [Joseph and the Bishop] rode Contento and Angelica. Father [Joseph] had forced his hand, but he was rather glad of it" (63).

Are the mules still a gift, either in the manner in which they were given or in the spirit in which they were received? Joseph does not ask for the mules with a sense of entitlement, but would it be entirely fair to say that he has only his bishop's and Manuel's interests at heart? Manuel is clearly bullied into relinquishing the mules, and yet he bears no resentment, nor does he seem concerned about any costs or penalties should he quite reasonably refuse Joseph's request. Are we to assume that the spirit of charity has overcome too prideful an attachment to these two lovely beasts? Or has Manuel in effect purchased both a putative spiritual reward and social approbation, the pride of knowing that the clerics will be riding *his* prize mules? What obligations, if any, do Manuel and Joseph now owe each other, or is there no presumed reciprocity beyond a continuing good will?[3]

Aristotle, Kant, Smith

Aristotle might be inclined to praise Manuel's action as generosity or even as magnanimity. For Aristotle, generosity is a virtue of character concerning material wealth. The generous man is moderate toward wealth insofar as he is willing to part with it in giving it to others, in his judgment of the goodness of the person to whom he is giving it, and in giving neither too much nor too little. He receives honor for this virtue of character and rejoices in acting in concert with the good. One might also see Manuel's gift as an act of Aristotelian magnanimity. It is a great deed reflective of a greatness of soul conducted nonetheless with a moderate sense of pride. Although giving two mules instead of one might be an unusual gift—even for a wealthy *ranchero*—Manuel's offering is not excessive, indiscriminate, or vulgar, and he takes pleasure in the giving. There is something fine and beautiful in how Manuel is portrayed, and he would seem to meet Aristotle's criteria of generosity and magnanimity (Nicomachean Ethics, V.4: 1119b20-1125a).[4]

There is one Aristotelian criterion, however, which is not met. The logic of generosity and magnanimity in Aristotle's account presupposes the superiority of the giver and inferiority of the recipient. It is, for Aristotle, better to give than to receive, but this is because the receipt of a gift carries with it an implicit, if not explicit, judgment of being in need or suffering a lack or deficiency (1124b10-20).[5] There is no hint of superiority or inferiority in Cather's portrayal of Manuel and Joseph. Indeed, their relationship, however recently formed, resembles more closely the equality of exchange which characterizes Aristotle's account of friendship. In this, Aristotle would seem to recognize a transcendence of the cycle of exchange and obligation in the relations which obtain between friends. That is, the fullest expression of giving is that which obtains between friends.

Aristotle follows his account of the virtues of character with a discussion of justice. His approach is not initially in terms of the classical Greek definition— rendering unto each what is due—but rather from its status as a virtue: What sort of mean is justice? What are the extremes between which justice is an intermediate? He acknowledges from the outset the difference between what is lawful and what is fair: both the lawful and the fair person will be just, but one can be unfair without violating the law. Yet neither category—fairness or lawfulness—would seem to apply to the giving-receiving we see with Manuel and Joseph. To use the terms of justice to understand Cather's scene would be to engage in a category mistake.

Aristotle's fruitful differentiation of four kinds of justice—distributive, corrective, proportional, and political—gives us a foothold for thinking about the relationship between what is charitable and what is just. As Aristotle understands them, the four kinds of justice aim at: the distribution of goods to effect equality; the corrective or proportional rectification or restoration of goods; and the political actions of ruling and being ruled. Charity as reflected in the relationship between Joseph and Manuel would seem to have no part of any of these. It does bear some resemblance, however, to a notion of justice as proportionate reciprocity. Reciprocal justice pertains to the proportional equality which should obtain in relationships of exchange where the relative values are incommensurable. That is, reciprocity in exchange requires a numerical equality facilitated by money, for all items of exchange must be reducible to an intermediate value. "Reciprocity that is proportionate rather than equal, holds people together," Aristotle says in

Nicomachean Ethics V.5, "for a city is maintained by proportionate reciprocity." This bond finds its strength in the presumption that there will be "a return of benefits received," for "when someone has been gracious to us, we must do a service for him in return, and also ourselves take the lead in being gracious again" (2000, 74).

How are we to understand the intermediate value of the exchange between Manuel and Joseph, if it is to be understood as an exchange at all? Presumably we could determine a price per prayer (either as a unit price or as a function of labor) and draw some equivalent with respect to the market price of cream-colored mules in mid-19th-century territorial New Mexico. But this would seem to be beside the point. In Aristotelian terms, Manuel's gift to Joseph is an act of virtue and so intelligible under principles of general justice, but not amenable to the principles of specific justice. Aristotle gives a nod in this direction with what is effectively a footnote (*Nicomachean Ethics* V.8) on the relation between decency and justice. In the same way that what is decent is just by subsuming the category of justice, so by extension one might view generosity as opening more widely than justice, transcending the category without being inconsistent with it.[6] That is, justice is fulfilled and transcended insofar as the very ground of justice is transformed.

In contrast to this Aristotelian approach, what if we were to view Manuel's gift from the perspective of Kantian duty? There is nothing in Joseph's suggestion that Manuel has a duty—spiritual or ecclesiastical—to give the mules, nor does Manuel see his actions in terms of duty, even a duty of reciprocity for the good that Joseph has performed on the *rancho* (acts which, properly speaking, are the duties of a priest). Manuel's joy in giving would disqualify his gift as a disinterested act. Further, one is left with some discomfort at the prospect of making Manuel's gift a principle of universal law (See Kant, *Foundations of the Metaphysics of Morals*, preface and Section I). It would seem unfair to enjoin—either through positive law or some principle of universal moral law—all people to give their prize possessions to a newfound, if worthy, friend. Moreover, the extreme particularity of the circumstances of Manuel's gift would seem to preclude universal generalization. Manuel's offer is prepared by his sense of gratitude at the accidental and rare arrival of a priest at his remote *rancho*, reinforced by the personal and mutual goodwill that develops between them, and spurred by Joseph's unselfconscious appreciation of something that Manuel too loves and deems beautiful. That is, the gift is highly particularized in time, place, personality, and circumstance. If any one of countless variables were to change, the nature of the gift in Cather's portrayal would be compromised.

What if we were to view Manuel's gift in terms of Adam Smith's theorizing about moral sentiments? Again, we do not see in Cather's portrayal of Manuel any calculation of costs and benefits, nor do we have a hint that he is making his decision in accordance with the view of an impartial spectator, either human or divine (See Smith 1982, II.ii.2 and VI.i). Manuel will not be known where Joseph and his bishop are riding the mules, there is no advertisement from which he would derive public esteem, nor will he receive a tax deduction for his gift. Though these ancillary benefits might accrue, they do not seem to lie at the essence of his gift. And although Manuel is hopeful of Joseph's prayers, the anticipation of God observing him favorably for his gift does not figure in Manuel's reflections. His pride in his gift is not inconsistent with the notion of an impartial spectator, but the validation of his action seems to derive from something other than social (or even spiritual) approbation.

Beyond Human Categories

We can certainly account for Manuel's gift in Aristotelian, Kantian, and Smithian terms, but individually and collectively those accounts seem not to capture the entirety of what transpires in the scene Cather has given us. Manuel's gesture (that very word is significant) is an act of charity implicated in a web of reciprocity which defies theorization, and it neither responds to nor can form the basis of a moral law. It is an act of virtue, of a character formed by habit, but it is not a response to duty or to an imagined judgment of the merit of the act.[7] Both the gift of the mules and their receipt is spontaneous and free. The exchange of mules and gratitude entails no obligation beyond that of good will (of which prayer is a special function). And although there is no explicit obligation, the two are obliged to one another in love. There is, properly speaking, a philanthropy defined not by the gift but of which the gift is itself a feature. The gift both expresses and extends in a new and special way a preexisting affection and good will. There is an expansion of their friendship, and as Aristotle says, "when men are friends they have no need of justice, while when they are just they need friendship as well, and the truest form of justice is thought to be a friendly quality" (2009, 142). The gift displaces us from the normal categories of human moral relations.

Aquinas addresses the failure of human categories fully to account for the nature of the gift by recognizing its dual valence: in terms of the virtue of charity and under the aspect of grace. True to his Aristotelian roots, Aquinas considers charity as a human virtue, embedded in benevolence and friendship. True to his

Augustinian roots, he also sees that any good can be simultaneously referred to nature and to God. For Aquinas, it is consistent with human nature to give of oneself. But the good of charity is grounded in God's goodness. That is to say, the capacity of humans to give is both natural and divine. The completion of the human act of giving is super-human and requires a super-natural gift, of which God is both the source and the example (*Summa Theologica*, 2a2aeQ27 art. 2, 3, 8). For Aquinas, to give truly is a kind of excess, a spilling over of love, having both its source and intelligibility in God. Thus Aquinas recognizes an overlap between a human and a divine logic of giving—an anthropological understanding of what it means to give and a theological one. A gift understood in terms of human virtue is not less meritorious, but it would seem to be less complete.

The distinction between the anthropological and theological understandings of a gift underlies a difficulty in contemporary phenomenology taken up by Jacques Derrida and Jean-Luc Marion. Derrida lays out a fundamental problem with respect to the very possibility of a gift. Leaving to one side the interesting and significant technical issues of phenomenology in his account, Derrida's argument is this: the moment either the giver or the recipient is conscious of the gift as such—i.e., *as a gift*—it ceases to be a gift. That is, the moment of self-conscious recognition cancels out the event of giving, and implicates it irretrievably in the logic of economy and exchange, of credit and debt. As a giver, I take credit in the currency of *amour propre* and am conscious of deserving some recognition of thanks, either from the recipient or from some third party.[8] As a recipient, I am conscious of being under some obligation to the giver, owing a debt of gratitude and, perhaps, responsible for some kind of reciprocal gift, however proportionate to my means. Where Aristotle saw bonds of benevolence, Derrida sees the handcuffs of the cycle of exchange whose moral currency can never find an equilibrium. Derrida does not—at least as a philosophical matter—deny the possibility of the gift in an absolute sense, but he does render highly problematic the possibility of anyone being in a position to observe the gift, insofar as the giver and recipient are ignorant of it. In the end, Derrida's account is a phenomenological transposition of the Kantian approach, recast as a problem of knowledge and self-awareness (Derrida 1994; 2008).

Jean-Luc Marion, by contrast, insists upon at least one participant's consciousness of the gift, but offers two putative ways out of the economy of exchange: anonymity and immaterial gifts. Where the giver or recipient is unknown, Marion argues, the horizon of exchange recedes to a vanishing point. Further, he says, we have many examples of immaterial gifts—gifts where no thing or object is given, but rather gifts of time, love, authority, and trust, for example. We clearly value immaterial gifts, but can we put an exchange value on them? Yes, Marion suggests (like Derrida), but in so doing we destroy their character as gifts. Marion continues:

> The gift does not always imply that something is given. Now this remains true, not only in daily life, but in the most important and meaningful experiences of human life. We know that, to some extent, if the gift is really unique, makes a real difference, cannot be repeated, then in such a case, the gift does not appear as something that could shift from one owner to another owner. Each genuine gift happens without any objective counterpart. When we give ourselves, our life, our time, when we give our word, not only do we give no thing, but we give much more. Here is my point: We can describe the gift outside of the horizon of economy in such a way that new phenomenological rules appear. For instance, the gift or the given phenomenon has no cause and does not need any. It would sound absurd to ask what is the cause of the gift, precisely because givenness implies the unexpected, the unforeseeable and the pure surge of novelty. And also the gift cannot be repeated as the same gift. So we discover with the gift, and to let it display its visibility according to its own logic, we have an experience of a kind of phenomenon that cannot be described anymore as an object or as a being (1999, 63-64, italics in original. See also Marion and Carlson 1998).

Several points are worth highlighting. First, the gift is a unique event in time and place which cannot be transferred or valued according to the traditional rules of economic exchange. Second, the gift has the character of spontaneity—it is free precisely because it emerges outside of a system of causality; it is not in its origin a reciprocating act. Third, it cannot be repeated, which is to say that by definition it cannot be systematized or taken to scale.

At stake in the debate between Derrida and Marion is the status of *grace*—the divine possibility of an absolutely free gift. Can the possibility of a free gift transcend the limits of law? Rather, as Hannah Arendt puts it, "Caritas fulfills the law, because to caritas the law is no longer a command; it is grace itself" (1996, 91). Or, in the words of St. Augustine: *Lex libertatis, lex caritatis est.* "The law of liberty is the law of love." The freedom of the gift thus understood transcends and so fulfills a legal, juridical notion of reciprocity, allowing an account of human giving which enriches the dignity of both the giver and the recipient. How relations are understood shifts from what Augustine called the *libido dominandi*, possessive desire, to the expansion of love beyond desire. Only in giving do we learn to possess lovingly. Just as the gift is spontaneous and therefore free in its origin, so too it is free in its acceptance—neither the act of giving nor the act of receiving includes an expectation of causal consequence; the gift is not intended to produce a result. It is not an exchange, nor is it intended to produce change—it is absolutely free.

And yet, change does occur. When we give, when we receive, we are changed—unpredictably. We are changed most by gifts that are unattended, unexpected by giver and recipient alike. Part of this change is the experience of being outside the horizon of economy altogether, the experience of being free with a super-natural logic of causality in which each act of giving or receiving ushers in something radically new and unpredictable. The currency of this new economy is love, and the conditions it produces are those of human flourishing.[9]

Transcending Exchange

In Cather's story, what is really being given? Manuel is only incidentally giving Joseph the mules. He is in essence, rather, giving a good that he loves and so gives a part of himself, enlarging his soul by parting with a beloved possession in favor of an overflowing of love which cannot be possessed. It is right that Manuel is attached to his mules. Were they not valuable to him, they would not have had the same value as a gift. In giving up the mules, he actually comes to possess them more perfectly. Joseph receives the mules, but in fact he receives the overflow of Manuel's love; in being the occasion of Manuel's expansion of love, Joseph is not made inferior but is equally expanded in his graceful receipt. What occurs is not an exchange but a creation, a refusal of a zero-sum horizon of economy.[10] As such, it is something of a miracle—something super-added to our common life that is not subject to the laws of human necessity and indeed might be at odds with those laws altogether.[11] "But if love can be measured by nothing other than itself," writes Hans Urs von Balthasar in a profoundly Augustinian vein, "then love appears as formless, transcending all creaturely determinateness and precisely for this reason is a threat to it" (2004, 125).

The gift which yields a miracle changes us. Cather herself puts it this way, in a passage just before that in which Joseph stumbles across the mules at Manuel's *rancho*:

> 'Where there is great love there are always miracles,' he [the bishop] said at length. 'One might almost say that an apparition is human vision corrected by divine love. I do not see you as you really are, Joseph; I see you through my affection for you. The Miracles of the Church seem to

me to rest not so much upon faces or voices or healing power coming suddenly near to us from afar off, but upon our perceptions being made finer, so that for a moment our eyes can see and our ears can hear what is there about us always' (1990, 50).

The miracle, for Cather, is a refinement of our perception, the enriching of our sensibility, an enlargement of our humanity, a recognition of the dignity of giver and receiver beside which the beauty of any cream-colored pair of mules cannot compare.

What are the implications of this account for philanthropy? The nature of the gift is best preserved when it is understood outside the causal cycle of reciprocity and the dictates of the moral law. This causal cycle would seem to include a sense of obligation (or *noblesse oblige*) to spend one's money well, and from a sense of trying to accomplish some anticipated good. This causal cycle can readily be seen at work when philanthropy seeks to borrow forms of accountability either from government, by employing bureaucratic rules and procedures, or from business, by seeking to quantify returns on investment. Similarly, it would seem that in such a causal cycle recipients would not only come to expect being given to but would also come to have no shame or sense of inferiority in receiving. The desire to alleviate potential shame for the recipient may also be what is at work in some efforts of philanthropy to move responsibility for "charitable" activity into the social welfare state or, alternatively, to insist that the market can wholly fulfill the demands of moral reciprocity through commercial exchange.

Anonymity, whether of giver or recipient, would seem to be one way of breaking the cycle of exchange and expectation, of credit and debt, and both bureaucratic social welfare provision and the flow of goods through market production and consumption can afford anonymity. At the same time, anonymity would seem to be at odds with another criterion of a gift in the fullest sense, namely particularity. If Manuel had given 1,000 pesos to the Mule Fund for Itinerant Priests, the same material object would have been achieved, but the nature of the gift would have been very different.

These two elements—standing outside the cycle of causality and embracing fully the particularity of time, place, and person—force us to think anew about two pressing issues in philanthropy: measurable impact and scale. One could measure Joseph's new mobility, but how would one calculate the increase of love, both individually and socially, which is the essence of the gift of the mules? And if the essence of the gift is in large measure the particular bond of love between giver and recipient, how are we to think about taking effective giving to scale?

Perhaps this closing example will help reframe these practical questions. Several years ago a friend quit his high-level European job to start an after-school program in the worst ghetto of a major Eastern-European capital city. The neighborhood around the school is a wreck, strewn with heroin syringes and garbage, plagued by unemployment and teen prostitution, and largely neglected by government and nonprofit institutions alike. Many of the state-sponsored classrooms do not function because of teachers' laziness and administrative corruption, and the after-school program is, for many children, the only safe place for study and tutoring, and its staff members have become a surrogate family in a very real sense. When the program received coverage by a national television station, the CEO of a major bank phoned to offer the bank's financial support. "When can you visit?" my friend asked. When the CEO replied that he was too busy to visit the ghetto, my friend thanked him for his concern, said he wasn't interested in the bank's money, and hung up. The CEO found time to visit, but the bank drew the line when my friend asked that funding be contingent upon bank officers volunteering regularly to tutor and play sports with the kids. My friend's insistence on human participation is an implicit recognition of the economy of love. In this case at least, the bank's financial support is a means, not an end, a condition for the far greater giving and receiving that occurs when human beings share the profound gifts of love, trust, resilience, and dignity.

There can be philanthropy without charity. And if this distinction has any value, we might say that philanthropy is measurable and scalable, but charity is not. Philanthropy can be the praiseworthy giving of one's self and one's means. Charity fosters the enlargement of the soul of the one who gives and the one who receives. Philanthropy aims to change others and their circumstances, and so operates in a material register. Charity, in having no aim other than itself, changes us, and so resounds in a spiritual register. Those whose souls are enlarged by charity are restored to themselves and to their communities.

Philanthropy can help establish the material conditions in which charity can flourish. Habits of philanthropy can nourish the soil in which seeds of charity may grow. But a truly good society will be full of miracles, in Cather's sense, a society in which each of us grows in love by giving of ourselves, becoming, however incidentally, the beneficiaries of a new creation. Those gifts are richest which are unattended, miracles of grace which shine with the beauty of the light of dawn.

NOTES

[1] Ludwig von Mises suggests that in exchange, each gives the less valuable for the more valuable. In this example, by contrast, Manuel gives what is most valuable in ignorance of what he will receive.

[2] The true valence of one's motives is always difficult to assess, and one can have an interest in being disinterested. T. S. Eliot underscores the problematic character of even the noblest of actions when his Beckett, in *Murder in the Cathedral*, exclaims, "The last temptation is the greatest treason:/To do the right deed for the wrong reason (1963, 44)." For a further exploration of the relationship between selfishness and self-interest in a theological vein, see C. S. Lewis, 2001. Dostoevsky's *The Idiot* (2003) portrays the conventional absurdity of purely selfless action.

[3] It is worth noting from the outset the cultural context of gift-giving. In Arab culture, I am told, admiring an object obliges the owner to give the object as a gift. In Indian culture, the recipient's response of gratitude for a gift is seen as redundant, even strange, since the giver is already grateful for the occasion the recipient has afforded in being the object of his giving. Manuel's gift may coincide with the first of Maimonides' eight levels of charity (1972, Mishneh Torah, Laws of Charity, 10:7–14: 135-138).

[4] Manuel's action would seem not to satisfy the demands of magnificence, which is generosity publically displayed and for a public good; a gift to the cathedral fund might, however, be so termed.

[5] See also Aquinas, *Summa Theologica*, 2a2ae Q27 art.1, where Aquinas reaffirms that loving is more proper to charity than being loved, though to be loved is also praiseworthy insofar as one is lovable. It is worth noting that the modern culture of individualism accentuates this sense of the inferiority of the recipient. Prizing as we do individual autonomy and self-sufficiency, being the recipient of a gift is often experienced as an insult of sorts, a reduction of dignity in being the object of paternal care, a recognition or creation of tacit inequality. Yet the inability or unwillingness to freely receive a gift may be as corrosive of human relations as the inability or unwillingness to give a gift. That is, modern autonomous individuals would do well to learn how to receive a gift gracefully and with joy. To receive a gift in such spirit, however, would require a revision of our dearly held embrace of autonomy as well as a recognition that there can be non-oppressive relationships of inequality. As givers and receivers we become more human.

[6] In a section on alms in Chapter 1 of *The Gift*, Mauss notes that the Arabic *sadaka* and Hebrew *zedaqa* originally meant justice exclusively, but later came to mean alms.

[7] The highly particularized character of the gift recalls Aristotle's definition of virtue: to do the right thing in the right way to the right person at the right time and for the right reason.

[8] One might see taxable deductions for charitable giving as a kind of third party recognition. Making a charitable donation primarily for a tax deduction would seem to implicate the gift in the cycle of exchange; taking advantage of a tax deduction as a secondary benefit would seem to be incidental and therefore less implicated in the horizon of exchange. To refuse to take a tax deduction to maintain a supposed purity of the gift as a gift seems to me a sensible but not strictly necessary position. One could argue, on the contrary, that taking a tax deduction as a secondary benefit simply reduces transaction costs, leaving more funds for use or distribution. On this argument, a system of taxation might provide deductions as an incentive for greater philanthropy in the hope of facilitating social conditions more conducive to acts of charity.

[9] John Locke, in the *Second Treatise*, makes it clear that he is ambivalent about money as a durable medium of exchange. Bartering makes goods liable to spoilage, but in so doing imposes a natural limitation on the desire for them. Money, by contrast, is a surrogate for the goods themselves, and is therefore an abstraction not subject to natural limitation when treated as an end in itself. The gift given and received by Manuel and Joseph is a concrete surrogate for the love they share (1980).

[10] Implicit, further, is a revision of our customary notion of property. In 17th and 18th century English, "property" and "propriety" were largely interchangeable terms, though propriety carries its sense of the *how* of an exchange rather than just the *what*. The valence of the latter term underscores an important element of what Manuel possesses—the *how* of his gift recalibrates the very nature of his ownership of the mules.

[11] Cf. Aeschylus, *Prometheus Bound* (one of the earliest occurrences of "philanthropy"), where the gift of fire is also an act of rebellion (1961).

REFERENCES

Aeschylus. 1961. *Prometheus Bound*. Trans. P. Vellacott. New York: Penguin Classics.

Aquinas, Thomas. 1948. *Summa Theologica*. New York: Benzinger Bros.

Arendt, Hannah. 1996. *Love and Saint Augustine*. Eds. J. V. Scott and J. C. Stark. Chicago: University of Chicago Press.

Aristotle. 2000. *Nicomachean Ethics*. Trans. T. Irwin. Indianapolis: Hackett Publishing.

______. 2009. *Nicomachean Ethics*. Trans. D. Ross. Oxford: Oxford World Classics.

Cather, Willa. 1990. *Death Comes for the Archbishop*. New York: Vintage Classics.

Derrida, Jacques. 1994. *Given Time: 1. Counterfeit Money*. Trans. Peggy Kamuf. Chicago: University of Chicago Press.

______. 2008. *The Gift of Death and Literature in Secret*. Trans. David Wills. Chicago: University of Chicago Press.

Dostoevsky, Fyodor. 2003. *The Idiot*. Trans. R. Pevear and L. Volokhonsky. New York: Vintage.

Elliot, T. S. 1963. *Murder in the Cathedral*. New York: Harcourt.

Godbout, Jacques T. and Alain Caille. 1998. *The World of the Gift*. Montreal: McGill-Queens University Press.

Kant, Immanuel. 1989. *Foundations of the Metaphysics of Morals*. Trans. L. W. Beck. New York: Pearson.

Lewis, C. S. 2001. *The Screwtape Letters*. New York: HarperCollins.

Locke, John. 1980. The *Second Treatise of Government*. Ed. C. B. Macpherson. Indianapolis: Hackett Publishing.

Maimonides, Moses. 1972. *A Maimonides Reader*. Ed. I. Twersky. Springfield, NJ: Behrman House.

Marion, Jean-Luc. 1999. "On the Gift." *God, the Gift, and Postmodernism*. Eds. John D. Caputo and Michael J. Scanlon. Bloomington: Indiana University Press.

Marion, Jean-Luc and Thomas A. Carlson. 1998. *Reduction and Givenness: Investigations of Husserl, Heidegger, and Phenomenology*. Trans. T. A. Carlson. Chicago: Northwestern University Press.

Mauss, Marcel. 1967. *The Gift: Forms and Functions of Exchange in Archaic Societies*. New York: Norton.

Smith, Adam. 1982. *The Theory of Moral Sentiments. Glasgow Edition of the Works and Correspondence of Adam Smith, vol. 1.* Eds. D. D. Raphael and A. L. Macfie. Indianapolis: Liberty Classics.

von Balthasar, Hans Urs. 2004. *Love Alone is Credible.* Trans. D. C. Schindler. San Francisco: Ignatius Press.

von Mises, Ludwig. 1962. *The Ultimate Foundations of Economic Science.* Princeton: D. Van Nostrand Company.

RESEARCH NOTE

"PHILANTHROPY," "NONPROFITS," AND THE IRS MASTER DATA FILE FOR MASSACHUSETTS

George McCully

A fundamental issue in contemporary philanthropic and nonprofit studies is the need for clarity, precision, and consensus on the meanings of two basic words and concepts we all use daily, and on which the validity of our scholarship and the productivity of our practice depend: "philanthropy" and "nonprofit." Scholars and professionals customarily use these words interchangeably, as if they were synonyms. The IRS Master Data File on "nonprofits," however, shows that not only are the two terms far from synonymous, but that outside the tax code (and state laws of incorporation, which relate to the tax code) they have nothing significant in common. Philanthropy is currently undergoing a classic paradigm-shift; this discovery should facilitate that process and help build the new, twenty-first century paradigm in philanthropy.

Internet and computer technology enables, and is pressing, philanthropic data to become systematic, universally accessible, and transparent. Since 1997, *The Catalogue for Philanthropy* has been studying and clarifying philanthropy for donor education, more influential professional scholarship, and both professional and amateur practice. In 2011, a grant from the Fund for New Philanthropy Studies at DonorsTrust helped us deepen our analysis of the IRS Master Data File for Massachusetts, and to develop a typology of non-philanthropic nonprofits which would clarify their differences from philanthropy—"private initiatives, for public good, focusing on quality of life, and engaging in public fundraising"—i.e., the

AUTHOR'S NOTE: We wish to thank the Fund for New Philanthropy Studies at DonorsTrust of Virginia, and Lenore Ealy, for grant support of the non-philanthropic nonprofit research for this project. We also gratefully acknowledge technical support for this article by Carl Mastandrea and Elizabeth Crawford of the Catalogue for Philanthropy.

McCully, George. 2012. "Philanthropy," "Nonprofits," and IRS Master Data File for Massachusetts. *Conversations on Philanthropy IX*: 153-163. ISSN 1552-9592 © The Philanthropic Enterprise.

philanthropic marketplace of private grants and donations. This research note reports on the background and findings of our work, still in progress.

Advancing Philanthropy through Transparent Data

The *Catalogue for Philanthropy* was launched in 1997 as part of a donor education initiative by a consortium of twenty foundations seeking to increase and improve charitable giving in Massachusetts. The *Catalogue* annually provided articles on philanthropy in general, reinforced by profiles of small to mid-sized charities exemplifying philanthropic excellence. This strategy produced, in eleven years, the most detailed and thorough portrait, analysis, and advocacy of philanthropy in a major philanthropic market (more than 900 charities listed), ever published. It also set a practical record of increasing charitable giving—in only four years, 1997-2000, the *Catalogue* initiative evoked a *doubling* of Massachusetts' giving, from $2 billion to $4 billion. (The increase was interrupted in 2001 by September 11th and economic recession, then resumed several years later. Giving nationwide also increased in those first years—income up by 39 percent, giving by 62 percent; in Massachusetts, income also up by 39 percent, but giving rose by 98 percent; the next-closest state's increase was well behind, at 80 percent. The Massachusetts increase was effected by the top income group of 250,000 taxpayers, which was the *Catalogue's* target audience; their share of total giving increased from 51 percent, which is why they were targeted, to 74 percent).

Along the way, our processes of charities selection and public presentation encouraged us to develop a new donor-friendly taxonomy of philanthropic fields and their charitable organizations. We first considered using the conventional National Taxonomy of Exempt Entities (NTEE), but found it counter-productive. It is not systematic (thus not a taxonomy in the scientific sense)—its ten basic fields bear no logical or ontological relations to each other and are not logically elaborated. Its vocabulary is idiosyncratic and thus awkward for donor education (it was not designed for donors), and its internal inconsistencies render it useless for systematic or statistical data collection and analyses. We therefore decided to create our own systematic taxonomy, which has developed over the years as it grew to handle thousands of charities, into more than two hundred distinct fields in four fundamental areas, covering all possible human relationships: Nature (our relations with the physical environment), Culture (our relations with what humans have created), People (our relations with each other), and "Promoting Philanthropy" (all of the above).

In 2005, as the *Catalogue* approached its tenth anniversary, we wanted to measure our coverage of Massachusetts philanthropy. We had at that point listed 600 charities, in all fields, all across the state, but we had no idea how adequately that represented the total number eligible (in all fields, with budgets below $3 million) or the totals in each field, or the distribution of charities among fields. These elementary numbers simply did not exist—neither academia, nor philanthropic professionals, nor the government, had ever attempted to compile them (indicating that the NTEE did not encourage such compilation). Thus for practical purposes, more than scholarly reasons, we consulted the IRS Master File Data for Massachusetts nonprofits, which lists them all and was by then freely downloadable from the Internet.

We were astonished to discover that on any page of the IRS spreadsheet so few "nonprofits" had anything to do with actual philanthropy as we had learned that it exists. Armed with a clear definition—"private initiatives, for public good, focusing on quality of life, and (for charities as distinct from foundations) engaged in public fundraising"—which we had tested and validated in ten years' experience with thousands of charities, we could easily exclude large groups of obviously non-philanthropic nonprofits—organizations that comprise much of so-called "civil society," and are in the public interest to exist (thus their privilege of tax exemption), but which are basically self-serving, self-supporting, or government-supported institutions—e.g., professional, trade, alumni and condo associations; credit unions and teachers' retirement funds; real-estate trusts; social, athletic, country, and yacht clubs; cemeteries; etc.

Of the more than 40,000 Massachusetts nonprofits, 75 percent are non-philanthropic, having little interest in, nor interest to, the donating public. Private foundations are philanthropic but do not fundraise from the public; churches are by law considered in the public interest to exist, and are often philanthropic for their members and others, but they primarily serve and are supported by their members, and do not seek grants and donations from the general public. In short, "nonprofit" status is an artifact of the tax code, and does not signify interest to donors and grant makers in general.

Of the remaining 25 percent of registered nonprofit organizations, approximately 15 percent—more than half—are what we have called "para-philanthropic"—in a zone graduating the transition between clearly non-philanthropic and clearly philanthropic. This is especially true at the local level, where private and public interest are blurred and sometimes blended. They include Little League teams, PTAs, various clubs, local land trusts, some churches, and the like. This group needs detailed scrutiny and discussion by scholars and professionals; for our purposes we examined them one by one, eventually pruning the list to approximately four thousand *bona fide* charities, in all fields, of potential philanthropic interest to donors and grant-makers. In sum, we found that in Massachusetts—a large state with a mature philanthropic community which we have no reason to believe is exceptional—only about 10 percent of the total number of nonprofits is straightforwardly and undeniably participating in philanthropy, defined as "private initiatives, for public good, focusing on quality of life, and engaged in public fundraising."

We concluded from this research that philanthropic and nonprofit scholarship and practice have fundamental problems of terminology, and thus of empirical accuracy, clarity and simplicity. To the *Catalogue* it meant that, working with this much smaller number, and with our systematic taxonomy and Internet technology, we could compile for the first time anywhere a purportedly complete, systematic, analytical, on-line directory of *all* the charities in a single major market (Massachusetts), providing information of interest to donors from the charities' IRS 990s and websites, and leading donors to those websites as in the long run the best source for up-to-date data and display of the charities' styles and values, with contact links for practical connections. This would be the first system opening all of philanthropy to the public—making the whole and all of its parts visible, understandable, and accessible for everyone—powerfully conducive to increased charitable giving.

Specifically, for Massachusetts as our research and development laboratory, we could readily sort the four thousand philanthropic charities into our two hundred philanthropic fields; from their IRS 990s we could additionally record their revenue sizes, dates of IRS authorization (indicating institutional maturity), and geographic locations (for digital mapping). From their websites we could glean program summaries and demographics of people served. These could then— for the first time—constitute parameters for *systematic* searches and analyses of groups as well as individuals. With interactive Web 2.0 technology, users—from beginners to professional experts—could combine these parameters, and specified ranges within them, according to their interests and purposes, for unprecedentedly powerful, advanced, thorough, searching, data-gathering, and analyses, accomplishing in minutes what had previously taken weeks. When donors found the charities they wanted, contact information would lead them to personal contact, for giving and volunteering. Thus was conceived in 2006 the *Massachusetts Philanthropic Directory* (*MPD*), which we launched as a prototype in 2011 (patent pending, for quality control; sharing for free).

Strengthening the Culture of Philanthropy

As noted above, the data show that roughly 75 percent of nonprofits are obviously not philanthropic. Although the existence of most of them is probably in the public interest, and many do good works, and almost all are "private initiatives" "focusing on quality of life," we found that their clearest empirical disqualifier from philanthropy—i.e., from donors' and grant-makers' interests—is simply that they themselves show no interest, in their 990s and on their websites, in seeking grants and donations from the general public—which is to say, the philanthropic market.

Why not? Especially when many 501(c)3 public charities—approximately 28,000 in Massachusetts—are authorized by the IRS to raise tax-deductible contributions from the public? The answer is that they don't need it—they are self-supporting without broader philanthropic support. Just as the public and most professionals mistakenly believe the word "nonprofit" to be synonymous with philanthropy, so also is it incorrect to believe it means financial dependency on the public.

Many have said, for decades, that using a negative word to describe a positive thing is not attractive and confusing to donors, as well as linguistically imprecise and stupid—like calling dogs "non-cats." To these sound but evidently unpersuasive arguments we can now add that it is also factually incorrect, and statistically misleading—exaggerating our numbers tenfold. Moreover, because "nonprofits" upon examination are so heterogeneous, they have nothing in common except their tax classification and related state laws of incorporation, so the word turns out to be meaningless apart from the tax-code, with no practical utility. <u>Scholars and professionals need now to stop and think about that, to look at the evidence, and to make their own informed decisions.</u>

In the sharpest contrast, the idea of "philanthropy"—the "love of what it is to be human"—is one of the most powerful and profound ideas in the history of Western thought, the core of a rich philosophical, educational, and moral tradition, rooted in classical antiquity and central to the great cultures of Periclean Athens, Republican Rome, the Renaissance, and the Enlightenment. It explicitly informed the birth of our own nation from the Colonial period through the Revolution and the Constitution. From its coinage in *Prometheus Bound* (line 11), it was associated "with **freedom** against slavery, **democracy** against tyranny; **civilization** against wildness or barbarism; with **education** as self-development and empowerment; with **optimism** and **progress** in history; and finally with the sense that these are all mutually interdependent and reinforcing...." (McCully 2008, 12, emphasis in original).

The term "nonprofit" emerged around the turn of the twentieth century, with little influence until it entered social science scholarship in the '60s, and increasingly thereafter became associated with the so-called "third sector" (neither government nor business), even being taken as synonymous with "civil society." That is not a problem for the *Catalogue*, except when it is confused with philanthropy. Our institutional mission is "to strengthen the culture of philanthropy"; therefore we oppose confusing influences, which we have found from donors and charities alike is diluting, enervating, and inhibiting.

To help clarify the vocabulary and dispel the conceptual fog in the philanthropic world, and as we were working with the data anyway for our own purposes, we developed for colleagues in other fields, and attempted roughly and tentatively to quantify, a typology of the much larger and more varied world of nonprofits. As a practical matter, we believe that the best prioritizing strategy for *philanthropic* studies is to focus on and learn what we can from the philanthropic 10 percent of nonprofit entities, the indisputable hard core of philanthropy—a very substantial body of perhaps 200,000 institutions nationwide, about which as a group almost nothing is known because they have been carelessly submerged in and confused with the overall nonprofit population.

By suggesting what kinds of non-philanthropic institutions inhabit the so-called nonprofit sector, we hope also to clarify *why* they can no longer be considered philanthropic. We do NOT consider this basic distinction between philanthropic and non-philanthropic institutions as <u>in any way an invidious value judgment.</u> There is nothing wrong with non-philanthropic nonprofits as a group; most of them can be construed to be in the public interest, meriting the privilege of tax exemption. Finally, we invite empirical correction—our goal is consensus terminology.

A Preliminary Typology of Non-Philanthropic Nonprofits, Based on Sources of Revenue

We have found that as a practical matter there is a close correlation between sources of revenue and the characters of organizations, which may seem obvious but has not yielded rigorous typology.

Apparently close to, but not quite, philanthropy

Some institutions give every appearance of being philanthropic, except that they are not engaged in the philanthropic marketplace of public fundraising for grants and donations—on their 990s they either leave that revenue space blank or insert a zero, and their websites, if such they have, show no interest in it (as does not having a website). This constitutes a surprisingly large number of institutions—in Massachusetts more than 8,000, or 20 percent of all nonprofits, fully twice as many as those entities reporting revenue from grants and donations. These organizations show no signs of trying and failing to raise funds. They could be entirely volunteer organizations, with no paid staff or overhead expenses (and no mention of volunteers on their websites?), in which case we would list them as philanthropic. It is conceivable that the people behind these organizations just don't know how to fill out 990s correctly or have useful websites, and if so, the recently simplified forms may help solve that problem. It is also possible that many of these entities are defunct (though still submitting 990s?); time will tell about that as well. Our methodology requires conclusive evidence of market participation for an institution to be classifed as philanthropic. We cordially invite them to provide such evidence, but until then we have taken the conservative course of not including them in philanthropy. Our database should be concretely and definitively positive.

In the public interest, but about themselves

Next closest to philanthropy are nonprofit organizations that do not address the general public but instead have so narrow, and often local, a focus as to suggest that they are basically self-serving. In Massachusetts and probably everywhere, there are many of these—13 percent of all nonprofits in the Bay State. These include Little League and other local community or school athletic teams, parent-teacher associations, small libraries or land trusts, and the like. They are private initiatives, and they do report some revenue from donations and even grants, but it is not clear that they or their grants and donations serve a *public* good—their fundraising appeals are largely to their members' self-interests; they do not fundraise from the general public, but from relatives, local businesses, and other interested parties. Here, too, we have taken the conservative position that to classify any of them as philanthropic requires stronger evidence of public benefit, on a case-by-case basis in which the size and scope of the public benefit beyond themselves will be determinative.

Self-supporting, self-serving organizations

Still further removed from philanthropy as ordinarily conceived is the largest single cohort—54 percent, more than half of all nonprofits—which are entirely self-supporting from revenue sources within their own organizations, neither seeking nor depending at all on any grants or donations from the outside public. They do not participate in the philanthropic marketplace. They are independent, self-supporting trusts or endowments, or membership organizations supported by dues and contributions of members only (such as social, country, and yacht clubs; condo, professional, and trade associations; alumni organizations, churches, etc.), serving primarily to benefit their own members rather than a broader public. It is common for such organizations not to have websites, and for their principal beneficiaries to be themselves, directly or indirectly. Claims to be serving public good are often unclear or secondary to their members' benefits. Whether individual institutions should be considered philanthropic is of course subject to correction on the basis of evidence, which we cordially invite. Our goal is a consensus list.

A special word is in order here about foundations. Community foundations are certainly philanthropic: they exist to promote philanthropy, at the interface between the donating public and the charities within their service areas and sometimes beyond (as in international philanthropy). They engage in public fundraising and so meet every criterion of "philanthropy." Most private foundations, on the other hand, do not invite public participation, and yet are entirely devoted to philanthropic activity, whether operating or grant-making—thus they are self-supporting but *not* self-serving. Because they are not of interest to donors, they have not been, but probably will be, included in the Massachusetts' and other states' *Philanthropic Directories;* they are included in our system's homepage for all of philanthropy in each state—in Massachusetts, *MassPhilanthropy.*

Quasi-governmental, quasi-commercial corporations

In numbers of organizations a surprisingly small percentage—3.5 percent—but in dollars a predictably very large percentage, is a group that resembles either business or government more than philanthropy. Some of these organizations support themselves entirely through earned income—as is the case of "nonprofit businesses" (as they style themselves) such as Blue Cross/Blue Shield in Massachusetts. Within this group, 0.3 percent are entirely dependent on government funding—in effect, they are quasi-government agencies. A single nonprofit in Massachusetts reports annual revenue of $1.4 *billion,* which it receives from a single government source—the National Security Agency; it has a noticeably large number of senior staff earning six- and seven-figure salaries. Another 0.3 percent of nonprofits are funded by a mixture of revenue sources— earned income, government grants and contracts—but *not* public fundraising of grants and donations. These can be very large institutions such as hospitals, with large revenues and assets. Clinical practices of physicians associated with hospitals are often incorporated as nonprofit and tax-exempt, with very highly paid staff who are not considered shareholders.

Conclusion

To our knowledge, the nonprofit dataset has not previously been described nor typologized in such detail by sources of income. Nonetheless, this data illuminates the nonprofit sector—its structure, operations, issues, and interests, especially in relation to government and the for-profit economy, as well as for refined concepts of civil society or the social sector.

The non-philanthropic nonprofit sector is by far the dominant cohort—quite varied but clearly distinguishable from the philanthropic nonprofits strictly construed, by reference to their disinterest in philanthropy and their viability from non-philanthropic sources of revenue. <u>These organizations are in no way dependent on the public, nor competing with philanthropies for philanthropic fundraising dollars.</u>

There are a few more lessons here. The sheer variety of nonprofits reveals that *tax-exemption*—through the federal tax code and state laws of incorporation subordinate to the tax code—*is the only feature these entities have in common.* To test this conclusion, we asked the nearly 1,400 subscribers to the ARNOVA List-Serve to suggest any other common trait, and none has emerged. If there is none, it means that common expressions such as "nonprofit management" are meaningless without further qualification—for example, by referring to specified cohorts, such as philanthropies, cemeteries, country clubs, real estate trusts, condo associations, teachers' retirement funds, black lung associations, trade unions, professional associations, etc.

Moreover, the federal tax-exempt classification system seems to us to need thorough review by the IRS and Congress. It is clearly a product of politics over decades, arising from conditions that may no longer apply in all cases. There may even be appreciable federal and state tax revenues to be gained by eliminating obsolete or inappropriate tax exemptions—especially useful today. We have found many cases in which the tax exemption's prohibition against distributing surplus revenues (profits) to private shareholders has been used to justify distributing those surpluses instead to top executives in the form of large compensation packages—six- and seven-figure salaries and other bonuses. In short, *the tax-exempt nonprofit classification structure seems to need thorough review.*

Furthermore, the meaning of the word *nonprofit* itself should be reconsidered, because times have changed and some current conditions were not foreseen by the tax code. To take only one outstanding example: when institutions with billion-dollar endowments earn annually in their investment yields more than they can possibly spend on their charitable purpose and institutional development (including hyper-compensations), or raise from philanthropic fundraising, and are prohibited from distributions to private shareholders, their only recourse is to plow the surplus back into the ballooning endowment, in an endless upward-spiraling, positive-feedback loop. If their public tax-deductible fundraising is no longer necessary, should such institutions remain tax-exempt and continue siphoning off from other beneficiaries philanthropic dollars that might truly "make a difference"? To designate as "nonprofits" such highly profitable (in ordinary parlance) institutions, such as many of our nation's "private" universities, is an obvious mislocution. Sustaining tax-exemption for these entities poses lost opportunities for local, state, and federal tax revenues and is an embarrassment to authentic philanthropy. What these institutions have become is hugely profitable businesses that mix public and private interests and benefits.

Finally, from a practitioner's standpoint this subject of nomenclature is not only a matter of academic importance which one may decide to accept or not in one's own scholarly work. Imprecise and unvalidated language in philanthropic and nonprofit studies does undermine respect for that scholarship, and has produced public confusion and negative impressions of philanthropy, which have seriously crippled charitable giving and thus our nation's quality of life. This is a matter of public urgency, as it diminishes our common weal as a nation and our standing in the world. We all—scholars and practitioners—have a serious teaching responsibility and job to do. Please join those of us in the field who are working to increase charitable giving and philanthropy as a quintessentially American lifestyle.

REFERENCES

McCully, George. 2008. *Philanthropy Reconsidered—Private Initiatives, Public Good, Quality of Life, A Catalogue for Philanthropy Publication.* Indianapolis: AuthorHouse.

SECTION TAX CODE	DESCRIPTION OF ORGANIZATION
501(c)(1)	Corporations Organized Under Act of Congress (including Federal Credit Unions)
501(c)(2)	Title Holding Corporations for Exempt Organizations
501(c)(3)	Public Charities and Private Foundations
501(c)(4)	Civic Leagues, Social Welfare Organizations, and Local Associations of Employees
501(c)(5)	Labor, Agricultural, and Horticultural Organizations
501(c)(6)	Business Leagues, Chambers of Commerce, Real Estate Boards, etc.
501(c)(7)	Social and Recreation Clubs
501(c)(8)	Fraternal Beneficiary Societies and Associations
501(c)(9)	Voluntary Employees' Beneficiary Associations
501(c)(10)	Domestic Fraternal Societies and Associations
501(c)(11)	Teachers' Retirement Fund Associations
501(c)(12)	Benevolent Life Insurance Associations, Mutual Ditch or Irrigation Companies, Mutual or Cooperative Telephone Companies, etc.
501(c)(13)	Cemetery Companies
501(c)(14)	State Chartered Credit Unions, Mutual Reserve Funds
501(c)(15)	Mutual Insurance Companies or Associations
501(c)(16)	Cooperative Organizations to Finance Crop Operations
501(c)(17)	Supplemental Unemployment Benefit Trusts
501(c)(18)	Employee Funded Pension Trusts (created before June 25, 1959)
501(c)(19)	Posts or Organizations of Past or Present Members of the Armed Forces
501(c)(20)	Group Legal Services Plan Organizations
501(c)(21)	Black Lung Benefit Trusts
501(c)(22)	Withdrawal Liability Payment Funds
501(c)(23)	Veterans Organizations (created before 1880)
501(c)(25)	Title Holding Corporations or Trusts with Multiple Parents
501(c)(26)	State-Sponsored Organizations Providing Health Coverage for High-Risk Individuals
501(c)(27)	State-Sponsored Workers' Compensation Reinsurance Organizations

The Man Who Sold America: The Amazing (But True!) Story of Albert D. Lasker and the Creation of the Advertising Century
By Jeffrey L. Cruikshank and Arthur W. Schultz
Boston, MA: Harvard Business Review Press, 2010.
382 pages. $27.95 US (hardcover) (ISBN 978-1591393085)

Reviewed by Martin Morse Wooster

If you were to compile a list of the most dynamic philanthropists of the twentieth century, Mary Woodard Lasker (1900-1994) would have to be included. Lasker's single-minded mission, for which she used the resources of the Albert and Mary Lasker Foundation for more than forty years, was to dramatically increase taxpayer funding for federal government medical research on heart disease, cancer, and stroke.

Lasker was brilliantly successful in her efforts. Her relentless lobbying, climaxing in the Nixon Administration's "War on Cancer," resulted in the National Institutes of Health being transformed from a tiny agency with a budget of $5 million in 1949 to a vast operation with a multibillion dollar budget in the 1970s. But her effort was based on a spectacularly faulty premise: that if the federal government spent enough money, "a cure for cancer" would somehow be found. She consistently held this view throughout her long career. In 1986, forty years after she began her one-woman lobbying effort, a reporter from *Business Week* asked Lasker whether the notion that a cure for cancer could be found if government funding were increased was unrealistic. She said, "Nobody knows the full picture about any of these diseases, so how does anyone know what's an unrealistic expectation and what's not?"[1]

The money Lasker used to fund her campaign came from a fortune created by her second husband, Albert D. Lasker. When he died in 1952, he willed $6 million to Mary and an additional $6 million to the Albert and Mary Lasker Foundation. But Mary said that she was simply continuing her husband's ideas. Was her claim true?

Until now, historians have had a limited amount of materials to work with. The only biography of Albert Lasker, John Gunther's *Taken at the Flood*, published in 1960, was an authorized biography over which his wife and children had editorial control. *The Man Who Sold America* is just the second Lasker biography. Its authors, Cruikshank, an experienced business historian, and Schultz, former CEO of Foote, Cone, and Belding, state in a postscript that Gunther's book was "closely edited" by Albert D. Lasker's widow and his children, and "we have reinstated details that the Lasker family removed from Gunther's manuscript" (381). In addition, Cruikshank and Schultz had two sources not available to Gunther: an oral history, ultimately amounting to more than 2,000 pages, that Mary Lasker gave to Columbia University beginning in 1962, and numerous transcripts of interviews that Boyden Sparkes conducted with Lasker and his associates in the late 1930s for a biography that was never published. (Columbia University Libraries has since posted the Mary Lasker interviews on the web.)

Cruikshank and Schultz are good writers, and *The Man Who Sold America* adds substantially to our knowledge of Albert Lasker's business achievements. Their chapters on his philanthropic career are less enlightening, but they do add some details to the limited information we have about Lasker's philanthropic goals.

Albert D. Lasker was one of the greatest advertising executives of the twentieth century. He was born in Galveston, Texas, in 1880. In 1896, Lasker graduated from high school and, as an aspiring journalist, acquired a scoop by convincing the prominent socialist Eugene V. Debs, in Galveston to resolve a union dispute, to give a brief but exclusive interview.

Lasker's talents were not in journalism but in advertising. In 1898 he went to Chicago and joined the advertising firm of Lord and Thomas as an apprentice. Lasker rose to become president of the firm and stayed with the company until it was liquidated in 1942. (Many of Lord and Thomas' employees and accounts were transferred to a successor firm: Foote, Cone, and Belding.)

Under Lasker's leadership, Lord and Thomas became one of America's largest advertising companies. Lasker and his employees convinced Americans to eat Sunkist oranges and Sun-Maid raisins, use Whirlpool washing machines, and smoke Lucky Strike cigarettes. As Lasker's career progressed, he often took stock as partial payment for Lord and Thomas advertisements; Lasker's holdings in these companies, including Pepsodent and Kimberly-Clark, substantially increased his fortune.

Lasker's influence on American society was not limited to advertising. He was majority owner of the Chicago Cubs for a decade, and had he not allowed his friend William Wrigley to claim the naming rights, the Cubs today could be playing in Lasker Field. Lasker also played a key role in the effort to clean up baseball after the White Sox gambling scandal of 1919.

In the 1930s, Lord and Thomas were among the first national advertisers to buy time on radio. Their efforts helped to create "Amos 'n Andy," the first radio comedy, and "The Story of Mary Marlin," one of the first soap operas. In 1938,

Lord and Thomas decided to end its sponsorship of "Amos 'n Andy." The authors argue that Lord and Thomas' radio department, headed by Lasker's son Edward, then discovered Bob Hope and created the platform that enabled him to become a national star.

Albert Lasker had long been involved in philanthropy in a limited way. In 1928 he created the Lasker Foundation for Medical Research with a $1 million grant. The foundation lay dormant for nearly a decade, making no grants, until in 1939 Lasker declared that the University of Chicago could use the funds for general operating support. Lasker made another gift to the University of Chicago in 1940, giving the university Mill Road Farm, his estate in Lake Forest, Illinois. In 1947 the university sold the land to developers who turned the property into postwar housing.

Mary Lasker transformed her husband in a variety of ways. Politically, Albert was initially an ardent Republican who was one of Warren Harding's key advisers. According to Harding biographer Francis Russell, in the summer of 1920 Lasker personally delivered a $20,000 payoff to Harding's mistress, Carrie Phillips, along with the gift of a round-the-world cruise that kept Phillips out of the country until well after the election. In the 1930s, Lasker supervised Lord and Thomas' successful efforts in California that caused Socialist Upton Sinclair to lose his 1934 campaign for governor. Two years later, Lord and Thomas successfully defeated a California initiative that would have imposed punitive taxes on chain stores because they could sell products more cheaply than independent stores could.

Under Mary's influence, Albert gave up baseball and golf and embraced psychoanalysis and art collecting. Although he never formally switched parties, Albert endorsed Franklin Roosevelt in 1944 and Harry S. Truman in 1948. And in philanthropy, he followed his wife's lead.

One early cause was birth control. In the 1920s, Lasker's two sisters had used a bequest from their mother to "help women" by giving it to Margaret Sanger to promote birth control. In a 1950 speech accepting an award from the Albert and Mary Lasker Foundation, Sanger said that this gift from Lasker's sisters enabled "our cause in those early days ... to go out into the field and be heard."[2] In 1939, Lasker authorized a Lord and Thomas corporate grant to promote birth control in Georgia.

With Mary's encouragement, the Albert and Mary Lasker Foundation gave much more to the movement for birth control. "The Birth Control movement is something far beyond the implications of its name," Albert wrote to Sanger in 1940 (343). Mary claimed that her husband coined the name "Planned Parenthood," saying he decided on it because "it sounded more constructive and would meet with less public opposition" than the organization's previous name, the Birth Control Association of America (343).

Fighting cancer was the Laskers' second chief philanthropic interest. In 1922 and 1923, Lasker gave two donations totaling $25,000 to the American Society for the Control of Cancer, in memory of his brother Harry, who had died from cancer in 1922. "The two gifts," the authors say, "represented almost the entire endowment of the Society in its first decade of operations" (352).

The society remained small until 1944, when the Laskers and their allies took over the organization, renamed it the American Cancer Society, and launched a national fundraising drive that transformed it from a tiny organization that distributed pamphlets into one of the nation's largest nonprofits. Lasker was personally responsible for a 1945 campaign where, for the first time, such popular radio shows as "Fibber McGee and Molly" discussed cancer as a disease that shouldn't be hidden but instead confronted and treated.

But there's little evidence that Albert Lasker was interested in his wife's crusade to devote billions of dollars in federal taxpayer money to anti-cancer efforts. The only evidence that he supported Mary's efforts in that regard was a statement she made in 1962 that when she said her primary philanthropic energies were devoted to lobbying for national health insurance and increased research for cancer and tuberculosis, Albert allegedly said, "For that, you don't need my kind of money. You need federal money, and I will tell you how to get it."[3] Cruikshank and Schultz offer no other evidence that Albert Lasker supported a massive increase in federal funding for research or was active in the American Cancer Society after 1946.

The Man Who Sold America is an important and engaging biography, but it fails to answer many lingering questions about Albert Lasker's motives as a philanthropist.

MARTIN MORSE WOOSTER *is a senior fellow at the Capital Research Center and a contributing editor to* Philanthropy.

NOTES

[1] Martin Morse Wooster, *Great Philanthropic Mistakes* (Washington, D.C: Hudson Institute, 2010), p. 67, quoting Sara Siwolop, "The Fairy Godmother of Medical Research," *Business Week*, July 14, 1986.

[2] *The Public Writings* and *Speeches of Margaret Sanger*, "Lasker Award Address," October 25, 1950, www.nyu.edu/projects/sanger/webedition/app/documents.

[3] Martin Morse Wooster, *Great Philanthropic Mistakes* (Washington, D.C: Hudson Institute, 2010), p. 44.

• • • •

The Two Narratives of Political Economy
By Nicholas Capaldi and Gordon Lloyd, eds.
Hoboken, NJ: Wiley-Scrivener, 2011.
506 pages. $49.95 US (hardcover) (ISBN 978-0470948293)

Reviewed by Art Carden

*"The two competing narratives are the **Lockean (liberty)** narrative (but made canonical by Smith) and the **Rousseauean (equality)** narrative (but made canonical by Marx)" (xxxii).*

In *The Two Narratives of Political Economy*, Nicholas Capaldi and Gordon Lloyd bring together a selection of readings on the two most important themes in political economy dating back to John Locke and Jean-Jacques Rousseau: liberty and equality. They have assembled what will be a very useful reader for courses in the history of economic thought, political theory, and social theory writ large. They also frame the debate in terms that should influence scholars who study the development of economic, political, and social institutions. To select, modify, and in some cases translate passages representing some of the central themes in the discussion as it proceeded over the eighteenth and nineteenth centuries represents a significant editorial contribution.

Capaldi and Lloyd divide the book into three parts: "The Emergence of Political Economy," "The Arrival of Political Economy," and "The Maturation of Political Economy." An uncollected fourth section—indeed how I think about this review— might have been called "The Completion of Political Economy" or "The Close of Political Economy," or perhaps, more self-consciously provocative (and hyperbolic),

"The End of Political Economy." I will say more on this missing section below.

The starting point for the editors' analysis is the emergence of political economy out of the domain of "household management" and into social analysis, a move that was effected in part through the writings of John Locke and Jean-Jacques Rousseau. With Locke and Rousseau and their successors the unit of analysis of political economy shifted from the individual acting within the confines of a household economy and to the "nation" acting in the context of a broader global economy.

From Locke and Rousseau, Capaldi and Lloyd take us through contributions from Smith, Tocqueville, Saint-Simon, Robert Owen, Friedrich List, Proudhon, J.S. Mill, Marx, Engels, and some of the documents surrounding the American and French Revolutions (the American Declaration of Independence, the French Declaration of the Rights of Man and Citizen, the French constitutions of 1791, 1793, and 1795, and other documents). Scholars who are interested in the causes and consequences of institutions—specifically in the sense in which they are defined by Douglass C. North as the formal rules, informal norms, and enforcement characteristics that define the "rules of the game"—will find the juxtaposition of the American state papers with the French Revolutionary documents illuminating. This is particularly so in light of the discussions from Locke, Rousseau, Smith, and Tocqueville that precede them. I can see a very interesting classroom discussion beginning with the principles expounded by Locke and Rousseau, the specific text of some of the documents presented, and an evaluation of the kinds of incentives inherent in those documents.

The introductory essays—including the general introduction and the introductions to each section—helpfully prepare the reader for what he will encounter. I learned much from them. The editors begin by discussing "the Technological Project," which they call "the most important historical development in the last four hundred years" (xiii), and what accompanied it: the free market economy, limited government, rule of law, and a culture of personal autonomy (they note that the latter is not a libertine "culture of self-indulgence"). One of the seismic shifts, according to the editors, was the view that all men (and eventually, women) are equal in the eyes of God and the law and that to erect "legal barriers in the economic realm was tantamount to thwarting God's plan" (xvi). From all this emerged "a new persona—the entrepreneur."

Unfortunately, and hence my wish for that missing fourth section of the book, they do not carry their discussion of the entrepreneur through the contributions of late nineteenth and early twentieth century scholars, particularly those working in the neoclassical and Austrian traditions. The editors assume up front that people have easy access to the twentieth and twenty-first century versions of the narratives, and thus the book ends with Friedrich Engels' *Socialism: Utopian and Scientific*. This choice of stopping place weakens the volume as a whole, as the marginalists and especially those who followed in the tradition of Carl Menger (most specifically Ludwig von Mises and Friedrich Hayek) provided concrete answers to some of the questions raised by the two narratives in the eighteenth and nineteenth centuries. Most specifically, the contributions of Mises and Hayek to the socialist calculation debate show that a socialist society cannot function as an *economic* system. The impossibility of economic calculation under socialism has important implications for how we evaluate alleged tradeoffs between liberty and equality.

William Stanley Jevons, Leon Walras, and Carl Menger independently contributed marginal analysis to the science of political economy even before Engels published *Socialism* in 1880. Marginal analysis enabled future generations of scholars to develop complete theories of money and prices that were absent from the work of the classical economists and unrefuted by Marxists. Reading through the book, I found myself frustrated by the fact that there are a lot of questions raised by the authors assembled in this volume that are answered by scholars such as Mises, Ronald Coase, Hayek, and others, who are not included in the volume. A section containing some of these contributions with an introductory essay like those that bring the reader into the other sections would have made for a more complete discussion.

Nonetheless, the book is impressive for its topical breadth. One particularly useful inclusion is John Locke's "A Letter Concerning Toleration." The letter is especially interesting in that it recognizes, as Hayek would later, that the animating contest of liberty is a search process whereby the institutions that work are discovered through trial and error. This passage from Locke is instructive as one considers the difference between pure religion (with an internal focus) and impure religion (with an external focus): "No way whatsoever that I shall walk in against the dictates of my conscience will ever bring me to the mansions of the blessed; I may grow rich by an art that I take not delight in; I may be cured of some disease by remedies that I have not faith in; but I cannot be saved by a religion that I distrust and by a worship that I abhor. ... In vain, therefore, do princes compel their subjects to come into their Church communion, under pretense of saving their souls. If they believe, they will come of their own accord, if they believe not, their coming will nothing avail them" (39). Intriguingly,

Rousseau argues in a different vein (foreshadowed by Hobbes) that the separation of church and state is disadvantageous because no man can serve two masters: in this case, the state and the church.

In the end, *The Two Narratives of Political Economy* helps us understand the major themes that have shaped the history and ongoing development of political economy. Presumably, modern nation-states were instituted among men in order to secure the blessings of liberty; their general historical failure to do this suggests that we might want to turn our attention to other social institutions to understand how liberty and equality are best secured. The twenty-first century version of the Lockean narrative, particularly as it is being developed by economists at George Mason University and elsewhere, is turning scholars' attention toward the mechanisms by which governance emerges from voluntary cooperation. In this light, I'll be very interested in seeing what an updated edition of this volume might look like in another decade or two.

ART CARDEN *is Assistant Professor of Economics at Samford University in Birmingham, Alabama and a Research Fellow with the Independent Institute. Previously, he was Assistant Professor of Economics at Rhodes College in Memphis, Tennessee. His research has appeared in journals like the* Journal of Urban Economics, Public Choice, *and* Contemporary Economic Policy, *and he is a regular contributor to* Forbes.com *and the* Washington Examiner.

• • • •

Ten Ways to Destroy the Imagination of Your Child
By Anthony Esolen
Wilmington, DE: ISI Books, 2010.
256 pages. \$26.95 US (hardcover) (ISBN 978-1935191889)

Reviewed by Tony Woodlief

In a recent survey of teenage girls which asked them to name their ideal careers, nearly 40 percent selected something in the arts and entertainment fields. When asked if they thought they would actually get their dream jobs, two-thirds said either that they "think so" or that they were "certain."

As another piece of evidence about the dream world which is modern adolescence, I offer what happened when I was asked to speak to high-school students about how to pursue a successful career. In the course of my remarks, I said something that seemed imminently sensible, but which evoked immediate rejection from a majority of my listeners, namely, that none of us can do anything he wants.

"You can," said a student in the back, rising as if with great effort from his slouch, "if you want it badly enough."

"I'd really like," I told him, "to play professional basketball. But I can't shoot, nor can I dribble, nor do I have the reaction time of the average player on a losing college team. No matter how much I'd like to be a point guard for the Chicago Bulls, it's not something I can do."

"Then you must not want it bad enough," my challenger retorted. He returned to his slouch, fortified by the approving nods of his classmates.

The imagination of young people, it would seem, is in no danger of going away; if anything, one might be forgiven for thinking it could stand a good backhand. Many adolescents, in fact, live in a world of fantasy that encourages stupid choices and, eventually, crushed expectations.

Anthony Esolen's *Ten Ways to Destroy the Imagination of Your Child*, then, seems a welcome tonic. It appears we need to do some imagination destroying, and to replace what we level with common sense.

But wait—Esolen offers his book Screwtape-style, with an authorial voice that encourages readers to truncate the dangerous imaginations of their young charges, lest they grow up to be independent adults. What emerges from Esolen's ironic treatment is a clarification that the baseless dreaming of the sort one often encounters among young people, as it turns out, is not imagination run amok, but a narcissistic self-absorption that crowds out genuine imagination, which Esolen might define as man's inherent tendency to understand his place in creation, to grapple for truth, and to craft beauty within the context of being himself a created being.

The modern daydreaming impulse is not a natural extension of this, but rather the Mr. Hyde to genuine imagination's Dr. Jekyll. It is a toxic consequence, in part, of immediate, pushbutton, mental masturbation. With a few keystrokes today's teenager can blow up alien cities, watch the copulation of actors bearing outsized body parts, and tell any number of people on the receiving end of his texts how much he loves or hates them, all before he finishes the bag of potato chips at his elbow. And all the while, so long as his test scores are adequate, we tell him he's bright and encourage him to reach for the stars. "We can do a fine job curdling the imagination by stressing 'creativity,' for the creative child is encouraged to think of himself as a little god, with all his bright ideas coming from within. The older tradition has the poet as hearer before he is a crafter of verses. The Muse comes to him" (200).

What patience can exist, then, for the labor of true creation? What intimacy can be forged where passion comes so cheaply? What humility has been cultivated that might activate the poet's "receptivity," as Esolen calls it, to a world filled with mystery, with a grandeur that encompasses us, yet does not originate with us?

The artifacts of our current culture—and the shoddy, corporatized educational systems in which they are embedded—invite us to turn inward. "Self-expression," Esolen writes, "is the finest antidote for a perky imagination ever invented" (88).

This book is much more, then, than an assessment of what saps the genuine imagination of children. It is a lament for what we have lost and are losing: honor, humility, non-eroticized love, truth, and faith.

Esolen is a Christian—in an older sense of that word, before the modern apostates and know-nothings and sentimentalists got a stranglehold on it—and so he has a Tolkienesque sense of hope even (especially!) in the darkest hour, and of fighting the enemy with an eye not toward self-righteousness, but toward victory. This means thinking strategically about exactly how Mordor might be laid low.

And the Mordor of our time, one gathers from Esolen, is a utilitarian educational culture administered by small-minded bureaucrats in thrall to materialism, scientism, and social conformity. Whereas traditional conservative critiques of education tend to be of public schools—and these for being populated by government employees who fail to impart a sufficient level of "core knowledge" to their charges—Esolen reviles all the attributes of mass-production schooling that is equal parts Henry Ford and John Dewey: age-segmentation, undifferentiated treatment, chockablock schedules that afford no time for individual exploration, and obsession with facts ("How long is the Mississippi?") over knowing ("What was it like to navigate the Mississippi?").

It's tedious work, Esolen notes in Screwtape style, of blunting the properly imaginative impulse, but the tedium has a purpose. It's all part of a process for churning out citizens who make things difficult neither for their educators nor their rulers, and who set themselves to the task of enhancing the national GDP, both as producers and consumers. Writes Esolen: "...everything you do as a child must be geared—I use the word 'geared' deliberately—towards that resumé which will gain you admission to Higher Blunting, followed by Prestigious Work, followed by retirement and death" (54).

An additional result of modern education practices, ironically (or purposefully, according to Esolen's authorial voice), is that it makes students understand less, even as they learn more. Worse still, it makes them care very little about any of it. The recipe is eerily familiar to anyone acquainted with middle-school science projects: "Demand drudgery, but not drudgery that has as its end the mastery of facts, or of an intellectual structure within which to retain and interpret the facts, or of a great work of imagination for which the facts of grammar or arithmetic or whatever are the doorkeepers. Keep them busy *and* idle at the same time. Put them in groups, to pull down the intelligent. Have them make posters full of unrelated data" (25).

This is a dangerous critique, because it applies not only to the underperforming, overspending, government-run holding pen posing as a school down the street, but to a good many private and charter schools as well. When Esolen writes that factories aren't "...popular destinations for school field trips, because they'd involve going to an infernally hot foundry or a noisy machine shop, or to a factory where People Who Have Failed in Life are working" (83), the chuckle fades in the throat of the good conservative. *Wait a minute—this guy isn't just criticizing Cesar E. Chavez Middle School, he's going after Friedrich A. Hayek Academy!*

There is in most schools, in Esolen's estimation, far too much obsession with what Nobel Prize-winning economist Vernon Smith derides as "knowing what versus knowing how." There is, further, a dangerous concession to materialists who believe science is only, in the words of Walker Percy, "the isolation of secondary causes in natural phenomena," rather than the original—and religiously sympathetic—aim of "discovery and knowing."

The net—and ironic—effect is that greater exposure to the machinery of the modern school yields diminished knowing, albeit hidden, in many cases, by a heightened command of disconnected and de-contextualized facts. Today's best students know the dates of more wars than their ancestors, but they can no more give an intellectual and moral defense for (or a case against) war than they can run a farm or build a river raft.

And this knowing *how* of moral questions is of a piece with the knowing *how* of mechanical questions. Acquiring either requires interaction with the world that moves beyond (but not in the absence of) theorizing—an experience modern schools, families, and churches are increasingly ill-prepared to impart.

It's an interesting question, whether the models currently popular among education reformers—most of whom are conservative and libertarian—namely charter schools, private schools following some version of a classical education philosophy, and home schools actually avoid the pitfalls Esolen traces in his book.

It helps, in considering this question, to separate his critique into pedagogy and content. In the former category we find Esolen attacking the acquisition of facts, the test-driven *knowing what* at the expense of *knowing how*—how to do things, how to experience the world, how to grapple with moral questions. We find as well the hour-stacked-upon-hour indoor confinement of schools, the relentless scheduling and adult supervision of every activity, the relegation of mechanics, work, and vocational training to a lesser track for dumb kids.

It's the rare private or charter school, it's safe to say, that isn't vulnerable to criticism on all these fronts. Home schools can be somewhat better, insofar as many of them are more rural, and in the context of large families, yielding at least the opportunity for self-direction, along with outdoor play and work.

Schools favored by reformers may fare better on content, but here Esolen identifies as additional enemies of imagination: the politicization of stories, the diminution of the heroic and patriotic, and the elevation of sex equality to a religious impulse. He adds to these the elimination—by dint of mockery, suspicion, and ignorance—of *philia* and *agape*, so that *eros* reigns supreme.

Set alongside all this the destruction of reverence for God (and forget theological education that can stand more than a rudimentary examination), and the modern, public-school educated youngster too often emerges with his world having been flattened and faded gray, his passion reduced to sexuality, and his curiosity transmogrified into occupational hoop-jumping.

There are expensive private schools that manage to achieve these same destructive ends, of course, and a great many elite universities actually revel in doing so. Even a modest focus on great books, one takes from Esolen, can have an ameliorating effect, if only because grappling with *The Odyssey*, for example, forces one to deal with a complexity of emotion and motivation (not to mention the full panoply of Greek loves) that undermines the two-dimensional political correctness enshrined in textbooks and lesser literature.

In their embrace of great books, then, and classical education, and their devotion to religious instruction, advocates of education reform have within their sights a set of remedies for half the problem identified by Esolen. But what to do about pedagogy? Might it be the case, as in many revolutions, that the reformers still carry within themselves the wrong worldviews of those they seek to depose? This might be a fertile question for everyone involved in the strategy and philanthropy of education reform, and one could find a worse starting point than Esolen's book.

Indeed, it might be best to start with Esolen himself because, besides a passion that occasionally comes to the surface so fully that his Screwtape conceit is undermined (a small and admirable failing), the greatest shortcoming of this book (insofar as leaving readers hungry for more may fairly be called a shortcoming) is its absence of pedagogical prescription. Avoiding political correctness, godlessness, and sneering nihilism goes without saying, but what to do with the incessant drive toward greater and greater knowing *what*, at the expense of *how*? Here this reader, at least, wants to hear more from Esolen. And perhaps we will.

TONY WOODLIEF *is a writer who lives in Arlington, Virginia.*

• • • •

Adam Smith's Marketplace of Life
By James R. Otteson
Cambridge: Cambridge University Press, 2002.
338 pages. $41.00 US (paperback) (ISBN 978-0521016568)

Reviewed by Samuel Gregg

While Adam Smith is well-known as the founder of modern economics, rather fewer are especially familiar with his work as a moral philosopher—an activity that preceded and postdated his book *The Wealth of Nations* (1776). Moreover, just as many modern economists will privately confess that they have never read *The Wealth of Nations* (after all, it contains no long mathematical equations, so why bother?); among professional philosophers knowledge of Smith's philosophical writings, most notably Smith's book *The Theory of Moral Sentiments* (1759), may well be even sparser. This absence of knowledge may help to explain why Smith's economic thought is often caricatured as that of a Randian *laissez-faire* economist, while his philosophical contributions are sometimes portrayed as essentially that of applied Humean ethics with relatively little originality on Smith's part.

Close study of the corpus of Smith's work soon shatters these misconceptions, especially once we begin to compare Smith's economic and philosophical ideas. In recent years, one of the best books to engage in precisely this form of intellectual inquiry is James R. Otteson's *Adam Smith's Marketplace of Life*. Published ten years ago, it marked the beginning of Otteson's emergence as one of the best of a new generation of Adam Smith scholars.

The key to the persuasive power of Otteson's book is the way that he explores

Smith's conception of morality and then shows how it relates to Smith's thinking about the nature of the modern commercial society then emerging in the West. Otteson also underscores the parallels between Smith's conception of the development of morality and the growth of market-oriented societies.

Consisting of an introduction, seven chapters, and a conclusion, Otteson begins by summarizing the then-existing state of the Smith scholarship, particularly concerning the issue of what is commonly called *Das Adam Smith Problem*. This is the view, especially as articulated by nineteenth-century German scholars, that there were fundamental tensions between *The Theory of Moral Sentiments* and *The Wealth of Nations*: the former with its attention to human sympathy was seen as difficult to reconcile with the self-interested being that apparently inhabited the world of the latter.

Otteson then proceeds to outline what he considers to be the essence of Smith's moral theory, especially his concepts of sympathy, the impartial spectator procedure, conscience, and human nature (Chapters 1 and 2). This is followed by a discussion of how Smith believed people become moral beings and develop the capacity to identify moral standards and make moral judgments (Chapter 3). At this point, Otteson presents what he calls a "market model" as the "underlying conceptual structure of Smith's account" (9).

Chapters 4 and 5 are devoted to *Das Adam Smith Problem*. Otteson makes the argument that many contemporary scholars may have been too quick to say that there is no problem. Otteson suggests that the picture of human motivation that emerges in *The Theory of Moral Sentiments*—most notably Smith's attention to the virtues of justice, prudence, benevolence, and self-command and Smith's pointed criticisms of Bernard Mandeville's decidedly egocentric vision of the way the moral world "really" works—does seem rather different from the portrait of human motivation outlined in *The Wealth of Nations*. Reading *The Wealth of Nations* as a stand-alone book, Otteson notes, would give even attentive readers little-if-any indication that its author had written *The Theory of Moral Sentiments*. Otteson goes into some detail to explain why he regards many contemporary efforts to resolve the apparent tension as unsatisfactory.

Otteson then provides his own resolution of the two books, based upon his conception of Smith's moral theory as detailed in chapters 1-4. To this end, Otteson suggests that "a single conceptual model for understanding the growth and maintenance of human institutions underlies both books" (171). The model, put simply, is one of a market in which free exchanges in pursuit of each actor's own interests (broadly defined) give rise to an unintended system of order. A second factor permitting reconciliation between the two texts is what Otteson calls "the familiarity principle," which unifies the two pictures of human motivation operative in *The Theory of Moral Sentiments* and *The Wealth of Nations*. These sections of Otteson's book repay close reading. This is especially true of Otteson's treatment of Smith's understanding of the origins and nature of government and its particular responsibilities concerning justice (177-181).

In this regard, a key phrase employed by Otteson to describe Smith's view of morality and markets is that of "unintended order." This is important, not least because it seems to ascribe a larger role for human choice and action in the development of social, political, and economic arrangements than is suggested by, for example, the phrase "spontaneous order" much popularized by Friedrich Hayek. To this extent, "unintended order" lends itself to two things. First, it allows greater recognition of the power of human agency in consciously shaping our immediate world, something often difficult to detect in the neo-evolutionist tendencies that seem to serve as a reductionist explanatory tool for everything in the minds of many contemporary classical liberals and free-marketers. Second, it does not make the mistake of denying that the unintended side-effects of human choice and action can contribute to shaping society in beneficial ways that seem beyond the comprehension of many modern liberals and those with a penchant for extensive government economic planning.

In chapter 6, Otteson's attention shifts somewhat to the issue of whether Smith's approach to morality is essentially descriptive or whether it also has strong normative elements. Different parts of *The Theory of Moral Sentiments* and *The Wealth of Nations* can lead readers to believe that Smith thinks that what matters are the "facts" rather than what might be called "non-empirical realities." Again, the tendency is often to view Smith as seeing morality as a question of contingency in the sense of relative efficiency (the implication being that those aspects of morality that are no longer "efficient" can be dispensed with). Otteson's analysis articulates a careful challenge of that view. Without denying the strongly descriptive element of Smith's thought, Otteson sides with those scholars who maintain that Smith's ethical framework also had a strong normative dimension.

When discussing this issue, Otteson does not skirt or dismiss the "God-issue." He maintains that Smith believes that "the oughts" of morality arise, ultimately, from God's benevolent design. Heuristic devices such as the impartial spectator operate in the marketplace of morality to produce a state of affairs that Smith regards as the true human happiness that God intends for everyone. "The core virtues of morality are not only common to all ages and cultures, but Smith," Otteson states, "wants to argue that it is no accident that they are such: God planned it that way" (255). To understand this position, Otteson maintains, we need to understand the ultimate meaning of the impartial spectator device. For Smith, Otteson holds, it "represents the fruition of the system of morality that God wants us to develop; the impartial spectator is thus the manifestation of God's will in us, the partial manifestation, even of God himself in us" (256).

Herein we find, Otteson goes on, perhaps the biggest difference between Smith and Hume's respective conceptions of unintended order. Hume's would appear to not include, entail, "or perhaps even allow a grand design by God" (256). Though there is certainly an element of rule-utilitarianism in Smith, Otteson maintains that, for Smith, learning and following the system of morality is also a matter of obedience to God's will.

Otteson turns in chapter 7 to providing further evidence that the market model does permeate Smith's corpus of writings. In his conclusion, Otteson illustrates how Smith's moral theory which, at least in *The Wealth of Nations*, permits people to follow their self-interest (within the bounds of Smith's conception of justice) in the market, can facilitate the development of affection for and benevolence towards others in ways not so obvious in non-market economic settings. He also, however, advances the claim that Smith's theory fails to adequately address the issue of moral deviancy, and then tries to build an explanation for such choices and actions that conforms to Smith's view of the nature and ends of morality.

But perhaps one of the most interesting side-effects of Otteson's book is what his study of Smith tells us about the Scottish Enlightenment. While the Scottish Enlightenment is invariably and correctly presented as helping to usher in the dawn of the modern social sciences, *Adam Smith's Marketplace of Life* demonstrates that one of its most important figures—like many others of the Scottish School—did not think that being descriptive and analytical meant believing that the normative dimension of human life was somehow "not real," or that morality had to be dismissed as hopelessly subjective.

Integrating the positive and normative aspects of human reality is not of course an easy exercise—especially when we are ceaselessly told by many contemporary social scientists and philosophers that the two have little to do with each other. Nor are attempts at integration always achieved in the most coherent manner. Adam Smith and much of the Scottish Enlightenment, however, do provide us with some ways to undertake such an enterprise, of which James Otteson's book is a very readable and intellectually coherent example.

SAMUEL GREGG *is Director of Research at the Acton Institute and author, most recently, of* Becoming Europe: Economic Decline, Culture, and How America Can Avoid a European Future (2013).

• • • •

Philanthropy in America: A History
By Olivier Zunz
Princeton: Princeton University Press, 2011.
396 pages. $29.95 US (hardcover) (ISBN 978-0691128368)

Reviewed by George McCully

Olivier Zunz' new history, *Philanthropy in America*, is a major contribution to philanthropic studies—thoroughly researched and documented, clearly narrated and argued, and illuminating a main theme in the history of twentieth-century American philanthropy: its development in civil society. Within the limits Professor Zunz has chosen, he has rendered a great service to the entire professional philanthropic community, both academic and practical, for which we should all be grateful.

That said, a full appreciation of this substantial study requires knowledge of both its content and its context—both the mountain of information and scholarship it so admirably synthesizes, and its chosen limits. Within those limits, this will be recognized as the standard, authoritative account for some time to come. Beyond those, however—contextually—is where the greater, more profound and influential history will ultimately be discovered.

The reason for this remarkable situation is that while this book was being researched, written, and published, its subject was being transformed. American philanthropy itself was—and still is—undergoing a classic paradigm shift. What this book describes so well is the period of the twentieth-century paradigm—now increasingly considered the "Old Paradigm," and being superseded by an as-yet inchoate New Paradigm, outside Zunz' purview. The book captures, in short, a kind of bubble within a longer and deeper "history" of "philanthropy in America."

Within the bubble, the book is excellent; in the larger context it is still very good, but increasingly *passé*, as philanthropy moves on into the future. The history of American philanthropy is turning out to have more numerous, more powerful, and more profound themes than the development of the twentieth-century academic, social-scientific constructs of an alleged "third sector" and "civil society."

Space here does not allow a detailed account of the many subjects Zunz covers so well; this summary will focus therefore on the broad themes and structure of the bubble itself—the narrative framework.

Summarizing his "Conclusions," Zunz writes: "As this history has shown, philanthropy in the United States is not simply the consequence of a universal altruistic impulse; it is also a product of the large organizational revolution that American managerial and financial capitalism orchestrated in the last century and a half" (294). Here he cites his own previous work, *Making America Corporate, 1870-1920* (1990), along with the well-known works of Alfred Chandler (*The Visible Hand*, 1977) and Naomi Lamoreaux (*The Great Merger Movement*, 1985). For the "universal altruistic impulse" he cites only Adam Smith's *Theory of Moral Sentiments*, and elsewhere Tocqueville—i.e., no Americans. "Americans...have turned a universal desire to do good into a distinct brand of philanthropy. They have learned to turn market profits and market methods into a philanthropic engine powerful enough to influence the course of their own history" (294). They "have come to think of philanthropy not as a gift only, but also as an investment....to openly combine ideas of managing the market and [charitable] giving in a single mechanism geared for social progress....providing for their own future" (295). As Tocqueville had noted, American generosity was "self-interest properly understood" (296).

He begins to unfold this story in the first chapter, "For the Improvement of Mankind," which opens with a striking fact: that in two decades following the 1870s in America, "more people made more money more rapidly than ever before in history, and made very large gifts to society" (8). In the seventies there were 100 millionaires; in 1892, 4,047; by 1916, over 40,000, of whom at least two—John D. Rockefeller and Henry Ford—were billionaires. With too much money to spend personally or to contribute to traditional local welfare charities, the "new rich" created a "genuine American invention," the "general purpose foundation" (22), involving "long-term alliances" with Progressive reformers trained in the social sciences to devise strategic investments in new institutions and programs aimed not at temporary symptomatic relief of social problems but long-term, fundamental, solutions to the root causes of those problems. Because these new institutions were intended to be permanent and to invest in research, new discoveries, and social engineering, they needed unspecified, strategic, general humanitarian mission statements. This required legal reform, to recognize and protect "open-ended" charitable bequests (e.g., "to the improvement of mankind") as legitimate "charitable uses."

In Chapter Two, "The Coming of Mass Philanthropy," Zunz describes how systems also arose to mobilize huge numbers of small gifts by ordinary Americans, initially for the fight against tuberculosis, later for the World War I effort and its recovery, then for community improvement and poor relief during the Great Depression. Giving through churches, workplaces, and federated giving programs of community chests and community foundations encouraged American families to budget for charitable giving, a kind of "public thrift" which "gave philanthropy its democratic imprint in America" (295). Charitable giving had become "a routine part of American life" (75).

The new foundations and "mass philanthropy" created, together and in partnership with government, a new and powerful system of civil society, whose conspicuous potency evoked federal government interest in defining the proper relationship of private philanthropy to public politics and government—a recurrent theme throughout the book, and "a distinctive feature of American society" (297). The work of civil society called upon a broad range of technical and managerial skills and led to an increasing professionalization of philanthropy. The dialectic between professional philanthropists and government regulators consolidated an increasingly influential "third sector"—neither government nor business, tax-exempt, and privileged to raise tax-deductible donations and grants. Zunz posits tax exemption as the essential core of the third sector:

> Tax exemption has not only nurtured philanthropy in society, it has entrenched it. Equally important, it encourages an otherwise very diverse group of institutions that have dispersed and/or solicited private funds for the public good to work together, in essence fostering a nonprofit sector of groups with similar interests and privileges.
>
> The nonprofit sector is the outcome of this unique encounter between philanthropy and the state. It is a hybrid capitalist creation that operates tax-free so long as profits are reinvested in the common good....[R]evenues are designated for the support of beneficiaries rather than for the profit of stockholders (4).

Zunz asserts that the nonprofit sector has thus "become a distinct and pervasive part of the American political economy" (4). Moreover, he posits that twentieth-century philanthropy "should be understood as part of the American Progressive tradition," mobilizing enormous energy across all social classes and resulting in a "network of foundations and community institutions [which] has enlarged American democracy" (7). This view summarizes what some today regard as the "myth" of the nonprofit sector, about which more below.

The next five chapters tell the story of how the new system and the federal government, through decades of war, economic depression, natural disasters, and international recovery from war, struggled to define the role of private initiatives in testing experimental approaches and providing technical assistance to governments in social problem-solving. "By the middle of the twentieth century," Zunz observes, "Americans had created a large philanthropic enterprise that was part of the fabric of their daily lives....The nonprofit sector as a whole provided a medium through which Americans channeled their excess income to help the poor, to enhance children's education, to promote cultural activities, to fund science, and to initiate agricultural reform in poor countries, all in partnership with government" (169).

The two last climactic chapters describe the full flowering of the "nonprofit sector" and its purported institutionalization in Independent Sector in 1980. "Most Americans acknowledged the existence of a 'nonprofit sector'" (232). Liberals "promoted a sector balancing public and private sources of support....their fear was that the third sector might otherwise be absorbed into government" (233). Conservatives believed the federal government ought to leave social problem-solving entirely to philanthropy and state and local governments. "For thirty years [they] fought to make their idea of the nonprofit sector the accepted view of civil society. The nonprofit sector as we know it today emerged slowly from this confrontation" (233). "The nonprofit sector has come of age." Supreme Court decisions "have made the nonprofit sector the institutional voice of American civil society....Conservatives and liberals, individually and collectively, made nonprofits worthy substitutes for the associations Tocqueville had heralded as engines of American liberty" (262-263).

The final chapter, "American Philanthropy and the World's Communities" purports to show how American civil society has become a global force promoting democracy by working around governments and through NGOs, by defining development as improvement in quality of life rather than simply economic metrics (e.g., Amartya Sen), by mobilizing mass philanthropy techniques, and by promoting itself as a model for the rest of the world. The Internet is finally mentioned in the last seven pages (292-299), where Zunz acknowledges that "[i]ronically, the Internet and related high-speed communications, which are the most impersonal of means [!], have brought personal financial participation in the global associational revolution within reach of practically everybody."

Zunz' narrative, then, describes an onward-and-upward trajectory leading to global success. This is a case, however, in which the Devil is not in the details, which are admirable as far as they go, but in the over-all conceptualization and rhetorical structure, which are in turn a function of Zunz' training as an American economic and business historian. He naturally sees twentieth-century American philanthropy in the context of his field and previous work, and within its own terms there is considerable merit and appropriateness in this orientation—which is why the book is as good as it is. Nonetheless, problems remain.

The main problems are: that the history of distinctively American philanthropy does not begin with the amassing of unprecedented wealth and the emergence of the social sciences at the end of the nineteenth century; that before then it was not confined to "universal altruistic impulse"; that recent and current empirical research has raised questions suggesting that the so-called "third" or "nonprofit sector" is not and never has been a coherent objective historical entity or phenomenon, much less "whose profits are reinvested for the common good," but an artifact of the tax code and related state laws of incorporation; that scholars have not bothered to examine the data on which this concept is based; and that when the data is examined, "philanthropy" turns out to be only a small part of, and not at all coextensive with, "nonprofits" or an alleged "third" sector.

To begin with, Professor Zunz is certainly to be excused for not knowing— because very few American historians have noticed it either—that the *locus classicus* for adequately understanding distinctively American philanthropy is to be found on page one, paragraph one, of the first *Federalist Paper*, in which Alexander Hamilton launched the Founders' argument for ratification of our Constitution, saying, "It is commonly remarked" that Americans were at a new place in history; that whereas previously governments had been the products of accident and force, Americans had the unique opportunity of choosing their own government. "This," Hamilton wrote, "adds the inducements of philanthropy to those of patriotism." He was not talking about rich people helping poor people, nor about a "universal altruistic impulse" of generosity, but about an educational and cultural tradition going back *via* the Enlightenment, the Renaissance, and Republican Rome, to Periclean Athens. He was saying that the United States of America was intended and designed to be a philanthropic nation, a gift to humanity, promoting democracy and freedom to be sure, but beyond even those, helping to make the world more fully humane in every sense of that word. An adequate "history" of "philanthropy in America" would therefore explore how Hamilton and the Founders got the idea of "the inducements of philanthropy" from the American and especially Scottish Enlightenments, and how they modeled the new government on the "voluntary associations" that Tocqueville would later observe had characterized Colonial culture, which were (in John Gardner's words) "private initiatives for...public good," which is to say the practical philanthropy of voluntarism and collaboration.

Armed with this knowledge, historians might apply it to the IRS Master Data File of so-called "third sector" and "nonprofit" institutions, where they would immediately find that very few have anything to do with "philanthropy." In Massachusetts the *Catalogue for Philanthropy* did this research and found that 75 percent of tax-exempt entities are primarily self-serving (supported by, and providing benefits for, their own members), only about 10 percent are indisputably "private initiatives, for public good, focusing on quality of life, and engaged in public fund-raising (the philanthropic marketplace)," and the remaining 15 percent are "para-philanthropic"—between the two. Current research, in other words, is calling into question, on the basis of evidence, the fundamental assumptions or controlling "myth" of Zunz' book cited above (4,7): that "philanthropy" and "nonprofits" are roughly the same, that there is a "nonprofit sector" which is beneficial for public good and supported by grants and donations, and that the history of philanthropy in America is about the political economy of that sector in relation to government in the twentieth century.

Discontent with the Old Paradigm had certainly been expressed during its rise and dominance, perhaps most eminently by Richard Cornuelle's *Reclaiming the American Dream* (1965). But by the end of the century a profound structural and strategic change was first heralded within the profession by two articles in *Foundation News*.[1] Paradigm shifts are total transformations of the governing models of mature fields of endeavor. While Zunz' book presents an excellent history of the rise of the paradigm which governed twentieth-century philanthropy, it is oblivious to the fallacies which have contributed to its current unraveling by the Internet, the globalization of the American high-tech economy, new demographics of wealth, social networking, and other factors. The twentieth-century vocabulary, conceptualization, rhetoric, technology, infrastructure, and modes of operation which have governed American philanthropy are all being transformed—superseded by new models which have not yet coalesced in a new paradigm, though that is inevitable.

Even taken on its own terms, the portrayal of philanthropy in this book is notably impersonal and bloodless—a matter of political economy academically considered, driven by large systems from the top down, focused on the interplay of national government with the so-called "third sector." The wonderful world of myriad smaller charities, struggling creatively, intelligently, and compassionately at the grassroots level, with meager resources to improve Americans' quality of life in the face of persistent and emergent public problems, is not Zunz' subject and does not inform the perspective from which this history is written.

We must be enormously grateful to Professor Zunz for his major contribution to our scholarly literature because, within its own frame of reference, it is excellent. It does not detract in the slightest from this book to suggest that other histories are also needed.

GEORGE MCCULLY *served for twenty years as professor of European intellectual and cultural history, from the Renaissance to the Enlightenment, and for twenty-five years as a professional philanthropist—fundraiser, strategic planner, executive director, trustee, and advisor to charities, foundations, families and individual donors. In 1997 he created the highly respected and influential Massachusetts* Catalogue for Philanthropy, *to promote charitable giving and strengthen the culture of philanthropy through donor education. His book,* Philanthropy Reconsidered *(2008), presents a comprehensive overview of the "vocabulary, conceptualization, and rhetoric" of philanthropy from the ancient coinage of the term in* Prometheus Bound, *to its essential role informing the American Revolution and Constitution, to the paradigm-shift transforming philanthropy today. His latest work is the* Massachusetts Philanthropic Directory—*an on-line, systematically taxonomized, analytical directory to all the philanthropic charities of (initially) Massachusetts, which comprise only 1/7th of the state's "nonprofits". This dramatically innovative Directory system will be extended nationwide over the next two years. He is also a contributing editor to* Conversations on Philanthropy.

NOTE

[1] George McCully, "Is This a Paradigm-Shift?" *Foundation News and Commentary* (March-April, 2000) 41 (2): 20-22 and "Are Foundations Being Marginalized? Further Notes on the Paradigm-Shift," Council on Foundations, Washington, DC (September-October, 2000) 41 (5): 30-31.

• • • •

The Information: A History, A Theory, A Flood
By James Gleick
London: Vintage, Random House, Inc., 2011
544 pages. $15.95 US (paperback) (ISBN 978-1400096237)

Reviewed by Heather Wood Ion

James Gleick writes in his Prologue: "We can see now that information is what our world runs on: the blood and the fuel, the vital principle." He has undertaken his task of writing the natural history of information with an audacious sense of adventure. For many chapters, the reader shares the excitement of discovery, of suddenly coming up over a hill to view a new horizon.

Initially we move from African drums to literacy and how writing changed our thinking to dictionaries and taxonomies of all kinds. These chapters raise some of the essential issues: how are messages transmitted with accuracy? Does writing change the way we think? How does language structure experience? Yet within these chapters the central dilemma of Gleick's work rumbles like thunder in the background: *information is not knowledge.*

Admirably, Gleick distills huge swaths of intellectual history to serve his theme, and he is witty as well as thorough as he does so. For the first third of the book: from drums and cave paintings to the use of the telegraph, each of the tools used to transmit information is examined both in its function and as an abstraction, or expression of a theoretical approach to information. Dictionaries and logarithmic tables become fascinating illustrations of human ingenuity. What we take, according to the author, is a journey from things to words, from words to categories, and from categories to metaphor and logic. Gleick treats this journey as inevitable linear progression, the goal of which is to unite logic and mathematics (39).

The premise is now clear, and the reader knows that Gleick is not telling the natural history of an idea, rather, he is showing where the technology and theories we use today have come from. He is looking back from the perspective of the successful tools of an information technology to examine the evolution of such tools. The early chapters of reflection on messaging and categorization move into heroic biography: Gleick is fascinated by the individuals who invented the tools.

One of the most moving of the stories he tells is that of Ada Byron King, Countess of Lovelace, who worked with Charles Babbage. Together they sought to 'abstract information away from its physical substrate' (109) in the quest to develop an analytic machine. The frenzy of activity of these nineteenth-century thinkers even astounds Gleick, but he is impatient to reach the real focus of the book, and that impatience shows in the discussion of the telegraph and its impacts on society.

Picture the pioneering and homesteading communities of Western America: with the introduction of the telegraph both the time horizons and the real horizons of those communities changed. Gleick concentrates his discussion of this stage in the story on the development of codes and of the compacting of information. The reader senses a much greater tale waiting to be told about the human aspects of this new capacity to share rapidly and at a distance. For Gleick, this is a story of Morse, and then of Boole, and of the advantages of abstraction.

With chapter 6, *New Wires, New Logic*, Gleick has reached the core of his book, a biography of Claude Shannon and the impact of his work at Bell Labs on the creation of our current state of information technology. Parts of the early biography are charming, and we come to care deeply about Claude Shannon. At times this reader wished that this biography was itself a book, not the central core embedded in a more ambitious, and less successful, text.

Often Gleick refers to the failure of imagination in the face of new technologies, and he illustrates well that the first evaluations—such as the telephone would primarily be of use to musicians—are both ignorant and confined to what is already familiar, not evocative of what can be. The author is particularly convincing as he recounts how quickly amusement turned to business possibility as *the users* of the telephone began to explore its efficiencies. The italics are mine, as it is important to understand that it is the users of technology who take the new technologies forward, not the initial inventors or theorists.

Within the several chapters on Shannon, Turing, Weaver, and others there are numerous stories of how mathematicians work, how abstraction can be explained, and why the evolution of abstractions of signal processing into binary logic revolutionized the transmission of information. For many readers this will be the most important and engaging aspect of Gleick's book. It requires a considerable amount of mathematical training to follow the logic which created the field of cybernetics. Even without that training it is intriguing to learn where the vocabulary we now take for granted—feedback, machine learning, and digitization—comes from, as well as what these thinkers anticipated.

The chapters on genetics, memes and quantum physics are far less engaging than the biographical chapters, and to this reader it seemed as if Gleick needs the engagement with a heroic figure like Shannon in order to become passionate about a subject. Certainly the reader understands that the whimsicality of quantum physics is less satisfying for a writer engaged in the translation of abstraction for a lay audience. However, by the conclusion of chapter 13, and the admission that there is no clear definition of 'bit' and therefore of what we now understand as information, the writer (as well as the reader) is exhausted.

On page 403 Gleick dedicates a few paragraphs to the issue of information overload, and equally briefly mentions that the key to this sense of overload must lie in the separation between information and knowledge. For the remaining few pages of the text, Gleick's hero is the fabulist Jorge Luis Borges and his fictional "Library of Babel." It is both strange and sad that after this very lengthy history, the author turns away from his theme of the logic of information to the dark fantasy created by Borges. Gleick reflects briefly that the technology now makes facts 'cheap' but wisdom and learning remain as rare as they have ever been. The audacious adventure comes to an end like a hiker returned from a mountain trek: the burdens of laundry and exhaustion seem far more important than any exalted experience just gained. There are another hundred pages of detailed notes, and an extensive bibliography.

James Gleick has accomplished a hugely difficult task in this book. He has written the history of the tools we use in our everyday lives, knowing that for most of us, the abstractions on which those tools depend are irrelevant to the ways we apply them. It is the abstractions and the scientists who conceived them which intrigue Gleick. But the rest of the story: how information becomes knowledge, and how we humans discover meaning, has yet to be written.

HEATHER WOOD ION *is a chief executive and cultural anthropologist who holds dual degrees from Oxford University and specializes in turning around troubled organizations. She currently serves with Athena Charitable Trust, is Founder of the nonprofit Epidemic of Health and is a contributing editor to* Conversations on Philanthropy.

Bad Students, Not Bad Schools
By Robert Weissberg
Piscataway, NJ: Transaction Publishers, 2010.
303 pages. $39.95 US (hardcover) (ISBN 978-1412813457)

Reviewed by George Leef

Political science professor Robert Weissberg has been writing iconoclastic books that challenge the conventional (i.e., predominately progressive) wisdom on social issues for many years, and with this book he focuses his attention for the first time on America's woeful public education system. He dares to say what many writers fear to—our educational beliefs and policies are for the most part delusional nonsense. That nonsense serves wonderfully the interests of the education establishment—teachers, administrators, non-teaching staffers, union officials, professors of education, program officers, our grant-making foundations, and so on—but it leaves students stuck in schools that just go through the motions of education. But to a large degree (and here is where the book reaches the pinnacle of iconoclasm), that suits the students fine because many couldn't care less about learning.

As the book's title implies, our schools do a bad job mainly because the students themselves are bad. Many are not the least bit interested in learning. They dislike reading (and are not good at it), disdain rigorous thought, and see no point in developing beneficial traits through discipline and work. While Weissberg may seem to relish the "liberal" sin of blaming the victim, his purpose is to expose the folly of just about everything called "education reform," including both progressive and conservative notions about how to "save" or at least improve our schools.

The essential problem is that those ideas share the false premise that all students can learn and want to. Great numbers of young Americans, especially those from "underrepresented minority groups," however, grow up in homes where education is not prized and among peer groups that not only ridicule studiousness but reward those who are best at "acting out." Adolescents like that can't be turned into even moderately successful students no matter how much money is spent on the schools, personnel, and programs meant to make learning seem more relevant and fun.

But this isn't only a "minority" problem. White youth culture is also quite inimical toward academic effort. Studying just isn't "cool." Weissberg writes, "An extremely high proportion of students fail to take school seriously—they spend countless hours 'goofing off' with friends, often cheat on tests or rely on the homework of others. For many, attending classes is just a nuisance—between a third and 40 percent admit they are not paying attention or not trying hard. Teachers routinely report having classes where half the students seem 'checked out'" (37-38).

Weissberg buttresses his argument that student attitudes matter far more than the schools they attend by pointing to the facts that a) many Asian students who come from lower-class families and attend public schools with bad performance records on the whole manage to excel academically and b) many black students from prosperous families who live in nice suburbs with "good" schools (e.g., Shaker Heights, Ohio) still do poorly on standardized tests. Having a positive attitude toward school and a family that supports learning appears to be both a necessary and a sufficient condition for academic success. The schools themselves are at most a marginal influence.

Nevertheless, education "experts" keep advancing panaceas for fixing the schools. The only idea they won't tolerate is that of encouraging indifferent and disruptive kids to leave so that the remaining students will have a much better learning environment. That idea is taboo, especially with President Obama telling us that it's vital for an increasing percentage of Americans to graduate from college. All the experts insist that we must devote more and more resources to student retention—that is, keeping disinterested and disengaged students in school with any gimmicks the educators can think of.

Perhaps the most infamous of the many "let's give poor kids great schools and they'll make progress" programs was the Kansas City, MO experiment begun in 1985 when a federal judge told school reform zealots to "dream big." They came up with a long and expensive list of improvements to inner-city schools so that the racial achievement gap (a *bête noire* that recurs again and again in the book) could be closed. The reformers drew up plans for Taj Mahal schools equipped with everything from Olympic-sized swimming pools to a model United Nations assembly complete with simultaneous language translations. (The judge ordered that taxes be increased to pay for this utopian vision of "good schools.") And the results? No improvements whatsoever in student achievement. If good—in this case, gold-plated—schools mattered, we'd have seen wonderful progress in Kansas City, but we didn't.

Weissberg makes a compelling case that bad students are the main reason why the country has such a low level of academic prowess. (The National Assessment of Adult Literacy (2003), for example, found that less than a third of *college graduates* were "proficient" in prose literacy.) We spend lavishly on "education" and get pathetic results. Weissberg doesn't lay the fault entirely on students; he also shows that many of our schools are also bad, with teachers who are indifferent or incompetent (but can't be fired thanks to union rules), materials and curricula that have been dumbed-down, programs that ignore gifted students but lavish attention on the weakest ones, and are susceptible to educational fads emanating from our "colleges of education."

Those topics take up most of the middle of the book. Weissberg, retired from the University of Illinois, now lives in New York City and writes with relish about the innumerable follies of public school reform in New York. The politicians, from Mayor Bloomberg on down, have to pretend that they're doing something to improve the schools—every politician needs to be able to say that he's "pro-education." In New York (and most other cities), elaborate deceptions surround school performance so that heavily publicized plans appear to be working. Of course, they don't work because nothing really changes. The students are still mostly uneducable, the teachers are still unmotivated and/or incompetent, and the system still encourages that students be passed even if they have learned nothing. The way the once rigorous New York Regents Exam has been watered down is emblematic of the problems that plague public education across the nation.

One of the author's prime targets is misguided philanthropy. Ever since the Ford Foundation decided that fixing public education would be one of its goals back in the early 1960s, foundations have been pouring money into education. The problem here is that supposed experts often convince foundation officials (who tend to be utopians, easily led into supporting "progressive" theories) to back their visions. For example, Weissberg notes that a lot of foundation (and business) money has gone into programs intended to increase the number of "minority" students in math, science, and engineering. If American businesses really need more home-grown talent (many positions requiring such expertise are currently filled with foreign workers), it would make far more sense to try recruiting them from populations where students are more likely to have the aptitude and interest that is necessary. But political considerations demand programs that aim at ironing out group inequalities, so we spend tons trying to make math and science appealing to black and Hispanic kids, few of whom have thus far shown much interest or ability.

Foundations could, Weissberg argues, do considerable good if they targeted their grants toward school programs to help our best students advance faster, but that won't happen because of the firmly entrenched egalitarianism at most of them. Many donors would rather bask in the glory of publicity for programs that sound good even though they are just flushing away money on ideas that have already failed.

As I mentioned above, Weissberg is not a fan of "conservative" school reform ideas either. He does not think that Milton Friedman's idea of expanding parental choice through vouchers will accomplish much good. That is because most parents already have a range of choices other than "their" public school. Even in the inner cities, parents who want their children to receive true education as opposed to the vapid *faux*-education given away in the public schools have choices. There are fairly low-cost private schools and tutoring services that could make up for the deficiencies of the government schools. Only a small number of parents spend the time and money to avail themselves of such choices. Weissberg comments, "Put bluntly, many poor parents must choose between extra academic help for junior versus cable TV or a cell phone, so to insist that they 'lack choice' only flatters their disdain for education" (210).

The book concludes with perhaps the author's most provocative argument of all, namely that our public education system has evolved into a branch of the welfare state. "Bloated, unproductive school payrolls," Weissberg writes, "exist as a form of socially-acceptable bribery for those otherwise incapable of achieving a decent middle-class life. Watered-down diplomas similarly provide the happy illusion of 'education' to youngsters who might otherwise be driven by mayhem" (262).

That, I think, is a very useful insight. In real markets, where people exchange money for value and can take their money elsewhere if they don't get it, scams and frauds can't long survive. Once we put politics into them, it's inevitable that savvy interest groups will attach themselves like lampreys and begin to parasitically feed off the flow of tax money. Americans have long had a hard time saying "no" to anything that is labeled "education" and have come in the past century to say "yes" to almost anything that promises "social justice." What might be admirable values when pursued through private institutions turn the public treasury into a lush field for grazing by our education establishment. And the worse its results, the more money it can demand, as long as it blames our culture of injustice rather than acknowledges its own failures to attract and engage students and help them attain a serious education.

After such a strong indictment of American education, it would be incongruous for Weissberg to end on an upbeat note. He doesn't. The book ends with a resigned shrug. Our education system has been wrecked—for the majority of students, at least—and the combination of interest group politics and the anti-education mentality that goes with welfare dependency will prevent any beneficial change. That is a depressing but realistic assessment.

Despite editing that leaves much to be desired, *Bad Students, Not Bad Schools* is an excellent book that counter-balances the profusion of happy-face books and reports saying that our education is good and only needs more funding to get better. It isn't good and we should stop throwing away money on political fixes.

GEORGE LEEF *is the Director of Research at the John W. Pope Center for Higher Education Policy. He holds a BA from Carroll University in Wisconsin and a JD from Duke University. He was on the faculty of Northwood University in Midland, Michigan from 1980 through 1989 teaching economics, business law, and logic and is the author of* Free Choice for Workers: A History of the Right to Work Movement (2005).

• • • •

Western Culture at the American Crossroads:
Conflicts Over the Nature of Science and Reason
By Arthur Pontynen and Rod Miller
Wilmington, DE: Intercollegiate Studies Institute, 2011.
412 pages. $34.95 US (hardcover) (ISBN 978-1935191742)

Reviewed by Troy Camplin

Philanthropy or, in Frederick Turner's (2005) terminology, the gift economy, is based on the love of the good, the true, and the beautiful. As such, the gift economy itself can be understood as constituting the moral order, the scientific order, and the artistic order(s), each of which have their own institutions, including those which conduct what we commonly think of as philanthropy proper. All true philanthropy thus arises out of love, whether it be the love of virtue, love of knowledge, or love of art. All of these are part of philanthropy itself—the love of mankind.

As such, Arthur Pontynen and Rod Miller's book, *Western Culture at the American Crossroads: Conflicts Over the Nature of Science and Reason* does in fact deal with the underlying concerns of philanthropy itself in the authors' discussion of the slow destruction of the West's ideas of the good, the true, and the beautiful, culminating in their explicit rejection by postmodern thought. The book is a densely philosophical, high-level discussion of art theory which argues against the hegemonic modernist/postmodernist paradigm we are now living under. Overall, a book that covers ontology, epistemology, ethics, philosophy of science, math and geometry, reason, truth, beauty, culture, history, theology, metaphysics, and art theory and history is necessarily difficult to summarize—even for an interdisciplinarian like myself. Yet at the same time, the authors' message is simple: we need to return to having a culture of wisdom. Being Augustinians, their preference is a Trinitarian culture, but they do acknowledge Hinduism, Buddhism, Taoism, Confucianism, etc. as wisdom cultures the world would be impoverished to lose, suggesting they are open to a more global classical-theological culture that is still, nevertheless pre-Modernist/Postmodernist.

In wisdom cultures there is concern with Being, a belief in an objective world to understand, and thus a belief in the actual existence of the good, the true, and the beautiful. Pontynen and Miller argue that modernist/postmodernist culture believes in only subjectivity and becoming and, thus, rejects wisdom, Being, objectivity, goodness, truth, and beauty. Insofar as this does in fact sum up postmodern culture, and insofar as we are living in a postmodern culture, this certainly has to have a negative effect on philanthropy.

Indeed, if we look to Europe (indeed, Pontynen and Miller discuss "European exceptionalism," which they identify with postmodernism, comparing it with "American exceptionalism," which they identify with the classical-Judeo-Christian Anglosphere), we see far less philanthropy and far more government involvement in morals, science, and the arts than we do in the United States. Yet the influence of modernism/postmodernism is moving the United States more towards Europe— something which Pontynen and Miller see as a problem—one which will lead to violent destruction. It would seem that they are right insofar as the more the United States moves toward postmodern culture, the weaker we see private philanthropy become and the stronger and more pervasive we see government become.

However, the values subjectivist may come away from this book thinking the authors are anything but their friends, especially when they say we should engage in "a willful dedication to the pursuit of objective truth and goodness" (148). Does this deny values subjectivism? Not at all. It may be that there are in fact a set of human values that are true and good—but that different people rank them different ways. Thus would values subjectivism be retained in the way it was always meant, recognizing the possibility of ordinal variety, without having to assert complete relativism. It would still be improper to assert your value rankings over others, even as some set of values is agreed to be proper, another improper. I doubt even the strongest relativist would agree that someone who values oppressing women, molesting children, killing people who look and believe differently than he does, and robbing people is but an example of the rich tapestry of humanity which we should therefore tolerate if not defend. The fact that such a person's values would not be defended suggests even the supposed relativist believes in some level of objective goodness and truth. We need to stop pretending otherwise. On this they are right that postmodernism is incoherent.

Pontynen and Miller further argue that postmodernists view everything as power relations, as Master-Slave relations (Hegel, Marx). Insofar as this kind of interaction is the kind found in the political economy, postmodernists view everything as necessarily political. As a result, everything becomes subsumed under the government. However, Turner identifies four human economies—the political economy, the gift economy, the market economy, and the divine economy—and each of these economies have their own kinds of interactions appropriate to those economies: value-creating market exchange in the market economy, reputation-creating love exchange in the gift economy, sacrificial exchange in the divine economy, and of course, power-creating master-slave relations in the political economy. As such, postmodern culture is in fact destructive of a wide diversity of human interactions, reducing complex human behaviors and interactions to the simplest, most destructive kind.

Thus, Pontynen and Miller lament the loss of Medieval conceptions of Truth, Goodness, and Beauty to Modernism and Postmodernism, which have reduced everything to a nihilistic, violence-promoting will to power. If one were to just read their book (and watch the news), ignorant of the recent work by Steven Pinker (2012) and Matt Ridley (2011), one would think we have grown increasingly violent since the collapse of the Medieval worldview. However, we have seen quite the opposite trend taking place: as we have moved from Renaissance to Modernism to Postmodernism, the world has become less and less violent. Whether this move is a result of changing culture, expanding free markets, or increasing population density making being polite a rational survival mechanism—or something else—the authors' claims about the violence inherent in the modernist/postmodernist system seem to show the tensions between systems that promote uniformity of values, as do some wisdom cultures, and those that allow for greater diversity. It may be true that a culture that values Truth,

Goodness, and Beauty is less violent than the one we have now—but such a claim could only be true if our world's loss of violence is due to the expansion of free markets, in spite of culture. It may also be that the pluralism, perspectivism, multiculturalism, and relativism of postmodernism have had a positive influence as well. A person 100 percent certain he has the Truth and that what he does is the Good can be much more easily convinced to harm others who endanger those values than can one who is never certain he has the truth or that he has a monopoly on the good. However, one who outright rejects truth and the good can equally be convinced to support just about any movement. And if all is but power relations, isn't it better for you to be in power than someone else? Certainty gave us the Inquisition; nihilistic political romanticism (that is, postmodernism broadly understood) gave us the French Revolution, Nazism, and the Russian Revolution/Stalinism.

The Romantic philosophy of Rousseau, Hegel, Marx, et al. (the line to postmodernism) gives rise to a Romantic politics realized in the French Revolution, the communist revolutions, and, in its explicitly racist, irrationalist version, Nazism. In this sense, Pontynen and Miller are correct that the modernist/postmodernist world view can lead to the worst kinds of violence, insofar as it leads to political romanticism married to bureaucratic efficiency (Milan Kundera, at least, agrees that communism is a version of political romanticism). Though the periods between eruptions of romantic politics have been relatively peaceful, I think they do make strong their implicit argument—and history has proven them on this—that Romantic politics is necessarily violent, brutal, and barbaric. Pontynen and Miller go so far as to equate Romanticism with sociopathy; in politics (in which they include progressivism as political Romanticism), at least, given the above examples, there is little question the equation is correct. Which should make one suspect the Romantic philosophers, the philosophers of will, as well. When you replace love with will, the world degenerates into violence.

"Will" is one of the central ideas Pontynen and Miller attack. Whether it be the will to power, the will of the people, the will of any given person, or, in what they see as a mistake made by Christianity itself, the will of God. For them, God does not do things because He wills it, but because God is the embodiment of Truth, Good, and Beauty. God thus does things out of love, not will. The universe exists not because God willed it, but because God is Love. They reject the notion of will because with will, one does not need reason, truth, goodness, love, or beauty as guides for one's actions. If one has enough force and power, one can impose one's will on others. Insofar as the gift economy promotes the good, true, and beautiful, their idea of will is in fact in opposition of the very idea of philanthropy. Indeed, if one combines will with, say, the good, you can see yourself as justified in imposing your idea of the good on others—an idea that suggests using the force and power of government rather than the voluntary nature of true philanthropy. Will, and thus modernism/postmodernism, thus destroys culture. This point bears greater contemplation in the context of discussions about the virtue of donor intent.

For Pontynen and Miller, the ideal culture is one that is classical, Judeo-Christian, and Anglosphere in its conception of tradition-informed cultural change. Those familiar with the work of Hayek on spontaneous orders will recognize what is meant by the latter. Common law, free markets, and even language are examples of this kind of tradition-informed cultural change historically promoted most explicitly in the Anglosphere. Indeed, I would argue that Hayek's spontaneous order is a more detailed explanation of Adam Smith's "Invisible Hand", and its explanatory power can be expanded to include social as well as market orders. What is typically thought of as the double-stranded DNA of Western culture—the classical and Judeo-Christian traditions—is improved with their addition of a third strand, the Anglosphere. They do warn us, though, that "Should the Anglosphere shift from the classical-Judeo-Christian to modernism-postmodernism, then the traditionalism of English culture, previously understood as the bearer of wisdom, is transformed into the bearer of willful preference. Government based on willful preference—of the few or the many—destroys human rights for all" (143). If Pontynen and Miller are not in fact calling for a retreat to Medieval thinking, it is only because they acknowledge the importance of the Anglosphere to the maintenance of culture. It is thus a shame, then, that though they mention the Anglosphere, they hardly deal with this strand of cultural DNA at all. As a result, one is mostly left with the impression that everything has been going downhill since the writings of Aquinas, and things would be best if we were all Augustinians. Why must we go back? Is there not a way forward?

Frederick Turner has frequently observed (1986, 2006, 2007) that sometimes, in order to create the future, you have to break with the past, and sometimes in order to create the future, you have to break with the present and look to the past. Modernism/postmodernism is an example of the former; we are in a time requiring the latter. However, there is a difference between looking to the past to retreat from the present, and looking to the past to build the future from the present. Pontynen and Miller can help us understand what we might want to recover from the past, but their message is one of retreat. As Turner has shown in works ranging from *Natural Classicism* (1986) to *Natural Religion* (2006), we do not have to retreat; rather, we can take these insights and build a new future with a new culture—one that accepts all our cultural insights, from past to present, and across cultures.

REFERENCES

Pinker, Steven. 2012. *The Better Angels of Our Nature: Why Violence Has Declined.* New York: Viking.

Pontynen, Arthur and Rod Miller. 2011. *Western Culture at the American Crossroads: Conflicts Over the Nature of Science and Reason.* Wilmington, DE: Intercollegiate Studies Institute.

Ridley, Matt. 2011. *The Rational Optimist: How Prosperity Evolves.* New York: HarperPerennial.

Turner, Frederick. 1986. *Natural Classicism.* VA: University of Virginia Press.

______. 2005. "Creating a Culture of Gift." *Conversations on Philanthropy* II: 27-58. ©2005 DonorsTrust.

______. 2006. *Natural Religion.* Piscataway, NJ: Transaction Publishers.

______. 2007. *The Culture of Hope.* New York: The Free Press.

TROY CAMPLIN *is an interdisciplinary scholar, the author of* Diaphysics, *and an adjunct professor at the University of North Texas at Dallas. He currently lives in Richardson, TX.*

THE
PHILANTHROPIC ENTERPRISE

Conversations on Philanthropy is a publication of The Philanthropic Enterprise, a research and education institute that works to strengthen our understanding of how philanthropy and voluntary social cooperation promote human flourishing. Through scholarly research, convivial exchange, and the discovery and encouragement of social traditions and innovations that produce joy, wisdom, and prosperity, The Philanthropic Enterprise seeks to demonstrate the crucial importance of independent philanthropy, voluntary activity, and spontaneous social orders in the formation of a free and humane society.

The Philanthropic Enterprise is an Indiana not-for-profit corporation. (Application for 501(c)(3) tax-exempt status is pending with the Internal Revenue Service.)

Contributions may be made payable to:
The Philanthropic Enterprise
PO Box 4449
Carmel, IN 46082

The opinions expressed in Conversations on Philanthropy are not necessarily the views of The Philanthropic Enterprise.

Correspondence may be directed to the Editor at
editor@conversationsonphilanthropy.org

CONVERSATIONS
ON PHILANTHROPY

Would you like to receive notifications when
Conversations on Philanthropy is published?
Be sure to join our Mailing List!

Complete and fax this form to 888-777-5164
OR
Subscribe online at www.conversationsonphilanthropy.org

Name ____

Title ____

Institution ____

Address ____

____

City, ST, Zip ____

Country ____

Email ____

Phone ____

Back issues of Conversations are available for $10 each.
Please send this form with your check made payable to
The Philanthropic Enterprise.

_______ **Conceptual Foundations (2004)**

_______ **New Paradigms (2005)**

_______ **Philanthropic Transformations (2006)**

_______ **The Legacy of Kenneth Boulding (2007)**

_______ **Philanthropy & the Pursuit of Happiness (2008)**

_______ **Identity, Interests, & Philanthropic Commerce (2009)**

_______ **Re-imagining Philanthropy: Myths and Opportunities (2010)**

_______ **Philanthropic Reflections (2011)**